Contents @ a Glance

Contents

Acknowledgments

John Cronan and Patricia Shepard did significant amounts of writing for this book. John wrote chapters 5 and 6 and part of 9, while Pat wrote chapters 3 and 8 and the other part of 9. John also technically reviewed all parts of the book that he didn't write. Both Pat and John are authors in their own right, and we are very lucky to have them work on this project. For this, for the ease with which we were able to work with them, and for their willingness to do whatever was necessary, we are most grateful. Thanks Pat and John!

The crew at Osborne, ably led by Joanne Cuthbertson in acquisitions and Nancy McLaughlin in editorial, with strong support from Gordon Hurd as editorial assistant, as always, made the project as easy as possible and in many instances even fun. Thanks Joanne, Nancy, and Gordon!

Publication Services did the editing and production of the book and we are grateful for their work. Kris Engberg, who was our principal coordinator, was always pleasant to work with and tried hard to implement our wishes.

Carole and Marty Matthews
July 1997

Introduction

The Office suite not only includes five full-featured productivity applications, but a number of utilities, all with many features, commands, and options. Office 97 represents a new level of sophistication and maturity in many of it components, although in the case of Outlook you have a brand new product with more than a few rough edges. It is therefore natural that you'll have many questions about how to use what is there, as well as how to handle situations when things don't go quite right. Between almost nonexistent documentation, online Help that never quite answers the question you are asking, and the hours you can spend waiting on a toll phone line to get tech support from Microsoft, there is a great disparity between the questions being asked and the answers that are available. The purpose of this book is to fill that void.

The many real-world questions that are answered here came from a combination of the authors' and their associates' many years of using Office, plus almost a year of using Office 97 beta and final releases, in addition to Stream International's experience in providing tech support to Office 97 users since the release of Office 97. The authors have virtually delved into every nook and cranny of the product and experienced a great many of the problems first hand. As a result, they have located practically every source of answers and have referenced many of them here.

The book then combines the "on the firing line" experience of a company providing tech support for Office 97 with about as much depth of experience in researching and using the product as you can have without actually being one of the programmers who wrote Office 97 (and the authors have spent a lot of time talking to the people behind Office 97).

Office 97 Answers is divided into 10 chapters, each of which covers a major subject. Within each chapter the questions and answers are further divided into topics. To find a particular answer, use the Table of Contents to identify the chapter and section in which it's located. You can then look alphabetically for the central topic of your question. Around your question, you'll find others that relate to it and will add to the answer you were originally seeking. You can also go right to a chapter and then look at the headings and alphabetical list of questions at the beginning of the chapter. Finally, you can use the Action Index to alphabetically locate a topic that doesn't pop out at you from either the Table of Contents or the Answer Topics at the beginning of each chapter.

Besides the questions and answers, there are many Tips, Notes, and supplementary sidebars throughout the book that give you insight into how best to do something that only considerable experience would otherwise bring. In addition to the Tips, Notes, and sidebars, there are a number of Cautions that point out actions that can cause considerable problems if they are not avoided. Each chapter (except for Chapter 1, "Top Ten FAQs") has an introductory section labeled "@ a Glance." These sections give you an introduction to the chapter's subject and how to address the issues related to it. Reading all of the "@ a Glance" sections will give you a broad understanding of Office 97 and answer many of your questions before you ask them.

Conventions Used in This Book

Office 97 Answers uses several conventions designed to make the book easier for you to follow. Among these are the following:

- ▷ **Bold type** is used for text that you are to type from the keyboard.

- ▷ *Italic type* is used for some labels and names (those that are not easily distinguished by capitalization) of fields and controls as they appear on the screen, and for terms or phrases that deserve special emphasis.

☞ Small capital letters are used for keys on the keyboard such as ENTER and SHIFT.

☞ When you are expected to enter a command, you are told to press the key(s). If you are to enter text or numbers, you are told to type them.

Top Ten
FAQs

Answer Topics!

How to **avoid automatic capitalization**

When you **can't find your address book
    and message file**

Compatibility with Word 6.0

How to **freeze columns**

Nonnetwork uses for hyperlinks

Page borders that don't print

**Preventing more than one person at a
    time from entering data**

Printing just one page in Landscape

Restoring the Office **Shortcut Bar**

Lightening and typing over **watermarks**

MOST FREQUENTLY ASKED QUESTIONS

1 **Whenever I type text that follows a period or text that I want to display in a list in lowercase only, the first character is automatically capitalized. Why is this? How can I avoid automatic capitalization?**

The default setting is uppercase for the initial character in text at the beginning of sentences and text at the beginning of lines. This is a feature of AutoCorrect. To turn off this feature, follow these steps:

1. Choose AutoCorrect from the Tools menu.

2. Select the AutoCorrect tab.

3. Click the option *Capitalize the first letter of sentence* (or *sentences,* in Word) to remove the check mark from the box, as shown here:

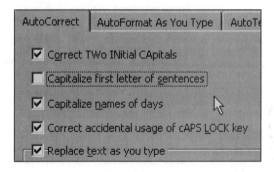

4. Click OK.

2 **I had been using the Windows 95 Inbox (Exchange client) for my e-mail until I installed Outlook. Now I can't find my address book and message file. Did they get wiped out?**

No, they're probably still there. In most cases the Office 97 installation will find your Windows 95 Inbox files, but not always. Your Windows 95 Inbox files are Mailbox.pab for your address book and Mailbox.pst for your messages. Both of these are located in the Exchange folder of your root directory. Outlook may create new files with similar extensions but different filenames (such as Outlook.pst) in the Windows folder. You can find and attach your original files to Outlook with these steps:

1. Within Outlook, open the Tools menu and choose Services to open the Services dialog box.

2. Click Personal Address Book in the Services tab, and then click Properties.

3. Click Browse to find your original file (it is probably in the Exchange folder). When you find the correct file, click Open and it will appear in the Path text box as shown here:

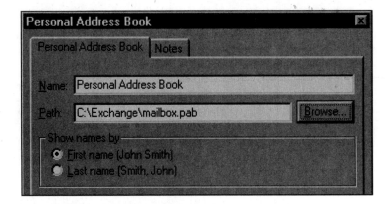

4. Click OK to return to the Services dialog box. Select Personal Folders, click Remove, and then click Yes. (You can't just change the file as you can for the address book.)

5. Click Add, select Personal Folders, and click OK.

6. Locate your existing file and its folder (it is probably Mailbox.pst in the Exchange folder) and click Open. The path will be displayed. Click OK twice. Your original address book and messages should now be available.

Tip: If you are entering a new address and there's any chance that you will want to use it again, then it is worthwhile to enter it in an address book, where it can be reused. It is not that much more work than entering the address directly in a message.

3 **I was unable to open a document created in Word 97 in Word 6.0. When I tried to open it, I got two error messages. The first message said that the file is not a Word for Windows document. I clicked OK and then saw a second message that said Word cannot open the document. Is there any way I can save a Word 97 document so it will be compatible with Word 6.0?**

Yes, when you are working on the document in Word 97, save the document in a Word 6.0/95 format. To do this,

1. Choose Save As from the File menu, even if you have already saved it as a Word 97 document.

2. Type in a new name if you want to keep the original as a Word 97 document.

3. Click the down arrow in the *Save as type* box, scroll down through the list of types, and select Word 6.0/95, as seen here:

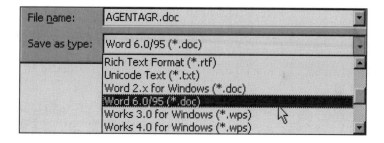

4. Click the Save button.

Tip: You can also choose Word 6.0/95 in the *Save as type* box to save a document that you want to open in Word 7.

4 **I have a table with more fields than will fit on a screen in Datasheet view. There is one field I'd like to remain on screen while I scroll horizontally. Is there a way to freeze a column?**

Yes. Click a record in the column you want to freeze. Choose Freeze Columns from the Format menu and the column will move to the leftmost side of the screen, identified by a heavy border along the right side of the column. Now as you scroll to see the fields off the right side of the screen, the frozen column will remain displayed.

▩▩▩▩   *Tip:*   You can freeze as many columns as you need to by repeating the process described above.

5   Are there **nonnetwork uses for hyperlinks?**

Usually you use hyperlinks to allow network users to quickly access other locations or references on either a network or the Internet; however, for a single user, selected text used as a hyperlink also can be inserted to open almost any file Word recognizes on your hard drive or LAN. You copy the material you want referenced and then paste it using the *Paste as Hyperlink* command. Then when you click the inserted hyperlink, not only will the referenced text be displayed, but also the document from which it was copied will be immediately opened. To insert a hyperlink to open a referenced document, do this:

1. Open both the document into which you want to insert the hyperlink and the document that contains text to be referenced.

2. Select the text to be referenced and click the Copy button to copy it to the Clipboard.

3. Move your insertion point to the place where you want to insert the hyperlink in the other document.

4. Choose *Paste as Hyperlink* from the Edit menu. The hyperlink is inserted as shown here:

These are the reasons we seek to encourage Space Camp for intermediate-school aged children:
    91% enrolled in more math, specifically algebra and calculus
    74% indicated they learned about career options;
    41% reported that their experience at Space Camp was a key element in choosing future curriculum; 87% chose courses supporting engineering, math or science;
    93% took more science courses primarily in physics and chemistry.
    It's easy to see why we're so excited about this extraordinary opportunity for the children of South Whidbey. We're asking for your help in making this trip more accessible for some children.

Now when you click the hyperlink text, the referenced document will be opened immediately, and the insertion point moves to the text that was selected for the hyperlink. For more information about hyperlinks see Chapter 9, "Using Office with the Internet and Intranets."

Tip: To quickly insert a hyperlink only, as seen below, choose Hyperlink from the Insert menu, browse to the file to be linked to, and click OK. When you click the inserted hyperlink, it will open the file in its appropriate application.

C:\My Documents\spacefunds.doc

6 I was glad to see that Word 97 has a page border feature, but I'm having a problem with page borders that don't print: When I add a border around the entire page, the border on the right side does not print. How can I correct this?

Many printers will not print text or borders that are at the edge, or near the edge, of the paper. The minimum distance you can print from the edge of the paper varies from printer to printer. You need to adjust the border.

To add a page border,

1. Choose *Borders and Shading* from the Format menu.
2. Click the Page Border tab and select the border style you want. Click OK.

Go to Print Preview to see if all borders will print. If not, do the following to adjust borders so they will be printed:

1. Choose *Borders and Shading* from the Format menu.
2. Click the Page Border tab.
3. Click the Options button. (See the sidebar "Page Borders" in Chapter 3 for more information.)
4. In the Margin section, adjust the point size for the side where the border is not printing, as seen in Figure 1-1, where the right margin needs to be increased. The Preview section shows the result of the change. Click OK twice to return to the document.

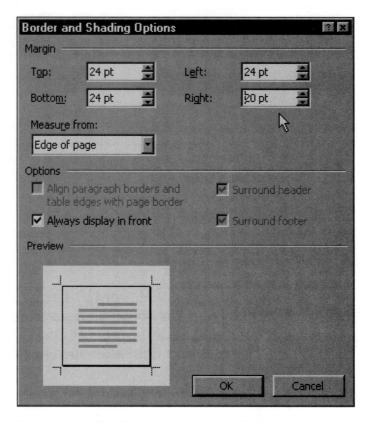

Figure 1-1: The Border and Shading Options dialog box

5. Click the Print Preview button (if you are not already in Print Preview) to confirm that the border will be printed.

Tip: If the border is still not showing, return to the *Border and Shading Options* dialog box from the Format menu, select Text in the *Measure from* box, and then adjust the point measurement in the Margin section.

7 **I don't want to go through the process of replicating a database in order to track potential entry conflicts; however, I want to avoid problems with conflicting data entry. How can I prevent more than one person at a time from entering data?**

When you or a member of your group is opening the database from the Open dialog box, shown in Figure 1-2,

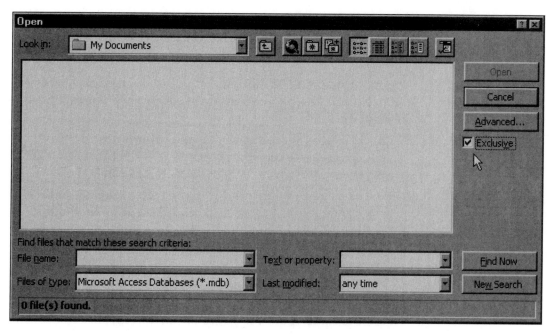

Figure 1-2: Select the Exclusive check box to prevent someone else from entering data

select the Exclusive check box on the right side of the dialog box, and click Open. If someone else tries to open the database they will receive the message shown here:

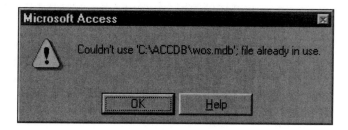

Exclusivity only lasts as long as the database is open. After the database is closed, it will again be available to be opened by anyone.

8 **In Word, how do I print just one page in Landscape? Only page 3 of my document should be printed that way, and all the others should print in Portrait.**

You must insert a Continuous page break on page 2 and then redefine the page orientation for page 3. Follow these steps to do it:

1. On the page before the landscape orientation (in this case, page 2), at the end of the page, select Insert, Break, and then *Continuous section breaks*. Click OK.

2. On the page to be printed in Landscape (page 3, in this case), select File, Page Setup, and then click the Paper Size tab.

3. Click Landscape and click OK.

▪▪▪▪▪▪ *Tip:* To view the Landscape orientation on screen, select View and Layout View. The header and footer for that page will remain the same as for the pages in Portrait layout.

9 **I installed Office 97 using the Typical Installation. Later when I looked for the office Shortcut Bar, I could not find it. How do I get it back?**

The Shortcut Bar is not installed as an active feature when you use the Typical Installation unless you installed it during a previous Office installation. To get it you need to use the Add/Remove Programs feature of Windows 95, as described here:

1. If you have Office applications running, you might take time to close them before continuing. Otherwise, the Setup process will stop and you will be prompted to do it.

2. From the Start menu select Settings and then Control Panel. Double-click the Add/Remove Programs icon. The Add/Remove Programs Properties dialog box will be displayed.

3. On the Install/Uninstall tab find the Microsoft Office 97 program on the list and select it, as shown in Figure 1-3. Click the Add/Remove button.

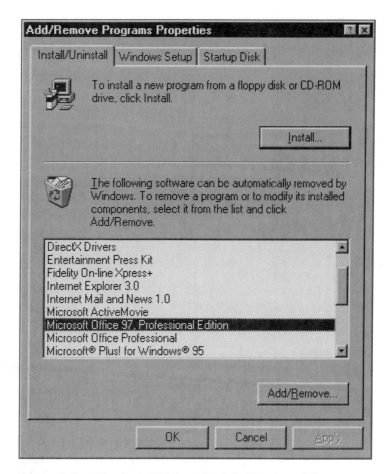

Figure 1-3:   The Install/Uninstall tab in Windows 95

4. If you have not done so, you will need to insert the Office 97 CD at this point. Click OK when you have done this. The Microsoft Office 97 Setup will begin.

5. In the Microsoft Office 97 - Setup dialog box, click the Add/Remove button to add a new component. Office will begin the Setup. Proceed as instructed. In the Microsoft Office 97 Setup dialog box, select Add/Remove.

6. In the Microsoft Office 97 - Maintenance dialog box, select Office Tools, and then click Change Option for the Office tool details.

7. In the Microsoft Office 97 - Office Tools dialog box, place a check mark beside Microsoft Office Shortcut Bar, as shown next. Then click OK.

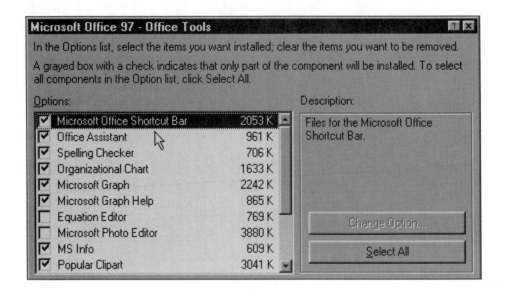

8. In the Microsoft Office 97 - Maintenance dialog box, click Continue to have the Setup program activate the Shortcut Bar. Click OK in the final Setup dialog box, and then in the Add/Remove Programs Properties dialog box click Cancel to end the Setup process.

9. You will need to reboot before the Shortcut Bar is automatically displayed on your desktop.

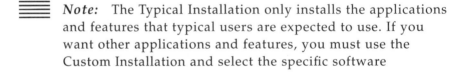 *Note:*   The Typical Installation only installs the applications and features that typical users are expected to use. If you want other applications and features, you must use the Custom Installation and select the specific software components you want.

10   As a Word 6 user I knew that when I wanted a **watermark** to appear on consecutive pages I had to insert the picture in a header. I did this in Word 97, but the picture was so dark that any text typed over it was not readable. Also, when I returned to the document window I could not type text over the watermark. What happened, and how do I correct it?

The watermark must still be inserted in a header or footer. After you insert the picture, do the following:

1. Display the Picture toolbar shown here, if it is not already displayed.

2. Select the picture.

3. Click the Image Control button, shown at the left, and select Watermark to dim the picture.

4. Click the Text Wrapping button, shown at the left, and select None so that you can type text over the watermark.

Now close the Header and Footer toolbar and you can type text over the watermark. If you are in Normal view, you will not see the picture. Change to Page Layout view or go to Print Preview to see how the watermark looks.

chapter

2 **Answers!**

Getting Started with Office 97

Answer Topics!

Office 97
@ a Glance

Office 97 consists of five applications:

▷ **Word,** for word processing tasks, such as writing letters, brochures, manuals, reports, or other text-related documents. New features included in Office 97 are free-form drawing; AutoShapes, with 32 predefined shapes available; document mapping for quick transfer to another part of a document via a Table of Contents displayed on the left of a split screen; Web page design capability and the ability to insert hyperlinks in normal Word documents, to other Web sites, or within your own computer; sticky notes; new fonts; and 18 toolbars.

▷ **Excel,** for spreadsheet tasks, where working with columns and rows of data allows you to more easily analyze, sort, chart, and otherwise work with numbers. New with Office 97 are page-break previews for viewing spreadsheet page breaks; using row and column labels to identify ranges; inserting hyperlinks for connecting to other Web sites or Excel workbooks; several new wizards, such as Lookup Wizard, File Conversion Wizard, and HTML Wizard; and the ability to track user revisions.

▷ **Access** (available only with Office 97 Professional), for database tasks, when you must organize data—either simple lists or very complex relational databases involving multiple linked tables and databases. New in Office 97 are date handling for the year 2000, a hyperlink data type, a Publish to the Web Wizard for posting

data to a Web page, a User Level Security Wizard for securing a
database, the ability to create forms with multiple tabs, design and
form enhancements, and more.

▷ **Outlook**, new with Office 97, is an information manager for
organizing your appointments, calls, messages, name lists, and
tasks. It provides a central place where faxes and intranet and
Internet messages can be viewed. It provides a scheduling calendar
that reminds you of appointments and to-do tasks. It provides
one place for address files, which can be grouped and organized
according to your needs.

▷ **PowerPoint**, a multimedia tool, creates presentations, from simple
overhead slides to powerful sound and video presentations with
animated graphics. Office 97 has added a Slide Finder for finding
slides in other presentations, Speaker Notes, enhanced animation
tools for creating custom motion effects, Custom Show to print
specific slides, Action Buttons to jump to any slide, Narration
for recording voices slide by slide, the ability to play CDs during
presentations, and more.

The power of Office 97 lies not only in the comprehensiveness of
each application, but in how they are integrated. Some of the ways this
integration is achieved are shown in the following list:

▷ **Common user interfaces,** including similar-looking menus and
toolbars, and common keyboard commands tie the five applications
together. When you have learned one application, you know much
about how to use the others.

▷ **Shared tools** also give commonality to the separate applications.
For instance, Spelling Checker and AutoCorrect allow you to
specify custom settings that are available to all the applications.
The Clip Gallery and Graph packages provide common clipart and
graphing features to Office applications, just as Office Art gives
consistent drawing and art capability between Word, Excel, and
PowerPoint. These are just some of the shared tools in Office 97.

▷ **Data compatibility** enables you to cut and copy data from one
application to paste into another, or to export and import from
one to another. For example, you can include an Excel chart and
an Access table in a Word document or a PowerPoint presentation.

▷ **Comprehensive help** comes in several flavors. First is the typical
Help system available with each application for looking up
subjects. New with Office 97 is the Office Assistant, which monitors
what you are doing and tries to guess what you are trying to do. It
offers tips on how to proceed. If you don't see the tip you need,

you can type your own question and get a list of options as it tries to interpret what you have asked. Finally, you can ask for online help directly from Microsoft's home page. You are given a list of destinations for the most likely reasons you might want to seek online help.

☞ **Linking and embedding** data, another way of integrating the applications, allows you to share data between files. Linking connects one file, or object within a file, to another. The connected file or object is displayed as part of the other file. The displayed object is actually the original file or object, not a copy. Therefore, when a linked file is updated, the updates automatically are reflected in the file containing the link. For instance, if you link a spreadsheet to a Word document, you don't have to remember to update the numbers in both documents. Embedding, on the other hand, inserts a copy of another object. When the original of that object is updated, the embedded copy is not updated.

☞ **Office Binder** can be best illustrated with the example of a team effort—when several people are working on one project. All the files related to the project are stored in a binder that is available to all members of the team. It can be revised and contributed to by many individuals, each uniquely identified. Schedules can be tracked and the project's progress can be monitored, because all team members share the contents of the binder.

☞ **Visual Basic for Applications**, the macro and programming language, can be used throughout Office to build short macros or complex applications based on the powerful Office applications.

INSTALLING OFFICE 97

 When I installed Office 97, my address book and all my e-mail and fax messages disappeared. The Inbox icon disappeared too. Where are they?

When Office 97 is installed with the Typical installation, the addresses for Exchange are switched to those for Outlook. The messages and address books used with Exchange are still there; they are just not being pointed to. There are two ways you can get your files back. The first method is when Office guesses that is what you need. The Office Assistant will help you get your messages. The second method is to do it yourself.

When Office 97 Offers to Help Get Your Messages

When you first bring up Outlook, the Assistant will display a menu of items to get you going. One of the suggestions is to *Import information from Schedule+ and other programs,* as shown here:

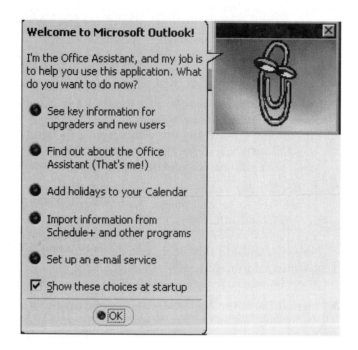

Follow these steps to get your information:

1. Click *Import information from Schedule+ and other programs.*

2. The Import and Export Wizard will lead you through selecting the specific information you need. Select *Import from a personal folder file* (.pst), and click Next.

3. In the *File to import* box, you must specify the address of the file to be imported. The Assistant's suggestion may not be what you want. If you used Exchange for your e-mail, for example, your data may have the following address:

   C:\ Exchange\ mailbox.pst

4. Click Next. The Import Personal Folders dialog box will be displayed, as shown here:

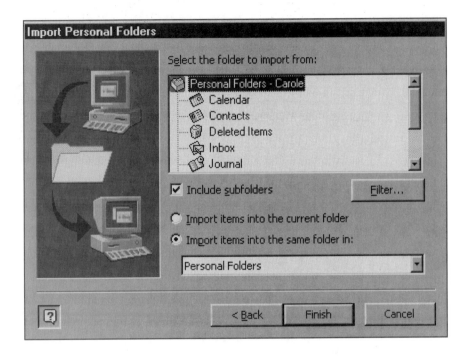

Data from the personal folder will be copied into Outlook. You will be able to see your previous messages.

You can select the specific information you want to import, or you can import it all by selecting Personal Folders.

5. When you have selected the data you want, click Finish.

When You Must Get Your Messages Yourself

You can direct Outlook to display messages from the Exchange files yourself. The Exchange messages are held in the \Exchange\mailbox.pst file, and the address book is in the \Exchange\mailbox.pab file. Outlook address book and mail files are in \Windows\Outlook.pst. To change Outlook to point to the Exchange files, follow these steps:

1. From the Start menu, select Settings and then Control Panel. Double-click the Mail and Fax icon.

2. Click the Add button for the list of *Available information services,* as shown here:

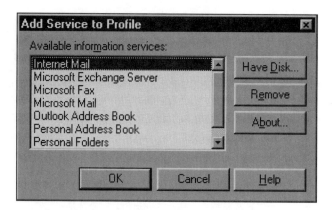

3. Select the service that you are missing, such as the Personal Address Book or Internet Mail. Click OK.

4. Depending on the option you choose, you will be shown another dialog box containing the address of the file. Check that the addresses are pointing to the files in the Exchange folder, such as this one for a Personal Address Book:

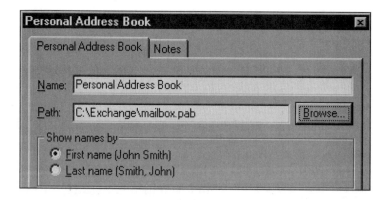

Tip: You may want to create more than one profile to handle the different types of services, such as Fax and Internet Mail.

How much **disk space** do I need to have available to install Office 97?

The space you need for Office 97 will vary depending on the product you select and the installation process you use. Here are the requirements:

Installation Process	Disk Space Required	RAM Required
Office Standard, Typical	102MB	8MB to run an individual application; more to run multiple applications simultaneously
Office Professional, Typical	121MB	8MB to run an individual application; more to run multiple applications simultaneously (12MB if running Access)
Office Standard, Custom	67 to 167MB	8MB to run an individual application; more to run multiple applications simultaneously
Office Professional, Custom	73 to 191MB	8MB to run an individual application; more to run multiple applications simultaneously (12MB if running Access)
Network Server, files on a local drive	52MB	16MB for individual applications
Network Server, files on a server	25MB	16MB for individual applications
Network Administrator	325MB	16MB for individual applications
Office Standard run from CD	51MB	8MB for individual applications; more to run more than one simultaneously
Office Professional run from CD	61MB	8MB to run an individual application; more to run multiple applications simultaneously (12MB if running Access)

By using a Custom Installation you can decrease the disk space requirements to some extent, depending on which applications and components you really need. If you are low on disk space you can experiment with selecting different components. You might, for example, delay installing some of the components you are not sure you'll use until you really need them, and then install them using Add/Remove Programs on the Control Panel.

You will also need 20 to 40MB of free disk space after installation for temporary storage in order for Office 97 to operate optimally.

Tip: If you are really short on disk space, you can run Office from the CD. To do this, select Run from CD-ROM as the type of installation rather than a Typical or Custom installation.

? I have both Office 95 and Office 97 on my computer and want to keep both. However, when I try to open an Office 95 document from the Explorer or My Computer, Office 97 is started. Why can't I get Office 95 to open the documents it has created?

When you double-click a document to start it, the last version you installed will be used to open it, regardless of whether or not it is the version that created the document.

▷ To always open a document with Office 97, install Office 97 last.

▷ To always have a document opened in the version of Office that created it, load that version of Office first and then open the document using the File menu Open option.

? I need to continue using a prior version of Microsoft Office with some of my documents. Will Office 97 overwrite my older version?

Only if you want it to. The default location for Office 97 is c:\Program Files\Microsoft Office, and for Office 95 it is c:\Msoffice. First, you will be asked if you want to change the folder name for storing Office programs, as shown in

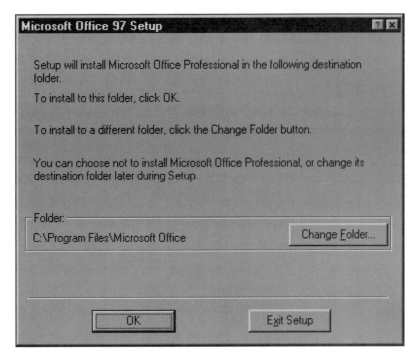

Figure 2-1: Preserving older versions of Office by changing the name of the folder that will contain Office 97

Figure 2-1. You can specify a folder name different from the previous installation. Then, during the installation you will be informed that Setup has found a previous installation of Office and asked if you want Office 97 to overwrite those files. You must answer No to retain the previous version. If you respond Yes, your previous Office programs will be replaced with Office 97; however, your data files will remain unchanged regardless of the method you use.

Caution: The default (and the recommended way to install) is for Office 97 to replace any older versions of Office, preserving the data files and user settings such as those in AutoCorrect. If you want to retain a previous installation of Office, you must respond *No* when asked if you want to overwrite the previous files with Office 97.

I used the Custom Installation to install everything. Now I find that my disk space is too cramped and I have several Office components, such as the Equation Editor, that I never use. How can I remove some of the Office components without affecting the others? (I'm not sure which files are required and which are optional.)

You will need to run Setup again and uninstall the components you do not want. To do this, follow these steps:

1. If you have Office applications running, you should close them before continuing. If you don't, Setup will halt the installation to suggest that you do.

2. From the Start menu select Settings and then Control Panel. Double-click the Add/Remove Programs icon. The Add/Remove Programs Properties dialog box will be displayed.

3. On the Install/Uninstall tab, select the Microsoft Office 97 program, as shown here:

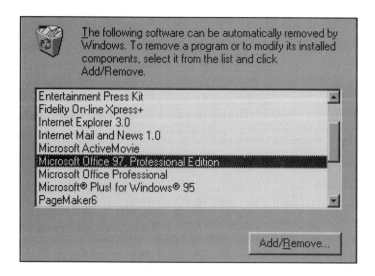

Click the Add/Remove button. You will need to insert the Office 97 CD at this point. Click OK when you have done this. The Microsoft Office 97 Setup will begin.

4. Click the Add/Remove button in the Microsoft Office 97 Setup dialog box to get a list of installed components.

5. In the Microsoft Office 97 Maintenance dialog box, scan the list and remove the check marks beside those components you wish to remove. When you select a component, the Change Option button will be available, as shown below; if you click it, you can see the details of the selected component. For some components (such as with Office Tools, with which Equation Editor is listed) you may only want to remove some of the options, not all of them.

6. Click OK when you have identified all components to be uninstalled and have removed the check marks beside them.

7. In the Microsoft Office 97 Maintenance dialog box, click Continue. The Confirm Component Removal message box appears. Click Yes if you are sure you want to remove the components.

8. In the final Setup dialog box, click OK, and then in the Add/Remove Programs Properties dialog box, click Cancel to end the Setup process.

Note: Be sure you run the Setup for the version of Office you are trying to modify.

? I used the Typical Installation for Office 97 on my new computer, but I did not get all of the same templates as with the Typical Installation in an older version of Office. How come? I really use some of them!

The Typical Installation does not always install the same wizards and templates as were used previously. The old templates can be manually copied from the old Templates folder to the Templates folder in Office 97. If you do not have the old templates on disk, you can use the Custom Installation or Add/Remove Programs, as described in the question on **removing Office components**, to retrieve them.

I have Windows 3.1. Must I upgrade to Windows 95 to install Office 97?

Yes, you must. Office 97 only works with Windows 95 and Windows NT 4.0.

 Tip: Disable any virus-detection utilities you may have before installing Office 97. These programs often use changes in system files to activate corrective procedures. If they detect Office 97 being installed, they could halt or otherwise disrupt the installation procedure.

CUSTOMIZING USER INTERFACES

 I want to create a new menu on my Menu Bar for tasks I do repetitively for a project I'm on.

To create a menu and place it on the Menu Bar, follow these steps:

1. Open the Office application that you want to add the new menu to.

2. Right-click on the menu bar or any toolbar (except the Office toolbar), and choose Customize from the pop-up menu.

3. Select the Commands tab.

4. Select New Menu from the Categories list, and then select New Menu on the Commands list, as shown here:

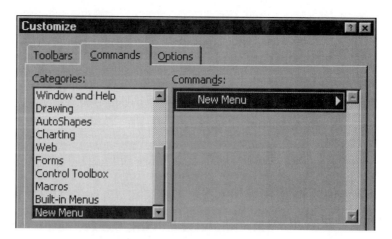

5. Drag the Command item to the Menu Bar on which you want the new menu.

6. To rename the menu, right-click on the new menu and drag the cursor over the New Menu name. Type in the name you want.

7. In the Categories side of the Customize dialog box, select the items you want on the menu (for a list of macros, select Macros). Drag the Commands on the right side of the dialog box to the menu and place them where you want them.

8. When you have finished placing the menu items, click Close. Figure 2-2 shows an example of a custom menu named Web Tasks that was created this way.

Tip: You can move the menu's items from one spot to another by dragging them. First make sure that the Customize dialog box is open, then place the pointer on the item, wait for a second until a rectangle appears, and move the rectangle to where you want the item placed.

? I want to **create a new toolbar** for my own tasks. How do I do this?

To customize or create a new toolbar for Office applications (except for Outlook, which doesn't offer customized toolbars), follow these steps:

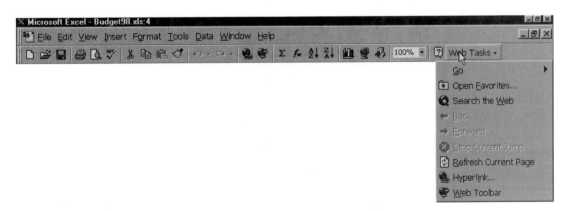

Figure 2-2:   Sample new menu

1. Right-click on one of the toolbars or the menu bar and choose Customize from the displayed menu, shown here (you can also select Customize from the Tools menu).

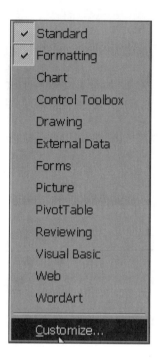

2. On the Toolbars tab, click New to create a new toolbar.

3. In the New Toolbar dialog box, shown next, type in a name for the toolbar. (In Word you also need to select the template to attach it to.) Click OK.

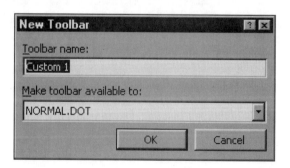

4. Click the Commands tab to select the buttons to be inserted on the toolbar.

5. To determine whether a button is what you want on the toolbar, click one of the Categories and then one of the Commands listed on the right. When you select a command, you will be able to see its description by clicking Description, as shown here:

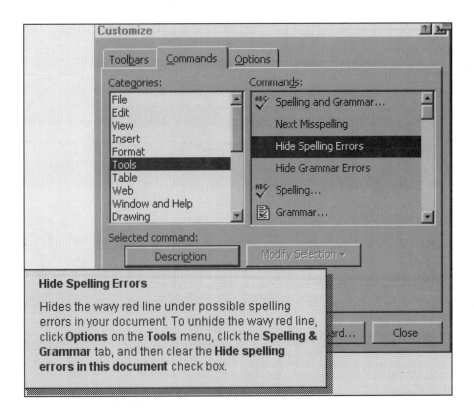

6. To create the toolbar contents you can perform one of these actions:

   ▷ To add a button, drag the button from the Commands list to the toolbar.

   ▷ To delete a button from the toolbar, drag it off the toolbar and release the mouse button, making sure you don't drop it into another toolbar.

   ▷ To copy the button once it's on the toolbar, press CTRL while dragging the button to another toolbar. To change the appearance of a button, either click the button and then click Modify Selection on the

Commands tab or right-click the button. Choose either Edit Button Image or Change Button Image to alter its appearance. (See the following section, "modifying a toolbar button," for more information.)

➤ To change the size of a toolbar, place the mouse pointer on the edge of the toolbar and drag it in the direction you want the edge to go.

7. When you have finished adding and changing buttons on a toolbar, click Close.

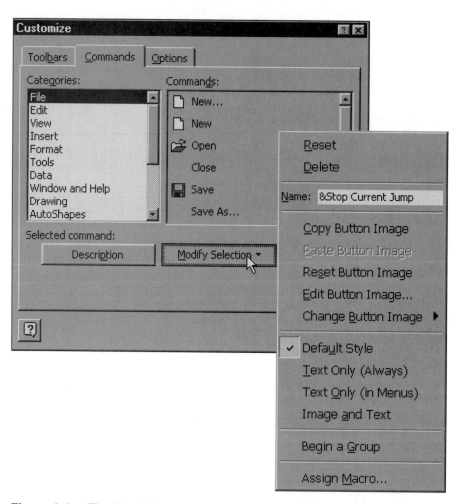

Figure 2-3:   The Modify Selection pop-up menu offers choices for changing toolbars.

Modifying a Toolbar Button

When you select Modify Selection or right-click a button, a menu is displayed with options for changing buttons on a toolbar, as shown in Figure 2-3.

Reset restores the original buttons to a toolbar if it has been modified.

Delete removes a button from the toolbar.

Name allows you to type over the displayed name of the toolbar.

Copy Button Image copies the image of the button into the Clipboard.

Paste Button Image places the image on the Clipboard onto the selected button.

Reset Button Image restores the original image to the button.

Edit Button Image changes the appearance directly by altering the pixels of the image, as shown in Figure 2-4. You can change the color by clicking a color and then clicking

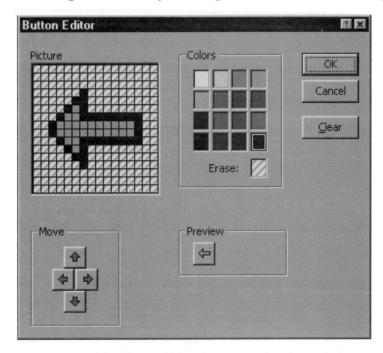

Figure 2-4:   The Button Editor lets you edit a button's image directly.

one of the pixels. You turn the colors of the pixels off one
at a time by clicking Erase and then clicking the pixels. You
can turn them all off by clicking Clear. (If you click Cancel,
it returns to its original image.) You can move the entire
design up, down, right, or left by clicking the arrow keys
in the Move box. Preview allows you to see what the button
will look like in its normal size on the toolbar.

Change Button Image displays a selection of images. You
can choose one of these images for a button by clicking the
image to select it, as shown here:

Default Style displays the button in the default style,
usually an image.

Text Only (Always) always displays a text label for the
button in toolbars or menus.

Text Only (in Menus) always displays a text label for the
button in menus.

Image and Text displays both an image and text.

Begin a Group groups menu commands together by placing
a divider on the toolbar, to the left of the button.

Assign Macro (in Excel) opens the Assign Macro dialog box
so that you can choose a macro for the toolbar.

Properties (in Access) opens the toolbar's Control Properties dialog box, which lists properties for each selected button (or control) in the toolbar.

How do I **make a toolbar button for an existing macro?**

To place an existing macro on a toolbar that is currently displayed requires several steps, depending on the application.

Placing a Macro Button on the Toolbar in Excel

In Excel, you must first place an unassigned macro icon in the toolbar, and then assign it to the macro of your choice. Then you can modify the icon to look like you want. Follow these steps:

1. Be sure the toolbar you want is currently displayed on the screen. If it isn't, display it by selecting Toolbars from the View menu. Click the name of the toolbar you want to be displayed.

2. From the Tools menu, select Customize.

3. On the Commands tab, find Macros in the Categories list box, shown here:

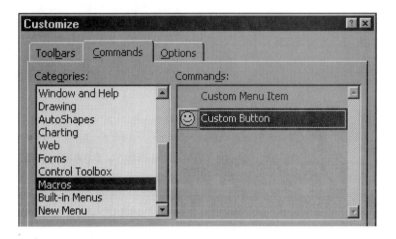

4. Drag the smiley-face macro icon from the Commands list to a blank spot on the toolbar where you want your own macro icon to appear, as shown here:

5. Click Modify Selection and a menu will appear:

6. To change the name of the custom icon, drag over the &Custom Button name and type in your own macro name.

7. Select Assign Macro to transfer your own macro functions to the custom button. A list of your macros will be displayed. Select the one you want for the button and click OK.

8. To change the appearance of the macro icon, click again on Modify Selection for the menu. Select one of the ways to change the appearance:

   ⊳ Text Only to just have the label on the button

   ⊳ Edit Button Image to directly modify the smiley face

   ⊳ Change Button Image to select another image supplied with Office 97

Placing a Macro Button on the Toolbar in Word

In Word, the procedure is slightly different. You first define a macro, place it on the toolbar, and then modify its appearance. Follow these steps:

1. Record your macro as usual, making sure to click the *Assign Macro to Toolbars* button.

2. Right-click on the toolbar and select the Customize option. Select the Commands tab.

3. Under Categories, find Macros. A list of the existing macros will be listed under Commands, an example of which is shown here:

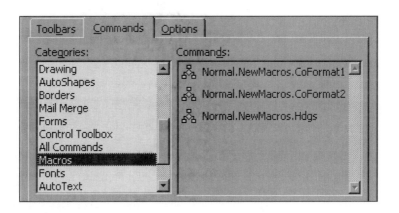

4. Select the macro you want and drag it to the toolbar (you will see an I-beam appear where the icon will be inserted). The whole name of the macro will appear on the button.

5. To change the name and appearance of the macro, right-click it to get the Modify Selection menu.

6. Use the guidelines listed in the section "Modifying a toolbar button" earlier in this chapter to change the image on the button.

▬▬▬ *Tip:*   You can also change toolbar buttons and menus from the Tools menu, by choosing Customize.

?   **I want to remove the Shortcut Bar from the screen when I am working in one of the Office applications. But I want it there when I want it. Is there a way to have it and yet not see it when I don't need it?**

You bet. You can cause the Shortcut Bar to be hidden most of the time. When you want it displayed again, you just move the mouse pointer over the blank space where it normally appears, and it will reappear. Here's how:

1. Right-click on an empty spot on the Shortcut Bar.

2. Select Customize from the pop-up menu.

3. Place a check mark next to *Auto Hide between uses*. Then clear the check mark next to *Auto Fit into Title Bar area*, as shown below, and click OK.

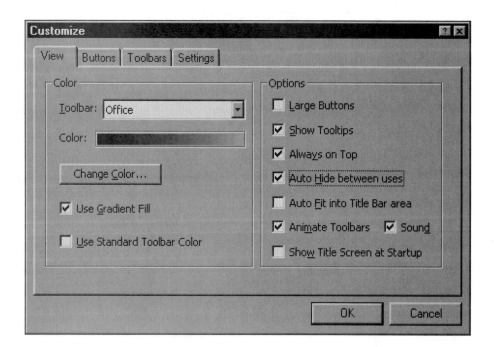

▒▒▒▒ *Tip:* To close the Shortcut Bar altogether, double-click the control menu icon, the leftmost button on the bar. The Shortcut Bar will reappear the next time Windows is started. To start it from the current session of Windows, select Start menu, Programs, Startup, and MS Office Shortcut Bar.

A previous employee modified a toolbar. We would like to restore the original toolbar. How do we do that?

You can restore the toolbar buttons by following these steps:

1. Right-click on an empty space on the toolbar and select Customize.

2. In the Toolbars list, select the toolbar to be restored.

3. Click Reset. In Word you can make the change to a specific document or template, or to all documents (Normal.dot).

4. Click OK if the Assistant asks for verification.

5. Click Close.

≡ *Note:* Toolbars cannot be customized in Outlook.

I want to be able to see several windows on screen at one time, each containing a different application with its own data so I can cut and paste from one to the other. How do I do that?

To see several applications simultaneously, create the different windows by starting the applications. Then simply right-click on the Taskbar and select either Tile Horizontally or Tile Vertically. Figure 2-5 shows an example of windows that were tiled horizontally and then rearranged for convenience.

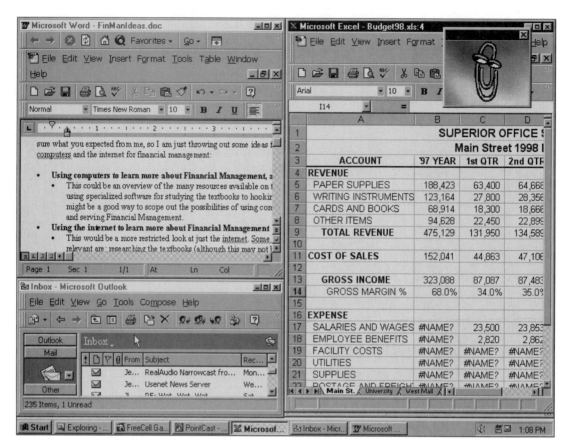

Figure 2-5:   Tiled windows running different applications.

FILE HANDLING AND COMPATIBILITY

?   **I find I have multiple name and address files, with some duplicated names. For example, I have an investment club list in Word, a customer list in Access, and my e-mail contacts in Outlook. How do I decide the best application to use for my name lists?**

Having multiple name and address files is not necessarily bad, depending on how they are used. However, there are some guidelines as to when to use one application rather than another for names and addresses. Word is probably not a good choice for name and address lists unless it is a very trivial list, and small and stable. The three tools for name lists within Office 97 are Outlook (the primary tool), Access, and Excel.

➪ Use Outlook for contacts when you want to manage multiple phone numbers, e-mail addresses, fax numbers, and addresses in one central location.

➪ Use Access for larger files when you are working with multiple, complex data files; for example, a customer database that is linked to Purchase and Accounts Receivable files. Access works well if you have several people working on these files simultaneously in a networked environment and reporting is important, as with Orders Outstanding reports or Overdue Accounts reports.

➪ Use Excel for situations in which a spreadsheet provides the best tools for analyzing the data related to a file. For example, perhaps you want to calculate salespersons' commissions by geographic area for the current quarter.

Tip: You can export and import lists between Word, Outlook, Excel, and Access by saving them as delimited files and then importing them into the desired application.

? How can I quickly **create a copy of an Office file?**

To open a copy of a file rather than opening the original, follow these steps:

1. In Microsoft Explorer, right-click the filename.

2. Select New (for an Access file, you will have to save the file under a new name) as shown next.

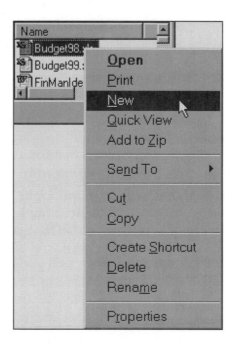

? I must retain both Office 97 and a previous version of Office on my computer, and documents created with Office 97 must sometimes be saved in the older version's format. What happens to the formatting created with features not in the earlier version?

Office 97 recreates the new features using the older version's tools. Although it may not be a perfect reproduction, it will be mapped as closely as possible.

? When I install Office 97, must I worry about my older data files that were created with a previous version of Microsoft Office?

Office 97 strives for compatibility between Office versions, so there is not much cause for worry. For example,

▷ If you install Office 97 over an earlier version, the data files will be preserved.

▷ You can read data files created with previous versions with Office 97.

▷ All data is saved from the Office tasks, such as Schedule+, Calendar, Task and Contact files, and e-mail sent and received.

▷ With Office 97, you can elect to save files in either the new or older format. So not only can you preserve the older file formats, but you can create new ones with Office 97.

? I need to transmit some of my Office documents to someone who doesn't have Office installed on her computer. Is there a way she can read Office documents without Office?

Yes. On the Office Web site you can download a free copy of Word Viewer 97, which allows you to read Word 97 documents without the Word 97 program. It is available on the Internet at http://www.microsoft.com/Word/Internet/Viewer

Other viewers are also available.

≡ *Note:* The viewers available on the Office 97 CD \valupack\Wordview and \valupack\ppt4view (which may also be available on the Web site) can only be read by files formatted in Office 95.

? I want to send my Office 97 document to an office with Word 6.0. How can they read my file without my saving it as a Word 6.0 file?

A converter utility that allows a Word 97 document to be read by Word 6 or Word 95 is available. You can download it from the Microsoft Software Library called *freestuff*.

≡ *Note:* The converter is also available on the Office 97 CD \valupack\wrd97cnv.

To download Converter,

1. Select Microsoft on the Web from the Word Help menu. (It also appears on the Office home page.)
2. Select *Free Stuff* to connect to the correct Web location.

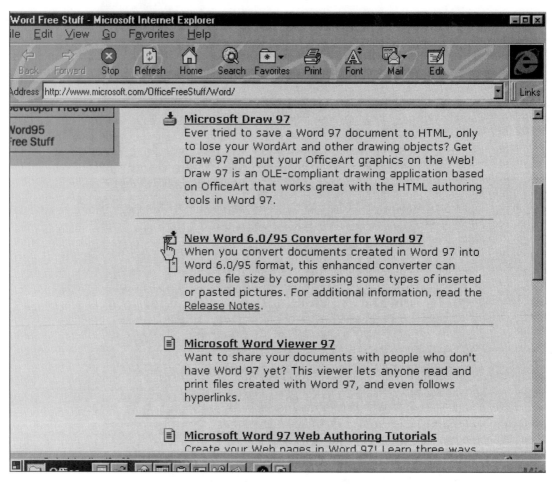

Figure 2-6:   Downloading Converter from Microsoft's Web site

3. When the Web site is displayed, click *New Word 6.0/95 Converter for Word 97,* as shown in Figure 2-6.

4. Click OK to save it to disk

5. Specify the folder location in the Save As dialog box and click Save.

Tip: There is a converter available to open Word 97 documents in any previous version of Word. It can be found at http://microsoft.com/word/default.htm.

In our office, some of our Access files were created with Office 97 and some with a previous version. I want to update the older database files so that they will be compatible with the newer file formats. Can this be done?

Although you can perform many functions on the older files without a problem (such as importing and exporting to and from Office 97 to the older version and cutting, pasting, and copying from 97 to the earlier version), you cannot redesign the older database files with Access 97 without first converting the files to the newer format.

To do this, open the older Access database in Access and the Convert/Open Database dialog box will open. If you choose Convert Database, the file is automatically changed to Office 97 format, and you have full use of 97 features, but there's no going back to the older format (which means that older versions won't open it). However, if you choose Open Database, you can view the database and add records, but you can't change the design of tables, queries, and so on.

USING HELP AND THE OFFICE ASSISTANT

 I would really like another Office Assistant animated icon. The paper clip is driving me nuts!

Easy to do! Office 97 comes with additional Assistant animated icons. To select another Assistant, follow these steps:

1. If the Office Assistant is displayed on the screen, right-click it for a menu, as shown here:

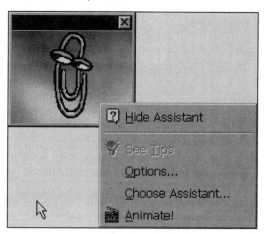

2. Select Choose Assistant and then select the Gallery tab.

3. Using the Next and Back commands, find the animated icon you prefer from these choices:

4. Click OK to select one.

 Note: Two of the Assistants (Mother Earth and Genius) require 256 colors. These two are available with the CD version of Office 97 or can be downloaded from Microsoft's Web page, as described below.

If you do not like any of the animated Office Assistant icons available with Office 97, you can download other animated and nonanimated Assistants from the Microsoft Office Web site. Follow these steps:

1. From the Help menu, select *Microsoft on the Web.*

2. Select Microsoft Home Page.

3. Click freestuff, as shown here:

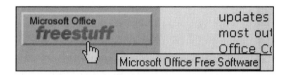

4. You may then be led through the process of registering with Microsoft. Follow the instructions given. You will need a password, your Internet name, and your name and address.

5. When you are finished with the registration, click Office Assistants for a list of Assistants. You can choose one or more to download to your computer.

Tip: From this same Web site, you can also download an animated cursor, sounds, and a screen-capture utility for creating movies.

Sometimes the Office Assistant is on the screen and sometimes not. How can I display the Office Assistant when I want it?

On the right of the Standard toolbar is the Office Assistant icon. Click it and the Office Assistant will appear, as shown here:

Tip: When you want to *hide* the Office Assistant, right-click it and select Hide Assistant.

? **When I place my cursor on an icon in a toolbar, I see no label showing what the icon does. I know this feature exists. How do I get it for Office 97?**

You must turn on the Toolbar ScreenTips with these steps:

1. From the View menu, select Toolbars, Customize, and click the Options tab.

2. Click *Show ScreenTips on toolbars* to turn on the feature as shown here:

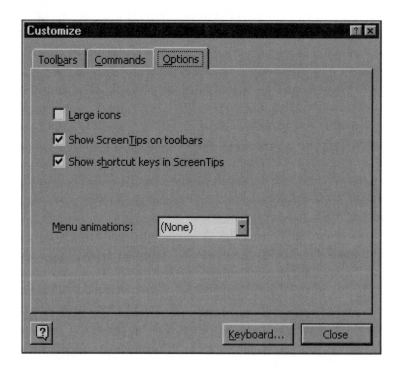

? **I like to use the shortcut keys but often forget what they are. Is there any help in Office for reminders for shortcut keys?**

To add the shortcut keys to the screen icon labels, as shown here,

follow these steps:

1. Right-click the Office Assistant icon in the toolbar.
2. Click Customize and then select the Options tab.
3. Place a check mark next to *Show shortcut keys in ScreenTips*.
4. Click Close.

> *Note:* Since you cannot customize dialog boxes in Outlook, this feature is not available there.

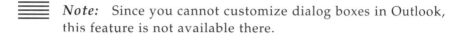 **I am finding that the Office Assistant frequently gets in the way. It is always asking to help when I don't want it, although there are times when I do find it helpful. How can I be more selective about when the Office Assistant appears?**

Office Assistant allows you to select some of the times when the Assistant is to appear. Follow these steps:

1. Right-click on the Assistant and select Options.

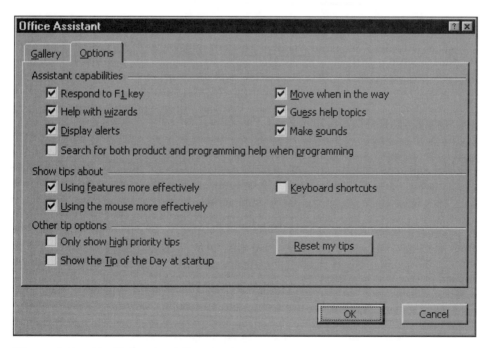

Figure 2-7:   Modifying the Office Assistant's "behavior"

2. Select the Options tab. You will see the dialog box shown in Figure 2-7.

3. Remove the check marks next to the situations in which you do not want the Assistant to appear.

MISCELLANEOUS

?

Sometimes I get a BEEP when recording a macro using the mouse. What's the problem?

The Macro Recorder cannot record some mouse movements. When you hear the error sound, try using keyboard commands instead of the mouse.

?

I thought the Spelling Checker was a shared component of Office, but when I add a new word to my custom spelling dictionary and then use another application, the second application does not recognize the word added to the dictionary.

You must close the first application before the added word can be recognized by other Office applications. The custom dictionary is updated with new words at the time the application is closed.

chapter

3 Answers!

Writing
with Word

Answer Topics!

(handwritten notes:) MYL HD SK7   M TRAINING   WS# 21325g.

Word @ a Glance

Word is the application in the Office Professional 97 package that is used for word processing. It is a sophisticated program that helps you produce the following:

➪ **Documents,** which can be created using automatic features such as AutoText, AutoCorrect, and AutoFormat. *AutoText* allows you to save a block of text that you use frequently (for example, an address or a closing), then insert it automatically by typing the name you gave the block and pressing F3. *AutoCorrect* corrects misspelled words automatically as you type. When you press the spacebar after misspelling a word, it is corrected automatically. Only words listed in the AutoCorrect dialog box are corrected; however, you can add your own words to this list. *AutoFormat* is used in two ways. You can format an entire document automatically, or you can automatically add formatting such as bullets, numbering, tables, and bold and underlining to text as you type.

Creating a document consists of typing text, inserting graphics or other objects, creating tables, formatting text with borders, and creating any other formatting that you want. The document is then named and saved by choosing Save As from the File menu, typing a filename of any length, and clicking the Save button.

☞ **Templates,** which are files that contain styles, graphics, and text that can be used to create documents. To create a template, choose New from the File menu, select the Blank Document icon, click Template in the Create New box, and click OK. In the Template window, you can create styles, insert graphic objects, and enter text. Save the template the same way you save a document, except save it as a Document Template rather than as a Word Document. Templates are stored by default in the Templates folder in the Microsoft Office folder.

☞ **Letters, labels, and envelopes,** which can be produced using the Mail Merge function. Choose Mail Merge from the Tools menu, and the Mail Merge Helper will help you produce any of these.

☞ **Newsletters, brochures, and flyers,** which can be enhanced by inserting a variety of pictures, ClipArt, WordArt, and automatic shapes. To create a newsletter, you can use the Newsletter Wizard in the Publications tab—choose New from the File menu and click the Publications tab. If this tab is not displayed, you can rerun Setup and reinstall Word, choosing to install the necessary components.

☞ **Master document files,** which can combine several smaller files. For example, if you are writing a book and you save each chapter in a separate file, you can then combine these files in a master document in order to produce a table of contents and an index that includes topics from all the chapters. The master document function also allows several people on a network to work on documents simultaneously. Choose Master Document from the View menu to work with these files.

☞ **Tracking functions,** which allow you to mark text, add highlighting, and insert comments. You can then create several edited versions of the same document, compare the versions, and quickly select or accept the marked changes. The Track Changes function is listed on the Tools menu.

CREATING AND SAVING
DOCUMENTS AND TEMPLATES

 When I first used Word 97 I was surprised that I didn't see that the document was being saved automatically as I had seen in previous versions. I looked in the Save tab in the Options dialog box and confirmed that fast save, AutoRecover, and background save were turned on. How can I be sure that autosave is working?

You were right to check the Save tab to be sure these features were selected. Also click the File Locations tab in the Options dialog box to see if a folder has been assigned for the AutoRecover files. If there is no folder in which to store these files, you will not see any indication that saving is taking place. To assign a folder for these files, do the following:

1. Choose Options from the Tools menu.
2. Click the File Locations tab.
3. Select AutoRecover files and click the Modify button to go to the Modify Location dialog box.
4. Click the down arrow in the *Look in* box and select the folder where you want the files to be saved. See the example in Figure 3-1.

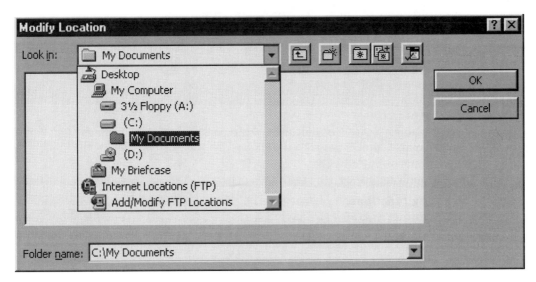

Figure 3-1:   The Modify Location dialog box

5. When you are done, click OK to return to the File
   Locations tab and click Close to return to the document.

? **In our office, we have created several different printed forms that can be filled in on paper, but we would like to create a form that can be filled in online. Can this be done? If so, how?**

Creating an online form is very similar to creating a printed
form that is filled in on paper, except that an online form
should be created as a template rather than as a document.
This allows users to fill in the form without changing the
original design. To do this,

1. Choose New from the File menu and click the
   General tab.

2. In the Create New box, select Template, as shown in
   Figure 3-2.

3. Click OK.

4. Create the form as you usually do, entering text,
   graphics, borders, and tables that may be needed.

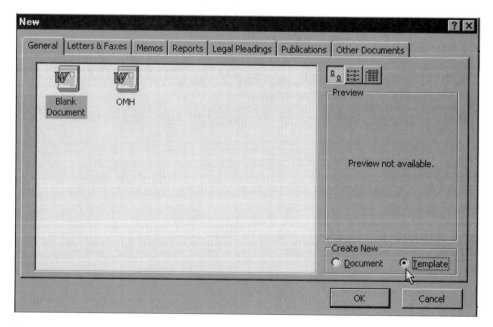

Figure 3-2:   The New dialog box

However, in an online form, you can insert fields that make it easy to fill in the form using the computer:

▷ **Text Form** fields, in which users can type text when filling in the form or you can enter default text so users do not have to type in text.

▷ **Drop-Down Form** fields, which display a series of choices. Users can scroll through the list to see all options and select the one they want.

▷ **Check Box Form** fields, which allow the person filling in the form to click a check box to turn it on.

To see a more detailed explanation of how to insert these, see the sidebar "Inserting Form Fields."

5. Display the Forms toolbar and click any of the form field buttons to insert the fields you want.

6. When done, click the Protect Form button, as shown here, to prevent changes from being made.

7. Save the template.

   To use the form,

1. Open a new document and select your form template as you would any other template. Your insertion point will be automatically positioned in the first field (if Protect Form was turned on when the form was created).

2. Fill in the field and press TAB to move to the next field, continuing until the form is filled in.

   ▷ When you are in a text box, type the text appropriate for that field. The box will expand to accommodate the text.

   ▷ When you come to a check box, type a character (*x*, for example) to fill in the box.

   ▷ When you come to a drop-down menu, click the down arrow to see all of the available choices and select the one you want.

3. When you are done, print the form. You can then save it as a document if you like, or you can close it without saving.

Inserting Form Fields

Display the Forms toolbar by right-clicking on any toolbar and selecting Forms.

Inserting a text form field

1. Move the insertion point to the spot where you want to place the field.
2. Click the Text Form Field button shown here. A shaded box is displayed. The size of the box will change as text is typed in when you use the form.

Inserting a drop-down form field

1. Move the insertion point to the spot where you want to place the field.
2. Click the Drop-Down Field Form button, shown here. A shaded box is displayed.

3. Double-click the shaded box to open the Drop-Down Form Field Options dialog box.
4. Type an entry in the *Drop-down item* box and click the Add button. The entry is then displayed in the *Items in drop-down list* box to the right:

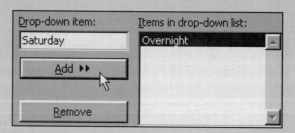

5. Repeat entering and adding items.

6. When you are done, click OK. The first entry is displayed in the box. When the form template is being filled in, the drop-down list will be displayed if the down arrow at the right of the box is clicked.

Inserting a check box form field

1. Move the insertion point to the location where you want to place the field.

2. Click the Check Box Form Field button as shown here. A shaded box will be inserted.

I do not see any templates that are exactly what I want in order to produce the types of documents that I sometimes create in Word. Can I edit the existing templates? Or can I create my own template?

You can do both. To edit an existing template, use the following steps:

1. Choose New from the File menu and click the tab that contains the type of template you want to edit.

2. Select a template, click Template in the Create New box (as was shown in Figure 3-2), and click OK.

3. Make your changes to the template and choose Save As from the File menu. If you want to keep the original template, give the new template a different name. If you save the template in the Templates folder, the next time you use it it will be located in the General tab rather than in the tab containing the original template that you opened and edited.

To create a new template, do the following:

1. Choose New from the File menu.

2. Select Blank Document, click Template in the Create New box, and click OK. A new template window is opened and contains only the styles from the Normal.dot template.

3. Create your styles and enter any text and graphics that you may want.

4. When done, choose Save As from the File menu.

5. Name the template and click the Save button. The next time you want to use this template, it will appear in the General tab in the New dialog box.

 ## How can I change the **default folder** for my Word documents?

≡ *Note:* Changing the default folder for documents in Word does not change the default folder for other Office 97 documents. If you click Open Office Document in the Office 97 toolbar, the default folder remains set at My Documents.

The default folder for all Office 97 documents is the My Document folder in Drive C; however, depending upon how you work you can easily change it by doing the following:

1. Click Tools in the menu bar and choose Options.

2. Click the File Locations tab to display the list of items and the folders in which they are currently stored.

3. Select Documents in the *File types* list, if it is not already selected.

4. Click the Modify button to go to the Modify Location dialog box (shown in Figure 3-1).

5. Click the down arrow in the *Look in* box and select the directory or folder you want.

•••••• *Tip:* If you double-click a drive, all the folders in that drive will be displayed. Then you can double-click a folder to display folders within it.

6. Click OK to return to the File Locations tab and click Close to return to the document window.

•••••• *Tip:* If you want to create a new folder in a different directory, select the directory you want in the Modify Locations dialog box. Then click the Create New Folder button, type a name for the folder, and click OK. To make this new folder the default folder for Word documents, select the name of the new folder, click OK to return to the File Locations tab, and click Close to return to the document window.

? **If I want to create a new document, when should I use the New button in Word and when should I use the New Office Document button in the Office toolbar?**

If you are working in Word, clicking the New button is the quickest way to open a new document window; however, it does not give you the option of choosing a different template. The Normal.dot template is attached by default. To open a new document window with a different template, choose New from the File menu, select the template you want from any of the tabs that are displayed, and click OK.

If you click the New Office Document button in the Office toolbar, you can select any type of document in any of the other Office applications—spreadsheet, database, presentation, or Word document.

? **Should I use a template or a wizard to create a document? It seems to me that a wizard is much easier to use.**

Using a template is faster than using a wizard, and with a wizard you are sometimes limited in the choices with which you open a document. When you open a new document with a template, you go directly to the document window and begin creating your document.

The wizard leads you through creating the document step by step, which can be very helpful. It provides you with various choices of styles, layouts, and information to be included. When done with the step-by-step procedure, you click Finish and the new document is opened. Depending upon the choices you make, new styles will be available, as well as the overall layout of the document. You can, however, make any changes you want when using a wizard, and then save the document as you usually do.

ENTERING AND EDITING TEXT

? **Is there a way to change misspelled words quickly that have been marked by Word?**

You can do one of two things, both of which are fairly quick:

▷ Move the insertion point to the marked word and right-click to display the list of spelling and grammar options that pertain to this word.

▷ Move the insertion point to the misspelled word and double-click the Spelling & Grammar Status button in the Status bar:

A list of options will be displayed, and you can select the one you want.

? Can I **create AutoText items** for my own logo and address? How do I do this?

The easiest way to work with AutoText is to first display the AutoText toolbar. To do this, right-click on any toolbar and select AutoText. The AutoText toolbar looks like this:

To create your own item in AutoText,

1. Type the text and, if you like, insert any picture, WordArt, or other type of graphic.

2. Select the text and graphic.

3. Click the New button in the AutoText toolbar to display the Create AutoText dialog box:

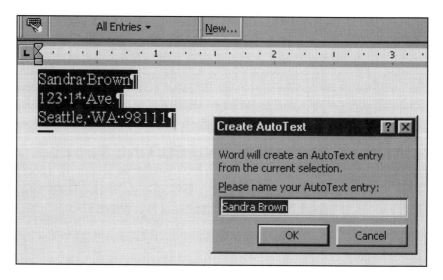

█████ *Tip:*   Another way to display the Create AutoText dialog box is to choose AutoText from the Insert menu and click New.

> The first several words of the selected text will be displayed in the dialog box; however, if the selection begins with a logo or other graphic, the text box will be blank.

4. Either accept the suggested name that is displayed by clicking OK or type a short name for the AutoText entry, and then click OK.

❓ I like the feature of having misspelled words marked as I type; however, I do not always want **grammatical errors marked**. Is there any way I can avoid this?

Yes, choose Spelling & Grammar from the Tools menu, and click the Options button in the Spelling & Grammar dialog box. The options that can be turned off or on are shown in Figure 3-3. Click *Check grammar as you type* to turn it off, and click OK. If you turn off both the spelling and grammar checking as you type, the Spelling and Grammar icon will not be displayed in the Status Bar.

█████ *Tip:*   You can also right-click the Spelling & Grammar Status icon in the Status bar and then click Hide Grammatical Errors. If you select Options, the dialog box in Figure 3-3 will be displayed.

❓ Is there a way to **insert AutoText quickly?**

A quick way to insert an AutoText entry is to move the insertion point to the place where you want to enter it, type the name of the entry, and press F3. If you are not sure of the name, click the AutoText button in the toolbar, select the entry from the list displayed in the AutoText tab, and click the Insert button.

█████ *Tip:*   Another quick way to insert text and graphics is to save it as AutoCorrect. To save an entry this way, select the text and choose AutoCorrect from the Tools menu. The selected text is displayed in the With text box. Type a short name in the Replace box, turn on Formatted Text if you want to save any

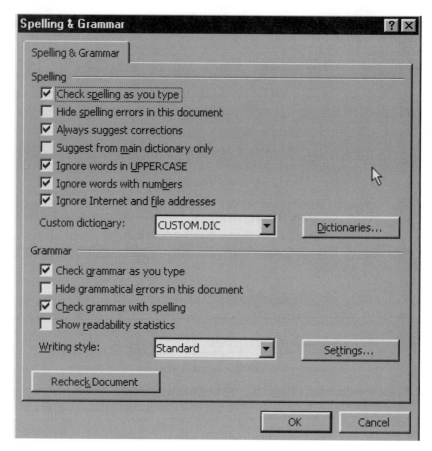

Figure 3-3:   The Spelling and Grammar options

formatting with the text, click Add, and click OK. When you type the name of the entry and press the spacebar, the text is inserted automatically.

? I work with large documents and would like to move quickly through them to see topics that are included; however, I do not usually use Outline view. I have heard that Word 97 has other ways to move around in a document easily. What are they and how do I use them?

Document Map is one of the new features, and the Select Browse button and scroll box in the vertical scroll bar are also available.

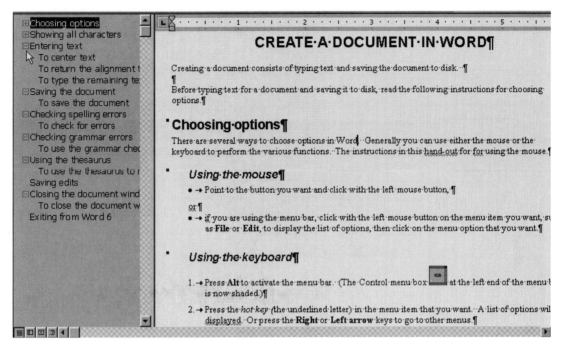

Figure 3-4:   The Document Map pane

To use the Document Map, click the Document Map button shown here:

When it is selected, an additional pane is displayed to the left of the document, as shown in Figure 3-4. This pane contains the current headings in the document. You can click any heading in this pane to move directly to that location in the document.

You can also change the display of headings in the pane:

▷ To collapse subheadings, click the minus sign that is displayed next to the heading.

▷ To expand subheadings, click the plus sign.

To remove the pane from view, click the Document Map button again.

Note: If you have formatted paragraphs in your document with styles other than heading levels, these paragraphs may also be displayed in the Document Map pane.

To use the Select Browse Object button to quickly move through the document, do this:

1. Click the Select Browse Object button in the vertical scroll bar at the right of the document window. A box showing various options will be displayed:

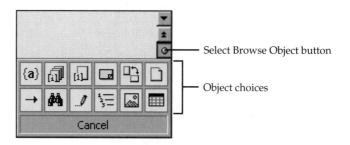

Select Browse Object button

Object choices

2. Move your pointer across each of the pictures to display a description of each type of object.

3. Click the one you want.

4. Click the Previous or Next buttons, shown here, to move immediately to that type of object.

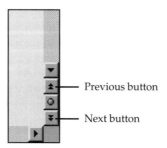

Previous button

Next button

To use the scroll box, do either of the following.

▷ Drag the box up or down in the vertical scroll bar. A page number will be displayed as you drag up or down, as well as the heading for the section in which the page is located.

▷ Click above or below the scroll box to move up or down one screen length.

? **I like to see my document in Print Preview to confirm overall layout of my document, because I can see up to six pages at once. However, I wish I could make changes such as adjusting page endings there rather than in Page Layout view, which only shows two pages at a time. Can I use Print Preview to edit text?**

Yes, you can. In the Print Preview window, click the Magnifier button, shown here, to turn it off. Turning off the magnifier changes the mouse pointer to an I-beam. Then you can make any editing changes you want. Click the Magnifier button again to leave editing and return to magnification.

? **I created a document in which I pressed ENTER three times to insert two blank lines after each paragraph. Later I decided the document would look better if there were only one blank line after each paragraph. Is there any way I can use the Replace function to make this change quickly?**

Yes, you can replace special characters by doing the following:

1. Choose Replace from the Edit menu.

2. Click the More button to display additional options if necessary.

3. With your insertion point in the *Find what* box, click the Special button and select Paragraph Mark. Do this three times to insert three characters in the *Find what* box, as shown in Figure 3-5.

≡ *Note:* The Special button is also available in the Find dialog box.

4. Tab to the *Replace with* text box, click Special, and select Paragraph Mark twice.

⋯ *Tip:* Once you know how any of the special characters appear in the *Find what* box after you have selected them from the Special menu, you can type them in directly; for example, ^p (SHIFT-6, *p*) for each time ENTER was pressed.

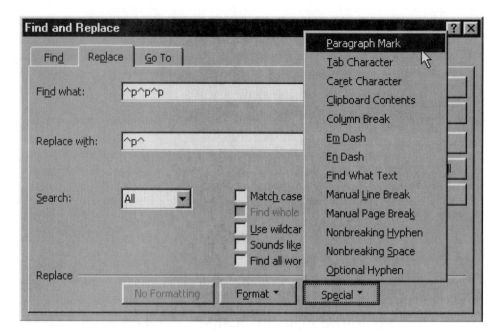

Figure 3-5:   The Replace dialog box

5. Click Find Next, and click Replace. If you are certain that you want this replacement throughout the document, click Replace All.

Tip: If you want to find or replace only formatting, click the Format button, and select the type of formatting you want. You can also instruct Word to find or replace text when it is formatted in a certain way. For example, if you wanted to locate a word only when it is formatted in bold, enter the word in the *Find what* box, click the Format button, and choose the type of formatting. The formatting characteristic will appear in the area below the *Find what* box.

? I notice that the view buttons are not displayed when I'm in Online Layout view. How do I restore them to the bottom of the window?

They are not available in Online Layout view. Click the View menu and choose any of the other types of views— Normal, Page Layout, or Outline. All of the view buttons will then be displayed.

Tip: If the button for Master Document view is not displayed, you can choose Customize from the Tools menu, select the toolbar in which you want to place the button, and click the Commands tab. In the Commands tab, select View from the list of Categories, and then locate and drag the Master Document view button to any position on the toolbar.

FORMATTING TEXT

I am confused about using AutoFormat. When I choose AutoFormat in the Format menu and click Options in the AutoFormat box, Automatic Bulleted Lists is selected in both the AutoFormat tab and in the *AutoFormat as you type* tab. However, when I type items in a list, they are not automatically formatted with bullets. How do I do this without using the bullet button?

Type any of the characters listed below, followed by a tab and text, and press ENTER. A different type of bullet will be inserted when ENTER is pressed, depending upon the character that you typed. The list below shows the results of typing different characters:

- Type an asterisk to display a round bullet.
- Type two hyphens to display a boxed bullet.
- Type one hyphen to display a hyphen.
- Type a greater than sign (>) to display a pointer.
- Type a hyphen and a greater than sign (->) to display an arrow.
- Type an equal sign and a greater than sign (=>) to display an outline arrow.

Note: The AutoFormat tab is used to turn on or off the features that are included in AutoFormatting, which automatically formats the entire document. The *AutoFormat as you type* tab is used to turn on or off the features that are automatically formatted as you enter text in a document.

?   **I am having a problem with some of automatic formatting's "overcorrections"; for example, typing text that begins with a capital letter followed by a period, a tab, and descriptive text. If I type "B. (TAB) Birth date" and press ENTER, Word displays a "C." on the following line. I want the next line after B. to be M. (TAB) Married. How do I do this?**

Typing a period following the capital letter automatically formats text in an outline form. You can do one of two things to avoid this:

➤ If you do not type a period following the letter, a subsequent letter will not be displayed when you press ENTER.

➤ If you want to keep the period, then you need to make changes to the Automatic Formatting options.

To turn off options that automatically format text,

1. Choose AutoFormat from the Format menu.

2. Click the Options button in the AutoFormat dialog box.

3. Click the *AutoFormat as you type* tab.

4. Turn off *Automatic numbered lists,* click OK, and click Close.

Caution: If you started typing the list and then decided to change the formatting using the steps just given, the outline formatting will be continued until you press ENTER twice after the last item. It is best to delete all the previous letters (you don't want them anyway), make the change in the AutoFormat box, and then type your list.

?   **I tried to use the mouse to change margins in the ruler, but I couldn't move anything but the indent markers. How do I use the mouse to change the margins?**

You cannot change margins using the mouse when you are in Normal view. You need to be in either Page Layout view or in Print Preview.

➤ To change margins in Page Layout view, point to the margin you want to change. A double-sided arrow will be displayed, as well as a ScreenTip that identifies the margin. Drag the margin to a new position. Notice that in Page Layout view a vertical ruler is displayed, which allows you to change the top and bottom margins, as well as a horizontal ruler to change the left and right margins.

▷ To change margins in Print Preview, click the View Ruler button as shown here:

Then point to the area directly above the margin— a double-sided arrow will be displayed. Drag the margin to a new position.

I have a list of numbered paragraphs. If I insert a note or comment that is not numbered, and I apply the numbering to the paragraph following the note, the numbering will begin with the number 1. Is there a way to change numbers in numbered lists?

Yes; do the following:

1. Move your insertion point to the list item whose number you want to change.
2. Choose Bullets and Numbering from the Format menu.
3. In the Bullets and Numbering dialog box, click the Numbering tab, and select Continue Previous List.
4. Click OK to return to the document window.

Tip: If you right-click on any bulleted or numbered item, a pop-up menu is displayed, and you can choose Bullets and Numbering to go to that dialog box.

I have problems using the indent markers. If I inadvertently drag them too far to the left or right, it changes the position of my text. Is it possible to restore it? How?

Drag the indent markers back to the position you want, or click the Undo button to return the indent markers to their previous position. Then, in the horizontal scroll bar shown here, click the left or right arrow or drag the scroll box and adjust the display on the screen.

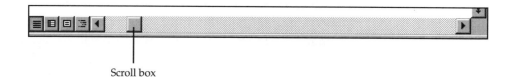

Scroll box

? **I frequently use the Shrink to Fit option in Print Preview, but there are times when the formatting changes are not what I want. For example, sometimes the font that is selected in Shrink to Fit is too small to be practical. How can I change back to the original formatting?**

Click the Undo button or choose Undo Shrink to Fit from the Edit menu. However, you must do this before making any other editing changes, otherwise this option will not be available to you. If this is the case, you will have to select the text and make any formatting changes that you want by using the Format menu.

Note: Shrink to Fit is a feature available in the Print Preview window that automatically reformats your document so it fits on a page. For example, if you have a document with text that extends to a second page, but you want it to be on one page, you can go to Print Preview and click the Shrink to Fit button, as shown here.

Formatting changes that are necessary to accomplish this are automatically applied to your document. If you have three pages, Shrink to Fit will reformat it so that the text will fit on two pages.

I created several styles to use in a document, and I would like to use these same styles in a different document, but I did not create a new template for the first document. Is there any way I can transfer styles in the Normal.dot template to other documents?

Open the document that does contain the styles you want to use and do the following:

1. Choose Style from the Format menu, and click the Organizer button.

2. In the Organizer dialog box, shown in Figure 3-6, a list of styles in the opened document is displayed at the left, and the styles in the Normal.dot template are displayed at the right. Select the styles in the box at the left and click Copy to add them to the Normal.dot template.

3. Click Close. When you open a new document window using the Normal.dot template, the added styles will be included.

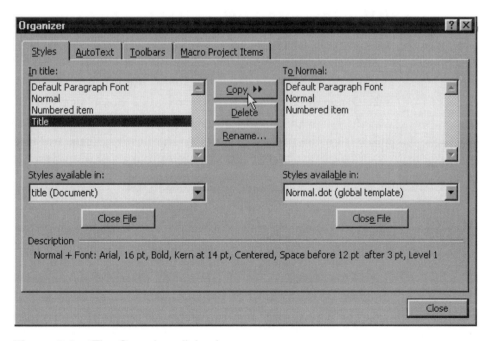

Figure 3-6:   The Organizer dialog box

INSERTING PICTURES AND OBJECTS

? **When I tried to insert .CGM ClipArt I was unable to; I got a message that Word was unable to import the file type. What can I do about this?**

You are probably missing the converter. To be able to use these files, run Setup and select the .cgm file type in the Graphics Converts option.

Tip: If you want to remove a picture from the Microsoft Clip Gallery, select it and press DELETE. This will remove the picture from the gallery, but it will remain in its original folder on the hard disk.

? **I have created a document that contains linked text boxes in which I have typed text that continues from one text box to the next one, which is on a different page. After I entered other text in the document, I wanted to place some of it in linked text boxes also. Is it possible to move existing text into a linked text box? If so, how do you do it?**

Yes, you can do this. Use the following steps:

1. Choose Text Box from the Insert menu.

2. Draw the boxes at the approximate position where you will want them in the final copy.

3. Move the insertion point to the first text box and click the Link button in the Text Box toolbar as shown here.

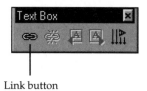

Link button

If the Text Box toolbar is not displayed, select the text box, then right-click on any toolbar and select Text Box.

4. The pointer becomes a pitcher. Move to the second text box and click to create the link. (The pitcher "pours its contents" into the second text box.)

5. Select the text to be placed in the text boxes and click Cut. Then move the insertion point to the first box and

click Paste. It may take a few seconds for the move to be completed.

6. To adjust the placement of the text boxes, point to them to show the four-sided arrow and drag each box to an appropriate position.

How do I **remove a border around a text box?**

You can easily remove the border as follows:

1. Display the Drawing toolbar.

2. Select the text box and click the Line Style button, shown here:

Line Style button

3. Select More Lines to go to the Format Text Box dialog box.

4. In the Line section, click the down arrow in the Color box to display a list of options, and select No Line. See Figure 3-7.

5. Click OK to return to the document window. Your box is now formatted without the border around it. You can't see the box, but if you click the area where it is located, handles will be displayed.

The AutoShape function is great; however, I want to type text within an autoshape I have created. Can I do this? If so, how?

First insert the autoshape you want. See the sidebar "Inserting an Autoshape" for specific instructions for doing this. Then use the following steps to insert text in the autoshape.

1. Select the autoshape and right-click it to show the shortcut menu. See Figure 3-8.

2. Click on Add Text and type text in the shape. You can type text in any autoshape except a line or a freeform shape.

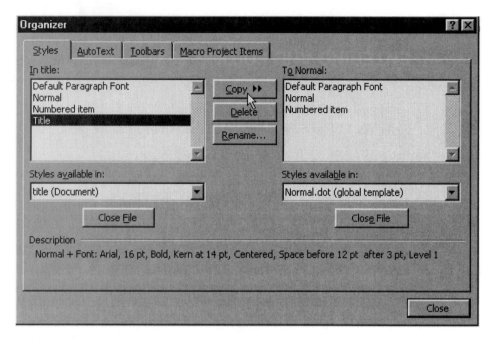

Figure 3-7:   The Format Text Box dialog box

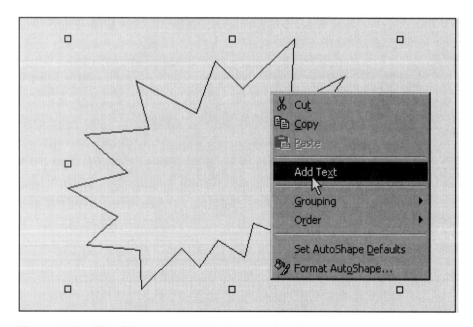

Figure 3-8:   The Shortcut menu for an autoshape

To edit the text, just right-click the AutoShape (not the text) to show the Shortcut menu, and select Edit Text.

• • • • • • • • • •

Inserting an AutoShape

1. Choose Picture from the Insert menu, and click AutoShapes. The AutoShapes toolbar is displayed, as well as the Drawing toolbar at the bottom of the window.

Tip: You can also right-click on any toolbar to display the toolbar menu and select Drawing.

2. You can use either of the following methods to select a shape:

  ☞ If you use the AutoShapes toolbar, click on a category and select a shape.

  ☞ If you use the Drawing toolbar, click on AutoShapes to display a list of categories. Select a category, and click the AutoShape you want to insert.

3. The pointer becomes a crosshair. Point to the place to insert the shape and drag to the size you want.

Note: To change the size of the AutoShape, select it to display the handles—these are eight small squares. Point to any of them and drag a side or corner to the size you want.

USING TABLES AND BORDERS

?

When I choose AutoFormat from the Format menu and click the Options button, I notice that Borders and Tables in *Automatic Formatting as you type* are turned on. How do you use these features?

To insert borders as you type, enter any of the following:

  ☞ Type three or more hyphens (-) and press ENTER to place a line above a paragraph.

  ☞ Type three or more underscores (_) and press ENTER to place a thick line above a paragraph.

  ☞ Type three or more asterisks (*) and press ENTER to place a dotted line above a paragraph.

▷ Type three or more number signs (#) and press ENTER to place a decorative line above a paragraph.

▷ Type three or more tildes (~) and press ENTER to place a wavy line above a paragraph.

▷ Type three or more equal signs (=) and press ENTER to place a double line above a paragraph.

Examples of each are shown in Figure 3-9.

To insert a table automatically as you type, do the following.

1. Type a plus sign (+) for the left side of the table.

2. Type hyphens (------) for the width of the first column.

3. Type a plus sign to begin the second column.

4. Type hyphens for the width of the second column.

5. Repeat for the entire table; for example:

    + -------- + ---------------- + --------

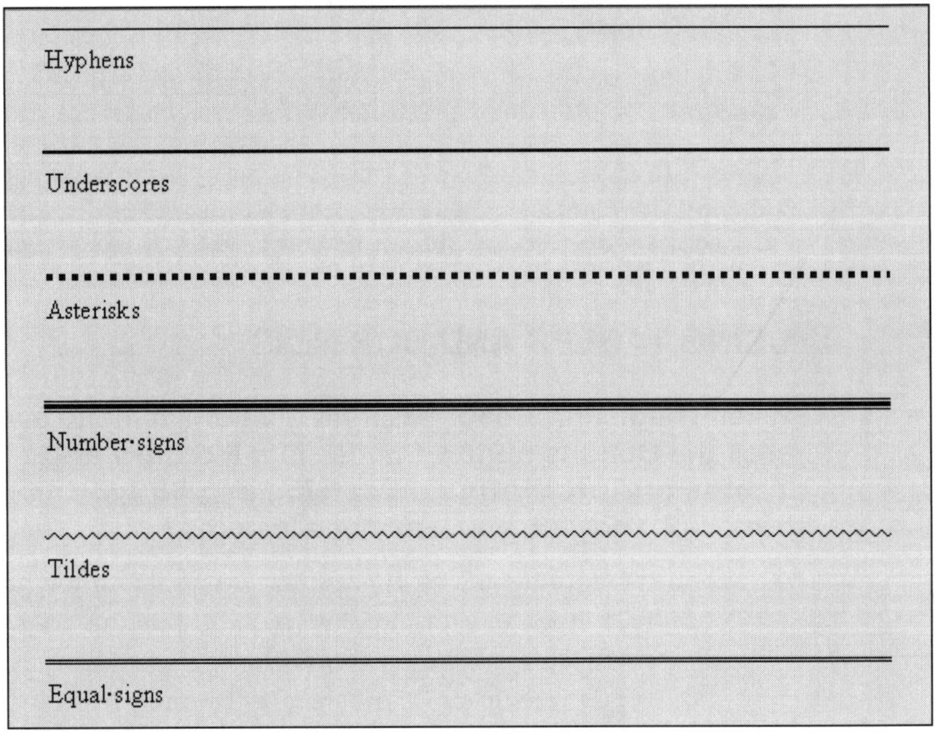

Figure 3-9:   Borders created with automatic formatting

6. To end the table, type a plus sign and press ENTER. Our example would look like this:

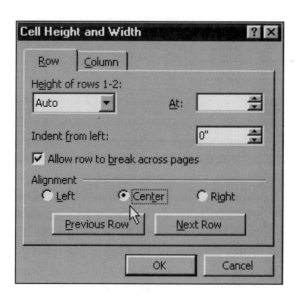

Tip: To add additional rows to the table, move the insertion point to the last cell on the right and press TAB.

? **I used the Insert Table button to create a table, and after reducing the size of the table I wanted to center it across the page. I selected it and clicked on the Center button, but that only centered the text in each cell. How can I center an entire table quickly?**

Move the insertion point to any cell in the table. Choose Cell Height and Width from the Table menu, then click Center in the Alignment section of the dialog box.

Click OK to return to the document window. Your table will be centered across the page.

?   **Recently, before converting text to a table, I selected several paragraphs. I wanted each paragraph to be in its own cell; however, the text was divided into many cells. How can I avoid this?**

To convert paragraph text to a table so that each entire paragraph is in a cell,

1. Select all of the paragraph text that you want in a table.

2. Choose Convert Text to Table from the Table menu.

3. Select the number of columns you want, if you want more than one.

4. In the Convert Text to Table dialog box there are several options in the *Separate text at* box. To keep each paragraph in one cell, turn on the Paragraphs option:

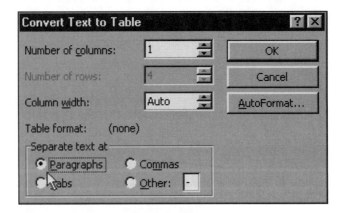

5. Click OK.

?   **I put a table with formulas in a template I created that would multiply a value in one cell by the value in another cell. When I used this template and entered values in various cells, I did not see the results of the calculation when I moved to the cell that contained the formula. What did I do wrong that prevented the formula from performing the calculation?**

To see the results of the calculation, move the insertion point to the cell containing the formula and press F9. If the cells containing formulas are in the same row or in the same column, you can select all of them and press F9.

Tip: If you only want to add values in a row or column, you can move the insertion point to the cell where the results are to be inserted and click the Sum button shown here. The result will be displayed immediately.

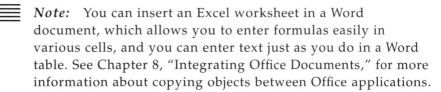

Sum button

Note: You can insert an Excel worksheet in a Word document, which allows you to enter formulas easily in various cells, and you can enter text just as you do in a Word table. See Chapter 8, "Integrating Office Documents," for more information about copying objects between Office applications.

MAIL AND OTHER MERGING

I want to print an organization name in uppercase that is on a line by itself in a merged document, but I do not want the name in uppercase in the data document because I will use it in other places where I want it in lowercase with initial caps. I tried to format the field in uppercase, but each time I merged, the formatting immediately changed back to lowercase. How can I format a field in uppercase?

When a field is on a line by itself, selecting it is different than if the field is within a line of text.

▷ If a field is on a line by itself and you want to change the case, select not only the field but also the chevrons that enclose it and the following paragraph mark. It is essential that the paragraph mark be selected. Then to change the case, choose Font from the Format menu, select *All caps,* and click OK.

Tip: You have to use the Font dialog box rather than the Change Case option to change the case so that the change will be permanent.

▷ If the field is within a line, select the field name and chevrons. Then choose Font from the Format menu, select *All caps,* and click OK.

Note: When you select a field in order to change the formatting, click the field name, then drag across it to include the chevrons. Notice that the field is then a shade darker than when you click it once. The darker shade indicates that you have selected it.

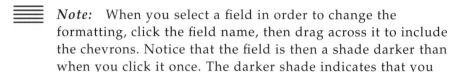

When I typed a letter and created an envelope for it, the address that I had typed at the top of the letter was displayed in the recipient's address box and the return address box was blank—the recipient's address was not displayed in the Envelope dialog box. Isn't there a way to insert addresses automatically?

To insert your address automatically in the Return Address box, choose Options from the Tools menu, click the User Information tab, and type your address in the *Mailing address* box. Then each time you create an envelope, your address will be in the Return Address box.

To insert the recipient's address automatically, move your insertion point to the beginning of the first line of the address. Then choose Envelopes and Labels from the Tools menu. The address will be displayed in the Recipient's address box.

I saved my merge output to a document file, then opened it using the Merged Documents command in the Tools menu, which I assumed is used for this purpose. When I did this, I saw a prompt: "Merged documents contain unmarked changes. Do you want to merge up to the first untracked changes?" What does this have to do with merged documents?

The Merged Document option is used to combine into one document the edits of documents that have been reviewed by several users. Generally these edited documents will be different versions of the same document that have been saved as separate files. These documents contain editing marks, highlighted text, and comments. Refer in this chapter to the questions in the "Collaborative Editing" section pertaining to editing and saving different versions of a document.

Mail Merge is used to send boilerplate documents, envelopes, and labels to a large mailing list. When you choose Mail Merge from the Tools menu, the Mail Merge Helper guides you through this process. See the sidebar "Mail Merge Helper" for more information.

● ● ● ● ● ● ● ● ● ● ●

Mail Merge Helper

To use the Mail Merge Helper,

1. Open a new document window, if necessary, and choose Mail Merge from the Tools menu. The Mail Merge Helper is displayed as shown in Figure 3-10.

2. Click the Create button under *Main document* and select the type of document you want to create.

3. Click Active Window to use the current window for the main document. If you click New Main Document, a new document window will be opened. The Get Data button is now highlighted.

4. Click Get Data and select Create Data Source if you need to create a new data document. If you already have a data document available, click Open Data Source and select the document you want, or you can extract data from one of several address books you might have by choosing Use Address Book.

5. If you click Create Data Source, a list of field names is displayed at the right. They will automatically be included in your data document; however, you can remove any of them. To do this, select the field you do not want, and click the Remove Field Name button. To add a new field name, type the name in the *Field name* box at the left and click Add Field Name. If you enter a space in a field name, you will not be able to use it—no spaces in field names are allowed.

6. When done, click OK. The Save As dialog box is displayed. Type a filename for the data document and click Save.

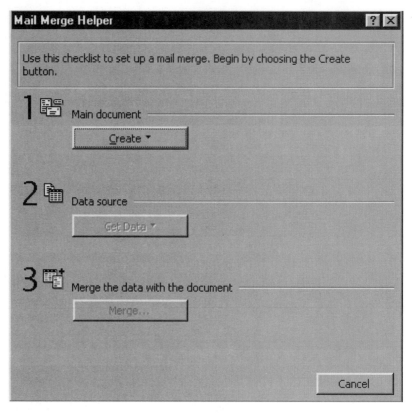

Figure 3-10:   The Mail Merge Helper

7. You can now go to either the data file or the main document; however, for our purposes here, click the Edit Data Source button. A data form will be displayed, and you can enter personal information for each record. Press ENTER after each entry, and also press ENTER when done with the first record to go to the next record. The number of records is displayed at the bottom of the dialog box. When you have typed in all entries, click OK.

8. You are now in the main document window. Choose Save As from the File menu, type a filename, and click Save. This is a good idea so that edits can be saved easily.

9. Now you can type the boilerplate text in the main document and insert fields. For example, if you are

creating a form letter, move the insertion point to the place where the inside address will be printed, click the Insert Merge Field button shown in Figure 3-11, and click Title to insert the title field.

Press the space bar once and repeat to insert the field FirstName, and so on. You can insert fields just as you do text—separate them by spaces and press ENTER to move to another line. Also, you can insert one field as many times as necessary in the main document. When you are done, save your changes.

10. In the main document, you can click the Edit Data Source button to switch to the Data Form. If you want to see the entire table, click *View source* in the Data Form dialog box. When you are in the data source table, you can click the Mail Merge Main Document button to switch to that window:

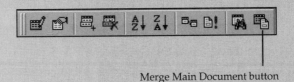

Merge Main Document button

11. In the main document, you can click the View Merged Data button to see what the merged output will look

View Merged Data button   Mail Merge Helper button   Edit Data Source button

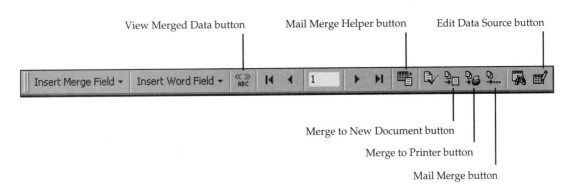

Merge to New Document button

Merge to Printer button

Mail Merge button

Figure 3-11:   The Mail Merge toolbar

like. Click this button again to see the fields. This is not the actual merge.

12. To produce the merged output, you can do one of the following:

➢ Click Merge to New Document to merge the data document with the main document and see the output in a new document window. You can then print the output from there and save the document as a new file. However, if you have a large database, this takes up a lot of disk space, which is not actually necessary as long as you have the main document and the data document.

➢ Click Merge to Printer to send the merged output directly to the printer.

➢ Click Mail Merge. This allows you to customize your merge with the following:

➢ Select to merge only certain records. For example, you can merge only records 10 through 20 using this option. Turn on From and type *10* in the first box and *20* in the second box.

➢ Click Query Options to enter specifications for a query or to sort the data based on select tables. The question on **selecting only certain addresses** gives more information on how to perform queries.

➢ Select to print or not to print blank lines that may be inserted if a field is empty.

13. When the merge is complete, save and close the main document and the data document.

To perform another merge using the same documents, open the main document. When you do this, the data document will be opened too, because it was attached when you created the main document. If you want to select a different data document, open the main document, click the Mail Merge Helper button, click Get Data, select Open a Data Source, and select a different data document.

I do not see any labels that are the size of the labels I usually use in mailings. How can I print custom-sized labels that are not included in the list of supplied labels that come with Word 97?

You can create a customized label by doing the following:

1. Select Envelopes and Labels from the Tools menu and click the Labels tab.

2. Click the Options button and then click the New Label button to go to the New Custom dialog box shown in Figure 3-12.

3. Type a label name and enter new measurements for the label size you want in the various boxes. Notice the Preview changes as you enter new measurements. Be sure to select an appropriate paper size.

4. Click OK when done to return to the Label Option box.

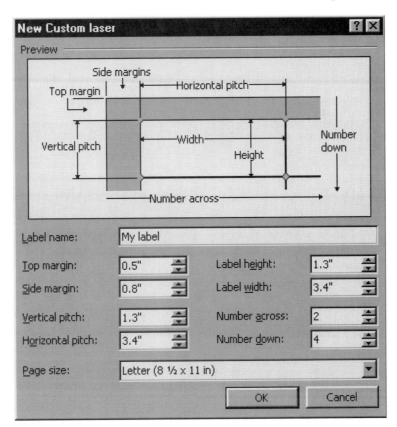

Figure 3-12:   The New Custom dialog box

5. Select the new custom label, now listed in the Product Number box, and click OK.

Tip: If you are not using merge to produce labels and you want to print a page of labels with different addresses on each label, choose Envelopes and Labels from the Tools menu, and click the New Document button in the Label tab. The blank labels will be shown in a new document window, and you can enter addresses in each. Press TAB to move from one label to the next.

When I print envelopes, I have to place each one in the center of the manual feed tray. There is not a precise guide on the tray, and many times the addresses are not placed correctly on the envelope. Can anything be done about this?

You can make changes to the way the envelope is inserted. To do this,

1. Choose Envelopes and Labels from the Tools menu.

2. Choose the Envelope tab and click the Options button.

3. Click the Printing Options tab:

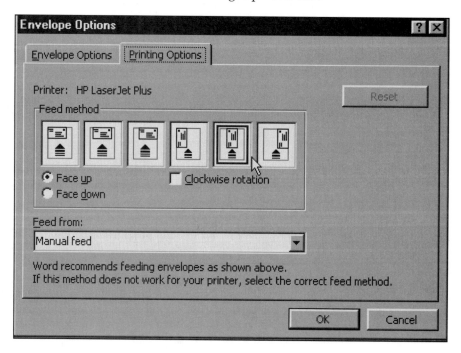

The default feed method is selected.

4. Select any other method and click OK to return to the Envelope tab.

5. Click Print.

••••••   *Tip:*   You may have to try several options depending upon the type of printer you are using before finding the one that works best for you.

?   **I opened my data document and wanted to perform a query to select only certain addresses (those in a particular city) to use in a merge. How can I do this?**

You can only perform a query in the Word data document if the main document that it is attached to is also open. Open the main document first, then do the following:

1. Click the Mail Merge button as shown here.

2. Click the Query Options button and select the Filter Records tab, shown in Figure 3-13.

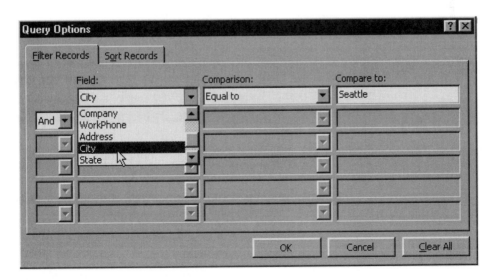

Figure 3-13:   The Filter Records tab

3. Click the down arrow under Field and select the field for the query. More than one field can be selected.

4. Move to the *Compare to* box and type the data to be selected for the query.

5. Click OK and then click Merge.

? **I created both my main document and my data document and performed a merge, which was successful, then closed both documents. I discovered an error in a name in the data document, so I opened the data document and edited the information. I then tried to merge again but the Mail Merge toolbar was not displayed. Also, I chose Mail Merge from the Tools menu, but that didn't have any option that I could use to start the merge. How can I start the merge function from the data document?**

You can't. You always have to open the main document to begin a merge. Once the main document and the data document are created, the main document has the data document attached to it automatically. See the sidebar "Mail Merge Helper" for information about using Mail Merge.

WORKING WITH LARGE DOCUMENTS

? **I know how to divide a large document into subdocuments in Master Document view. However, now I would like to combine several documents in a master document. Can I do this? If so, how?**

Open a new document window and choose Master Document from the View menu. The Master Document toolbar and the Outlining toolbar are displayed. To insert existing documents in the master document, do the following:

1. Click the Insert Subdocument button as shown here.

Insert Subdocument button

2. The Open Subdocument window is opened. Select the file you want to insert and click the Open button. The file is inserted in the master document at the insertion point, which is at the end of the first document.

3. Repeat clicking the Insert Subdocument button and selecting additional documents.

4. When you are done, choose Save As from the File menu, type a file name for the master document, and click Save.

 Note: Refer to the sidebar "Creating Subdocuments" for information about dividing large documents into subdocuments.

Creating Subdocuments

If after creating a document you decide that it would be easier to work with it if it consisted of several small documents, you can easily change it to a master document. To do this,

1. Choose Master Document from the View menu.

2. Select the portion of text that you want in a subdocument and click the Create Subdocument button. When you do this, the text is saved in the same folder as the original document, and an icon now appears at the far left:

When the subdocument is saved it is automatically saved as an RTF file, with the first letter or first word used as the filename. You can open any of these subdocuments separately and work on them. If you want to change the filename of a subdocument, go to the Save As dialog box, right-click the filename, select Rename, and type a new filename.

❓ What happened to the **concordance file** in Word 97?

The concordance file that was used in earlier versions of Word is still available, and the procedure for using it is also the same:

1. Create the concordance file. (See the following section, "Creating a Concordance File," for specific steps.)

2. Choose Index and Tables from the Insert menu and click the Index tab:

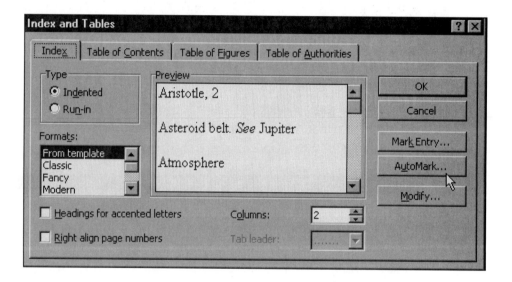

3. Click the AutoMark button, select the file that you are using as a concordance file to automatically mark text for the index, and click Open. The entries will then be marked automatically for the index.

4. Move the insertion point to the place where you want to insert the index.

5. Choose Index and Tables from the Insert menu, go to the Index tab again, and click OK to create the index.

Creating a Concordance File

A concordance file contains a list of words or phrases that you want to include in an index. It is used to automatically mark these words as index entries. When the index is created, they are inserted automatically with their corresponding page numbers. To create this file,

1. Open a new document file.

2. Insert a two-column table and type in the left column the words to be included in the index, exactly as they appear in the document. They must be case sensitive. In the right column, type the entries as you want them to appear in the index. Here's an example:

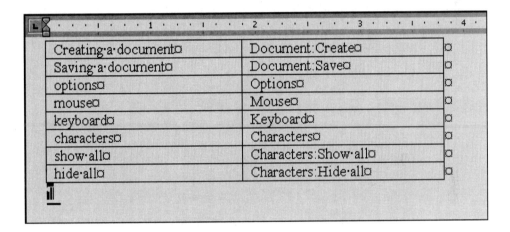

3. Choose Save As from the File menu, name the document, and click Save.

4. Close the file.

Tip: You can also press TAB after typing the word to be marked, then type the entry the way you want it to appear in the index. However, it is much easier to use a table; if the entries are in a table, you can easily rearrange them, edit them, or select only certain ones.

?   **Can I move outline levels from one subdocument to another in Master Document view? If I do this, will it change my original documents?**

You can easily move a section of text in a master document. Click the Expand Subdocuments button shown here if the subdocument text is not displayed.

Then do the following:

1. Click the plus sign to the left of the heading and text to be moved to select the block of text.

2. Point to the plus sign, hold down the left mouse button, and drag to the position where you want to move the text. As you drag, a horizontal line will be displayed, indicating the position of the block of text.

3. Release the mouse button when the text is where you want it.

If you save the changes made by moving text from one subdocument to another, this will change the original documents. When you open one of the subdocuments as a file by itself, you will see the changes.

?   **I inserted page numbers in separate subdocuments that I have now combined in a master document. What happens to these page numbers when I create a table of contents in the master document?**

Appropriate page numbers will be assigned to each page in the master document, and the table of contents will show them. You can save the master document, and these page numbers will remain as in the master document. However, if you open each subdocument individually, you will find that the original page numbers have not been changed. For example, if the last document had page numbering starting with the number 1, it will remain that way when that document is opened by itself, and not as part of the master document.

COLLABORATIVE EDITING

? **I have compared different documents using the Track Changes box, but I would like to compare different versions of the same document. Can I do this?**

In order to compare different versions of the same document, you need to save a version with a different filename. To do this,

1. Open the document containing saved versions, and double-click the File Versions button in the Status Bar, or select Versions from the File menu.
2. Select the file version you want, and click the Open button.
3. Save the document with a different filename.
4. Then go to the document that is saved with multiple versions, choose Track Changes from the Tools menu, and select Compare Documents.
5. Select the new filename and click Open.

? **I would like to keep an original version of a document, but I also want to edit it and save the edits. How can I do this?**

You can save several versions in the same document file by using the following steps.

1. Open the document, display the Reviewing toolbar, and, if necessary, choose Track Changes from the Tools menu, select Highlight Changes, and click *Track changes while editing*.
2. Edit the document and then click the Save Version button in the Reviewing toolbar:

3. Enter comments, if you like, and click OK.
4. After saving the edited text as a new version, reject all of the edits in the original document. To do this choose Track Changes from the Tools menu, select Accept or

Reject Changes, select the type of view, and choose Reject All.

5. Save and close the document. When you open the original document, it will not contain the edits. They are saved in the new version.

? **I have been told that reviewers can mark edits as they are added to documents. How do you do this?**

To mark edits as they are entered,

1. Choose Track Changes from the Tools menu.

2. Select Highlight Changes to display the Highlight Changes dialog box shown here.

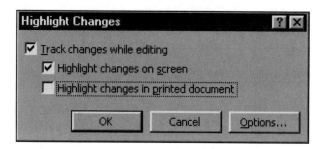

3. Select both *Track changes while editing* and *Highlight changes on screen*. You may leave *Highlight changes in printed document* turned on, if you like, or you can turn it off.

4. Click OK.

Or another way to mark text, if Highlight changes on screen is turned on, is to

1. Display the Reviewing toolbar shown here. To do this, right-click on any toolbar and select Reviewing.

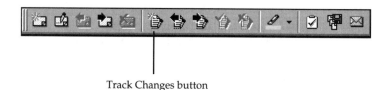

Track Changes button

2. Click the Track Changes button. TRK is then turned on in the Status Bar:

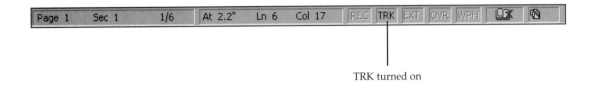

TRK turned on

3. Type any new text. It will be underlined to indicate added edits. If you delete text, it will be formatted with strikethrough to indicate a suggested deletion.

See the sidebar "Revision Marks, Highlighting, and Comments" for more detailed information about these functions.

Revision Marks, Highlighting, and Comments

If you want others to review your document, they can suggest edits without changing the original document. Any or all of the following functions can be used.

▷ Revision marks can be added to edits as they are entered, as discussed in the answer to the question about **marking edits as they are added** to documents.

▷ Highlighting can be added to text to call attention to it.

▷ Comments can be inserted. Comments do not change the text but are ideas or suggestions by a reviewer.

Note: Comments are what used to be called Annotations.

To add highlighting to text

1. Click the Highlight button in the Formatting toolbar shown here. The pointer becomes a drawing tool.

Tip: If the Highlight button is not displayed in the Formatting toolbar, display the Reviewing toolbar.

2. Drag the drawing tool across all of the text that you want to highlight.

3. When done, click the Highlight button again to return the drawing tool to an I-beam.

Tip: You can change the color of the highlighting. Click the down arrow at the right of the Highlight button. A palette is displayed, and you can select the color you want.

To insert a comment

1. Display the Reviewing toolbar.

2. Move the insertion point to the place where you want to add a comment.

3. Click the Insert Comment button shown here.

4. Text will be highlighted and followed by your initials and a number in brackets. A Comments From pane appears at the bottom of the document window, as shown in Figure 3-14.

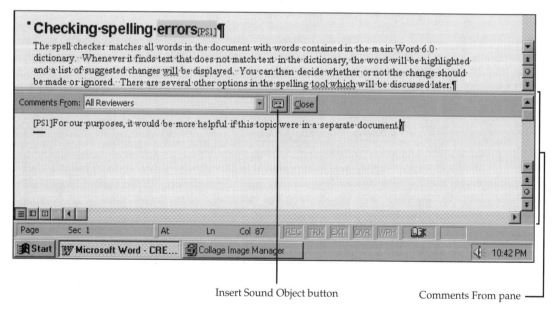

Insert Sound Object button   Comments From pane ─

Figure 3-14:   Inserting a comment

5. Type your comments in this pane and click Close when done.

Tip: If you have a microphone, you can click the Insert Sound Object button and enter your comments verbally.

To read a comment in a document

Move the pointer over the highlighted text. The comment and the author's name will be displayed automatically as shown in Figure 3-15.

To remove a comment

1. Display the Reviewing toolbar.

2. Click anywhere on the highlighted text.

3. Click the Delete Comment button in the Reviewing toolbar:

? **Our office produces large documents that include files created by several people. We lock the subdocuments, but anyone can open the master document and remove the lock on the subdocuments. Is there any other way to prevent unwanted changes to subdocuments?**

The best way to prevent unwanted changes to documents is to save each subdocument with a password. First, open a subdocument. You can do this by either opening it as a

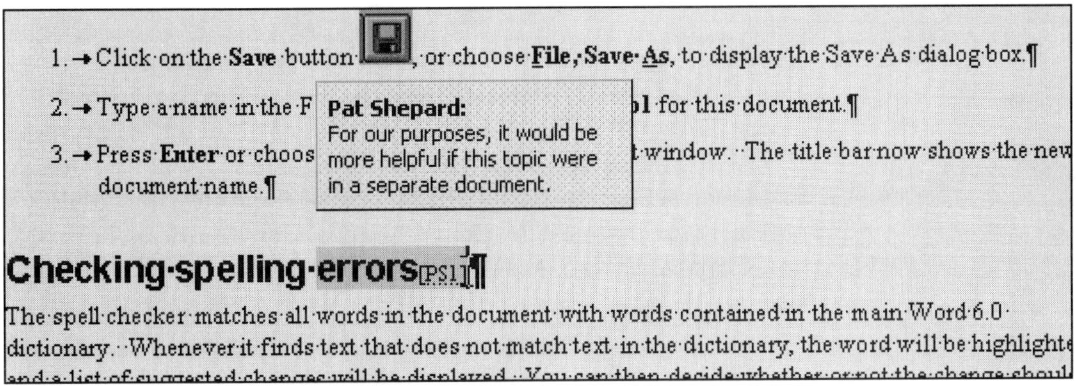

1. → Click on the **Save** button , or choose **File, Save As**, to display the Save As dialog box.¶

2. → Type a name in the F | **Pat Shepard:** | l for this document.¶
   For our purposes, it would be more helpful if this topic were in a separate document.

3. → Press **Enter** or choos | window. The title bar now shows the new document name.¶

Checking spelling errors[PS1]¶

The spell checker matches all words in the document with words contained in the main Word 6.0 dictionary. Whenever it finds text that does not match text in the dictionary, the word will be highlighted and a list of suggested changes will be displayed. You can then decide whether or not the change should

Figure 3-15: Viewing a comment

separate document, or, in the master document, collapse all documents and click the subdocument that you want to open. Then do the following:

1. Choose Save As from the File menu.

2. Click Options.

3. Type a password in the *Password to modify* box and click OK. The Confirm Password box shown here is displayed.

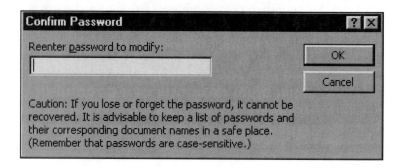

4. Type the password a second time in this box and click OK.

Caution: Be sure you remember the password. A good idea is to write down the passwords for documents that you are using and keep them in a safe place. If several people are going to be working on the same document, be sure each of them knows the password for the document.

5. Click Save.

Note: If others review the documents, but you want to control the types of changes they can make, turn on Protect Document and specify the type of changes allowed. To do this, choose Protect Document from the Tools menu. A dialog box is displayed where you can turn on any of the following to allow only certain changes: Tracked Changes, Comments, or Forms. You can also enter a password that will be required to open the document.

You can save the master document with the *Read-only recommended* option selected; however, this will not prevent the individual files in the master document from being opened and edited by anyone on the network. To save the master document as read-only, do this:

1. Choose Save As from the File menu.

2. Click the Options button to go to the Save dialog box.

3. Click *Read-only recommended.*

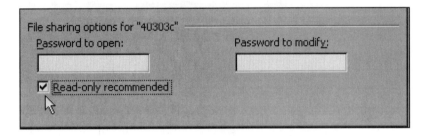

4. Click OK and then click Save.

? **I find that the revision marks can be distracting when I am not ready to edit. Can I turn off the highlighting and revision marks?**

Choose Track Changes from the Tools menu, select Highlight Changes, and click *Highlight changes on screen.* Click OK.

? **When I open a document that I know contains several versions, I open only the original version. How do I know what other versions of a document have been saved, and how can I open them?**

Open the document and double-click the File Versions button in the status bar.

 Note: If no versions have been saved, the button will not be displayed.

A Versions dialog box will be displayed. You will see the date and time a version was saved, who saved it, and any comments that were entered:

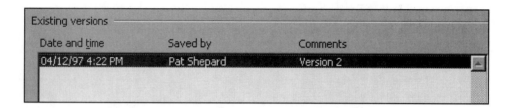

You do not necessarily have to enter comments. Select the version you want, and click the Open button.

****** *Tip:*   If the Status Bar is not displayed, choose Versions from the File menu to see the versions that have been saved.

4 Answers!

Analyzing with Excel

Answer Topics!

Excel @ a Glance

Excel is considered the worksheet component of Office, yet Excel can
perform three separate functions:

➡ The **worksheet** function, which displays and analyzes text and
numbers in rows and columns

➡ The **database** function, which manipulates lists of information

➡ The **chart** function, which produces charts that graphically depict
data

Each function is really just a different way of looking at and
interacting with data that has a common structure based on rows and
columns. This common structure is the worksheet.

The worksheet function of Excel, shown in Figure 4-1, provides for as
many sheets as you can hold in memory, each containing 256 columns
and 65,536 rows. The intersection of a row and a column on a single
sheet is a *cell*, which can contain up to 32,767 characters.

Excel's worksheets are stored in files called workbooks ("books" for
short). Think of a workbook as a file of worksheets ("sheets" for short),
although it can also contain charts and programming pages.

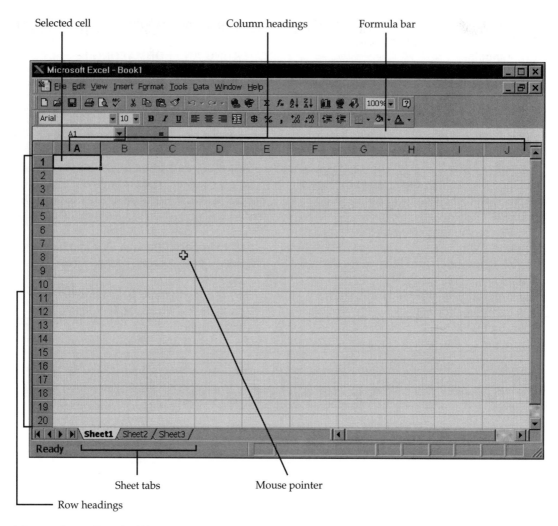

Figure 4-1:   Excel's Worksheet window

The three-dimensional structure of rows, columns, and sheets provides a powerful framework for financial analysis. Consider a company's financial plan or budget, an example of which is shown in Figure 4-2:

▷   Each row is an account—an element of revenue or expense.

▷   Each column is a period of time—months, quarters, or years.

▷   Each sheet is a unit of the company—a store, plant, office, or division.

▷   Summing across columns you get the total for an account.

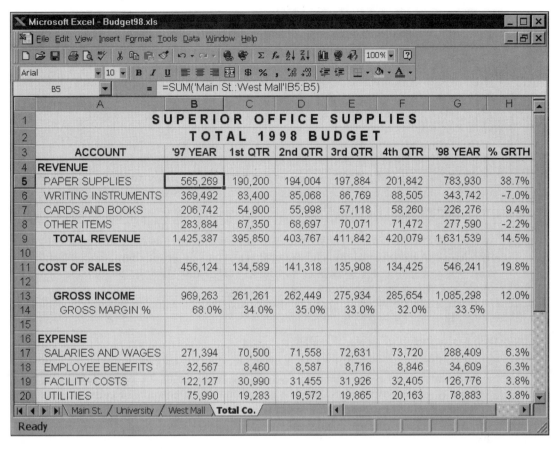

Figure 4-2: A company's financial plan

➤ Summing down rows you get the total for a time period.

➤ Summing through the sheets you get the total for the company. Excel identifies where information is located on a worksheet by

➤ Numbering rows 1 through 65,536

➤ Labeling the 256 columns A through IV (A through Z, then AA through AZ, BA through BZ, and so on through IV)

➤ Identifying sheets initially as Sheet1 through however many sheets you have, but allowing you to rename them anything you want with up to 31 characters

When information is entered on a sheet, it is stored in a specific cell or location. You know what that location is by the row, column, and sheet in which the information is placed. Using Excel's identification, you can give an address to the information you stored; for example, column D, row 7, Sheet1. Excel addresses are written with the column reference first, followed by the row. Using this convention, you can write the example address as D7. To add a sheet reference to this, you place the sheet name and an exclamation point in front of the column and row—for example: Sheet1!D7. A sheet is addressed from A1 for the cell in the upper-left corner to IV65536 for the cell in the lower-right corner.

The information in a cell may be either numbers or text. Numbers, which include formulas that evaluate numbers, can be formatted in many ways, including dollars, percentages, dates, or time. Text can include numbers and can be used as titles, row and column labels, and comments on a sheet. The primary difference between numbers and text is that you can perform arithmetic calculations on numbers but not on text. Think of numbers as arithmetic values and text as everything else. You can format numbers in several ways as you enter them. For example, you can enter **3.25, 3.25%, $3.25, 3 2/5, 32.5E-1,** or **3,250,325.25,** and Excel will format the numbers accordingly.

A range identifies one or more cells for use in a formula or in an instruction. A range can be

▷   A single cell address like D14.

▷   A group of cells identified by multiple cell addresses such as C5:E12, which is the rectangle extending from C5 in the upper left to E12 in the lower right. Such a group may be a column of cells, a row of cells, or a block of several rows and/or columns.

▷   A name or names that refer to one or more cells, like *Salaries*.

USING AND CHANGING A WORKSHEET

?   **I know I can drag the intersection between rows and columns to change their size, but what if I want to change the size of several rows or columns to be the same height or width?**

Select the rows or columns you want to size by clicking their headings. If you want to change several contiguous rows or columns, press and hold SHIFT while clicking the first and last headings. If you want to change several rows or columns that are not next to each other, press and hold CTRL while clicking each heading. Once the headings are selected, drag the heading intersection of any selected row or column, and all selected rows or columns will be sized the same as the one you dragged.

You can size a group of rows or columns more precisely by selecting them as just described and then choosing Row Height or Column Width from the Format menu and entering the width or height you want.

Tip: You can auto-size each column to its best fit by double-clicking on any header border within the selected columns (except the leftmost border).

I don't use some of the buttons on the Standard toolbar and there are others that I would use if they were there. How do I make changes to the toolbars?

You can add or remove tools from the toolbar by choosing Customize from the Tools menu, and then clicking the Commands tab. To remove a button, simply drag it off the toolbar while the Customize dialog box is open. To add buttons to the toolbar, select the category and command that the button will perform, and then drag that command to the location on the toolbar where you want the button.

Note: In Excel 97, unlike earlier versions of Excel, you can customize the worksheet menus with the exact same steps used to customize a toolbar. In fact the worksheet menu is now called the Worksheet Menu Bar.

If you remove a default toolbar button or menu option, you can quickly return it to its original location by clicking the Toolbars tab in the Customize dialog box, choosing the toolbar or menu you want to restore, and clicking Reset. You'll then be asked to confirm that that is what you want to do. A problem with using Reset is that you will lose any buttons you've added.

Is there a way to enter the **date and time** in a cell without typing them?

Yes. Press CTRL-; to enter the current date, and press CTRL-: to enter the current time. These can be placed in the same cell with a space between them, or in two separate cells. See the sidebar "Edit Keys" for more information.

● ● ● ● ● ● ● ● ● ● ●

Edit Keys

The functions of the keys you can use to edit a cell are shown in this table:

Key	Function
ALT	Activates Menu bar
ALT-ENTER	Inserts carriage return into cell
ALT-BACKSPACE, CTRL-Z	Undoes previous action
BACKSPACE	Deletes the character to the left of the insertion point
CTRL-LEFT ARROW or CTRL-RIGHT ARROW	Moves the insertion point one word to the left or right in the entry
CTRL-DELETE	Deletes text from the insertion point to the end of the current line
CTRL-'	Inserts the formula from the cell above the active cell at the insertion point
CTRL-`	Switches between displaying formulas and displaying values in all cells
CTRL-"	Inserts the value from the cell above into the active cell at the insertion point
CTRL-;	Inserts the current date in your computer at the insertion point
CTRL-:	Inserts the current time in your computer at the insertion point
DEL	Deletes the character to the right of the insertion point
END, CTRL-END	Moves the insertion point to the right end of the current line of the entry
ENTER	Completes editing, making any changes entered and leaving the active cell where it was originally
ESC	Cancels any changes made during editing, closes the edit area, and returns the original contents to the active cell
F2	Activates the cell and edit area so you can do a character-by-character edit on the active cell

Key	Function
HOME, CTRL-HOME	Moves the insertion point to the left end of the current line of the entry
INS	Switches between Insert mode, in which newly typed characters push existing characters to the right, and Overtype mode, in which newly typed characters replace existing ones
LEFT ARROW or RIGHT ARROW	Moves the insertion point one character to the left or right in the entry
UP ARROW or DOWN ARROW	Moves the insertion point between lines in the edit area if the entry occupies more than one line; otherwise moves the insertion point to the beginning or end of the line
SHIFT-LEFT ARROW or SHIFT-RIGHT ARROW	Selects the previous character or the next character
CTRL-SHIFT-RIGHT ARROW or CTRL-SHIFT-LEFT ARROW	Selects the next or previous word if the insertion point is in a space between words. If the insertion point is in a word, this action selects to beginning or end of the word.
SHIFT-TAB	Completes cell entry and moves to the cell to the left
TAB	Completes cell entry and moves to the cell to the right

 I can't remember all the function key combinations. What is a good reference for this?

Choose Contents and Index from the Help menu, click Index, enter **Function Keys,** and click Display. A list of most of the keys will be shown. Table 4-1 is a little more complete.

Table 4-1:   Function Keys and the Functions They Perform

Key	Name	Function
F1	Help	Opens the Excel Help window or the Office Assistant
SHIFT-F1	What's This	Displays context-sensitive help
ALT-F1	New Chart	Creates a new chart
ALT-SHIFT-F1	New Sheet	Inserts a new sheet
ALT-CTRL-F1	New Macro	Creates a new Excel 4 macro sheet
F2	Edit	Activates the Formula bar for editing
SHIFT-F2	Comments	Allows entering, editing, or deleting a comment that is to be attached to the active cell
ALT-F2	Save As	Opens the File Save As dialog box
ALT-SHIFT-F2	Save	Saves the active document
ALT-CTRL-F2	Open	Opens the Open dialog box
ALT-CTRL-SHIFT-F2	Print	Opens the Print dialog box
F3	Name	Opens the Paste Name dialog box to paste a cell's name into a formula
SHIFT-F3	Function	Opens the Paste Function dialog box
CTRL-F3	Define Name	Opens the Define Name dialog box
CTRL-SHIFT-F3	Create Name	Opens the Create Name dialog box
F4	Absolute	While editing, makes a cell address or range name absolute, mixed, or relative
F4	Repeat Last	When not editing, repeats the last action taken
SHIFT-F4	Find Next	Repeats the last Find command
CTRL-F4	Close	Closes the active document window
ALT-F4	Exit	Closes the application
F5	Go To	Opens the Go To dialog box to move the active cell to a cell address, a range name, or a file that you enter
SHIFT-F5	Find	Opens the Find dialog box
CTRL-F5	Restore	Restores the size of the active document window

Table 4-1:   (*Continued*)

Key	Name	Function
F6	Next Pane	Moves the active cell clockwise to the next pane
SHIFT-F6	Last Pane	Moves the active cell counter-clockwise to the previous pane
CTRL-F6	Next Window	Moves the active cell to the next document window
CTRL-SHIFT-F6	Last Window	Moves the active cell to the previous document window
F7	Spelling	Checks spelling
CTRL-F7	Move	Sets up the active document window to be moved with the direction keys
F8	Extend	Toggles the extension of the current selection
SHIFT-F8	Add	Allows the addition of a second selection to the current selection
CTRL-F8	Size	Sets up the active document window to be sized with the direction keys
ALT-F8	Macro	Opens the Macro dialog box
F9	Calculate All	Recalculates all open worksheets
SHIFT-F9	Calculate Current	Recalculates the active sheet
CTRL-F9	Minimize	Minimizes the active workbook
F10	Menu	Activates the Menu bar
SHIFT-F10	Context Menu	Displays the context menu for the active cell
CTRL-F10	Maximize	Maximizes or restores the active workbook
F11	New Chart	Creates a new chart sheet
SHIFT-F11	New Sheet	Creates a new sheet
CTRL-F11	New Macro	Creates a new Excel 4 macro sheet
ALT-F11	VB Editor	Opens the Visual Basic Editor window
F12	Save As	Opens the File Save As dialog box
SHIFT-F12	Save	Saves the active document
CTRL-F12	Open	Opens the Open dialog box
CTRL-SHIFT-F12	Print	Opens the Print dialog box

Are there **keystrokes to move from one sheet to another?**

Yes. CTRL-PG DN moves down one sheet (from Sheet1 to Sheet2) and CTRL-PG UP moves in the opposite direction. The sidebar "Direction Keys and Their Functions" provides the complete list of all direction keys.

Direction Keys and Their Functions

Key	Moves the Active Cell
LEFT ARROW or RIGHT ARROW	Right or left one column
UP ARROW or DOWN ARROW	Up or down one row
PG UP or PG DN	Up or down one window height
ALT-PG DN or ALT-PG UP	Right or left one window width
CTRL-UP ARROW or CTRL-DOWN ARROW	Up or down to the first intersection of blank and nonblank cells
CTRL-RIGHT ARROW or CTRL-LEFT ARROW	Right or left to the first intersection of blank and nonblank cells
HOME	Left to column A in the row with the active cell
END	Turns on End mode. When a direction key is next pressed, the active cell moves to the last occupied cell in the direction of the arrow (same as CTRL-ARROW keys above).
CTRL-HOME	To cell A1
CTRL-END	Down and/or to the right to the lowest and rightmost cell representing the corner formed by the rightmost occupied cell and the lowest occupied cell
END-HOME	Same as CTRL-END
CTRL-PG DN	Down one sheet (from Sheet1 to Sheet2)
CTRL-PG UP	Up one sheet (from Sheet2 to Sheet1)

? Why is the Format toolbar button that used to be called Center Across Rows now called **Merge and Center**?

The new Merge and Center button makes one cell out of the selected cells, which may contain several rows, and then centers in that large cell any text that was in the upper-leftmost cell. Excel considers all the merged area to be one cell and *any data in the other selected cells will be lost.* In previous versions of Excel the individual cells remained and the information in the leftmost cell just covered the other cells, which were limited to a single row.

Tip: To center text across rows without merging the cells and losing their content, choose Cells from the Format menu, click the Alignment tab, select Center Across Selection in the Horizontal drop-down list, and click OK.

? How can I **select multiple cells that are not contiguous**, since I can't just drag across them?

Hold down CTRL while clicking individual cells or dragging across two or more independent ranges of cells. For example, all of the highlighted areas here were selected by hold down CTRL while dragging across them.

All of the selected areas will be formatted alike if a particular format is chosen while these areas are selected.

? **My status bar disappeared.** Where did it go and how do I get it back?

Somebody probably turned it off. To get it back, open the Tools menu, choose Options, and make sure the View tab is selected. Then click *Status bar* to turn it back on.

Tool Bar Menu, choose options ? make view Tab is Selected or Status bar to turn on

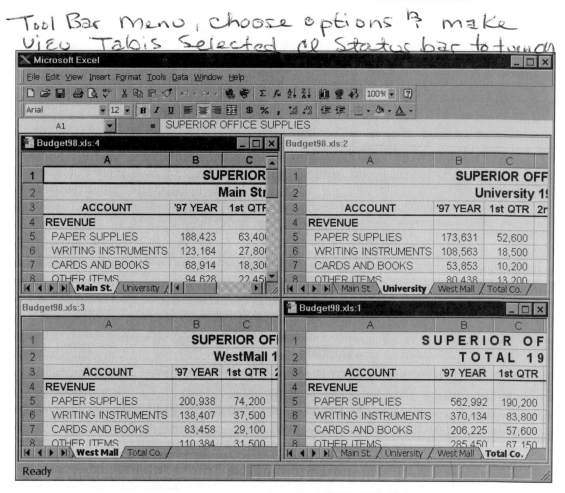

Figure 4-3: Multiple windows displaying different sheets

? **I would like to just see the total of a set of numbers without entering a formula to permanently create the sum. How is that done?**

Select the set of numbers, and then look in the status bar at the bottom of the window to see the sum:

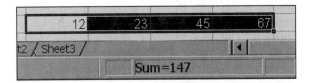

? **I like having multiple pages or sheets, but I want to see them all at the same time. How do I view multiple pages?**

With the multiple-sheet workbook open in Excel, open the Windows menu and choose New Window. Repeat this for all the additional sheets in the workbook. When you have created a window for each sheet, again open the Window menu and choose Arrange, then click Tiled and click OK. In each window, click a different sheet tab. You should now be able to see a portion of each of your sheets at the same time, as you can see in Figure 4-3.

ENTERING AND CHANGING INFORMATION

? **When I finish an entry I press ENTER and go to the cell beneath my entry. What I really want is to go to the cell to the right. How can I change where ENTER takes me?**

First, if you press TAB instead of ENTER to complete the entry, you'll go to the cell to the right instead of the cell beneath the entry. Second, you can change what ENTER does by opening the Tools menu, choosing Options, clicking the Edit tab, and selecting Right from the drop-down list, as shown next.

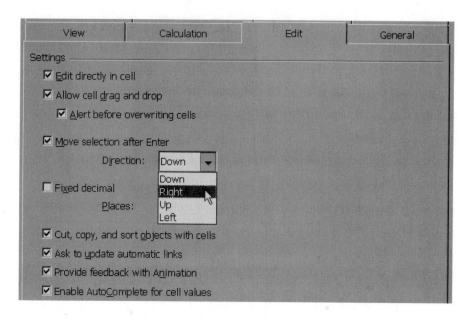

?   **Is there an easy way to delete information in a cell?**

If you haven't completed the entry by pressing ENTER, TAB, or an arrow key or by clicking the Enter button on the Formula bar, press ESC, and the information will be removed. If you have completed the entry, select the cell or cells and press DELETE. You can also either click Undo or open the Undo drop-down list and undo any of the last 16 actions you have taken, as you can see here:

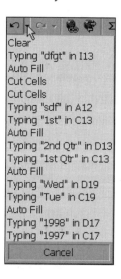

? I want some numbers to be numbers and I want some to be text. How do I get Excel to treat some numbers as text?

Based on what you type, Excel determines whether your entry is a number or text. If you type only numbers (0 through 9) or one of the following numeric symbols in the appropriate place, Excel considers your entry a number:

+ − ( ) . , : $ % / E e (in scientific notation)

If you enter a date or time value in one of Excel's built-in formats, it is considered a number. Finally, a recognizable formula that results in a number is treated as a number. Everything else is text. If you want an entry that would normally be a number to be text, place an apostrophe (') on the left of the entry. (The apostrophe won't be displayed.)

? How do I repeat an entry in a number of cells without retyping?

If you want to copy an entry you have typed in one cell into immediately adjacent or contiguous cells, place the mouse pointer over the fill handle in the lower-right corner of the cell, so that the pointer becomes a plus sign. Then drag the cell to the other cells you want filled with the entry, like this:

If you want to repeat the entry in widely separated cells, select the original cell and press CTRL-C to copy it, then right-click each new cell and choose Paste. When you are done, press ESC to turn off the Copy selection.

? Is there an easy way to create a series of numbers or words?

Yes. Type the first two entries, select them, and then drag the fill handle, as shown next.

This works with any number series, as well as with days of the week, months of the year, and dates. You can also select Fill Series from the Edit menu to open the Series dialog box for other options.

?   Excel doesn't have an Insert Symbol like Word, so how do I enter special characters?

Use these steps:

1. Open the Windows Start menu and choose Programs, Accessories, and Character Map. (If you can't find the Character Map—it's not part of a Typical Windows 95 installation—you will need to install it from your Windows 95 CD or disks.)

2. In the Character Map dialog box, select the font you are using, double-click the character you want, click Copy, and then click Close.

3. Return to Excel, right-click the cell in which you want the special character, and choose Paste from the context menu that opens.

   If you want the special character in a string of other text, double-click the cell (or select the cell and press F2), move the insertion point to where you want the special character, and then press CTRL-V to paste it in.

Tip: If you use a special character often, remember the keystroke for that character, which is shown in the lower right of the Character Map dialog box, and then use that keystroke when you need the character. For example, if you use the English pound symbol (£) a lot, you can easily get it by pressing and holding ALT while typing **0163** on the numeric keypad on the right of your keyboard.

ENTERING AND USING FORMULAS AND FUNCTIONS

? **Isn't there an easy way to enter the formula for adding a column of numbers?**

Select the cell beneath the column of numbers (or to the right of a row of numbers) and click the AutoSum button in the toolbar. The numbers to be summed will be selected:

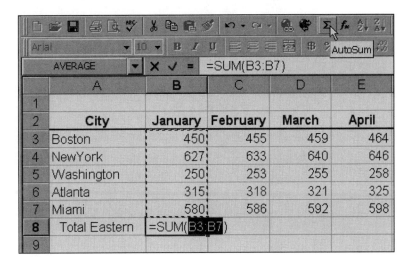

Press ENTER to accept the default selection, or use the mouse to drag over a new selection and then press ENTER.

You can also enter formulas for a range of cells under several columns of numbers or to the right of several rows of numbers and click the AutoSum button to automatically create all of the formulas in the range.

? **I can never remember the arguments in functions. How can I easily find these?**

Use the following steps to see the list of arguments and have them explained as you enter them:

1. Select the cell in which you want the function.

2. Click the equal sign in the formula bar to begin the formula entry process.

3. Open the function drop-down list that appears on the left of the formula bar.

4. Select the function you want to use.

5. Use the dialog box that opens to fill in the arguments that are needed. As you select each of the arguments, you'll see an explanation of it in the lower part of the dialog box, as shown here:

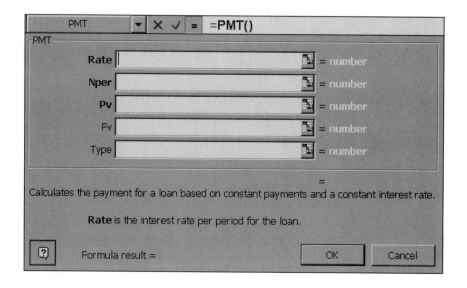

Tip: Open the Paste Function dialog box (either by choosing More Functions from the Formula bar list or by selecting Insert Paste) to view all of Excel's functions.

❓ Excel is **calculating one of my formulas incorrectly.** The formula is =D1+E1*F1. What's the problem?

You are probably expecting to add D1 and E1 before multiplying by F1. Excel, though, will multiply first and then do the addition. The reason is that Excel has a specific order of calculation, and in that order, multiplication is done before addition (see the sidebar "Order of Calculation"). You can change the order of calculation with parentheses, so your formula would give you the answer you want if it were written like this: =(D1+E1)*F1. Parentheses must always be added in pairs and may be nested more than 25 levels deep.

Order of Calculation

Excel calculates or evaluates a formula in a particular order determined by the precedence number of the operators being used and the parentheses placed in the formula. The following table describes each operator and gives its precedence number:

Operator	Description	Precedence
:	range of cell	1
,	union of cells	2
(a space)	intersection of cells	3
–	negation	4
%	percentage (/100)	5
^	exponentiation	6
*	multiplication	7
/	division	7
+	addition	8
–	subtraction	8
&	concatenation	9
=	equal to	10
<	less than	10
>	greater than	10
<=	less than or equal to	10
>=	greater than or equal to	10
<>	not equal to	10

Operations with lower precedence numbers are performed earlier in the calculation. When two operators in a formula have the same preference number, Excel evaluates them sequentially from left to right.

Tip: Excel has a very handy feature that shows the matching left parenthesis as you enter the right parenthesis. That way you know your parentheses match without having to count them.

? **I want to make my formulas more readable.** Is there an easy way to do that?

Yes; by entering row and column headings, you can use those headings in formulas to refer to the numbers immediately below or to the right of the headings. You do *not* have to define the rows or columns as named ranges. You can see this here:

SUM	▼	X ✓ =	=SUM(Washington)					
	A	B	C	D	E	F	G	H	I
2	**City**	**January**	**February**	**March**	**April**	**May**	**June**	**Total**
3	Boston	450	455	459	464	468	473	2768
4	NewYork	627	633	640	646	652	659	3857
5	Washington	250	253	255	258	260	263	=SUM(Washington)
6	Atlanta	315	318	321	325	328	331	1938
7	Miami	580	586	592	598	604	610	3568
8	Total Eastern	2222	2244	2267	2289	2312	2335	13670
9								

? **How do I freeze an address in a formula** so that it does not change when I copy it?

You can make an address absolute, where both the row and column are fixed, by typing a dollar sign in front of each part of the address or by pressing F4 after typing the address. For example, C3 is an absolute address. You can also have various combinations of fixed and relative addressing called mixed addresses. To get a mixed address, press F4 repeatedly to cycle through all four possible combinations, as follows:

If you have	pressing F4 will give you	which is a(n)
C3	C3	Absolute address
C3	C$3	Mixed (fixed-row) address
C$3	$C3	Mixed (fixed-column) address
$C3	C3	Relative address

 Note: F4 always cycles through the alternatives in the same order, regardless of which you start with.

? I have a really big worksheet, and every time I make an entry it takes forever to recalculate the whole sheet. How can I specify manual calculation?

Open the Tools menu, choose Options, select the Calculation tab, and click Manual. Once you have chosen manual calculation, your worksheet will not be recalculated until you press F9.

Tip: If you use manual calculation a lot and want a tool or menu option for it, choose Customize from the Tools menu, and in the Commands tab select the Tools category and drag Calculate Now to either a menu or a toolbar.

? Can I specify a range that is disjointed or not rectangular in a formula or function? If so, how?

Yes. Many formulas or functions that take ranges as arguments will allow nonrectangular and disjointed ranges using one of these range operators:

Operator	Name and meaning
:	Range, a rectangular group of adjacent cells
,	Union, the combination of two ranges
(space)	Intersection, the cells common to two ranges

For example, if you wanted to add two disjointed ranges, you would do so by summing the union of the two ranges with a formula like =SUM(B7:E7,E9:E12). If you wanted the average of the cells that were common to two ranges, you would use a function specifying the intersection of the ranges, as shown here:

AVERAGE ▼ ✕ ✓ =	=AVERAGE(H7:K11 H9:L9)					
	G	H	I	J	K	L	M
5	=AVERAGE(H7:K11 H9:L9)						
6							
7		35	23	67	83		
8		46	24	38	78		
9	23	78	18	95	45	53	
10		93	37	17	12		
11		24	45	73	62		

▪▪▪▪▪▪ *Tip:*   When you enter a function or a formula, do so with lowercase letters. If Excel properly interprets your formula or function it will change all the characters to uppercase, telling you your entry is OK.

COPYING AND MOVING INFORMATION

? Can I **copy a cell to a range** of cells?

Yes. There are four copy-to-range methods that work:

➤ Copying a single cell to another single cell, to a row of cells, to a column of cells, or to a block of cells. The destination (what you select to paste into) is another cell, a row, a column, or a block.

➤ Copying a single row to a range spanning one or more rows. The destination is a single cell or a part of a column—the leftmost cells of the receiving rows.

➤ Copying a single column to a range spanning one or more columns. The destination is a single cell or a part or a row—the uppermost cells of the receiving columns.

➤ Copying a block to a second block. The destination is a single cell—the upper-left cell of the receiving range.

Figure 4-4 shows these four copy range combinations.

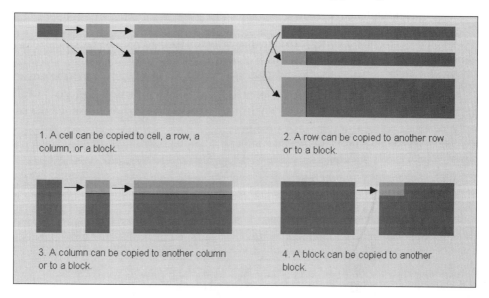

1. A cell can be copied to cell, a row, a column, or a block.

2. A row can be copied to another row or to a block.

3. A column can be copied to another column or to a block.

4. A block can be copied to another block.

Figure 4-4:   Four copy-to-range options

? I know I can *move* the contents of a cell by dragging the cell border, but isn't there a way to copy information without using Cut and Paste in the Edit menu?

Yes, several ways. The easiest is to hold down CTRL while dragging the cell border; this copies instead of moves the cell contents. You can also select the cell to be copied and press CTRL-C to copy it, select the receiving cell, and press CTRL-V. You can also right-click the source and receiving cells and select copy and paste, respectively, from the context or shortcut menu.

? Sometimes when I am copying or moving cells I want to insert cells above or to the left of existing cells instead of just pasting them over the existing cells. How is that done?

Select the range to be copied or moved. As you begin to drag the border of the range, press and hold CTRL if you want to copy the range, and then additionally press and hold SHIFT to insert it between other cells. As you continue to drag the range you'll see a bar appear between cells, showing where the range will be inserted, like this:

12	23	45	67
a	s	d	f
z	x	c	v

C10:F10

When you are happy with the placement of the bar, release the mouse button and only then release SHIFT and CTRL. You can also use Cut or Copy, select the cells below which or to the left of which you want the new cells inserted, and then select Copied Cells from the Insert menu or Context menu.

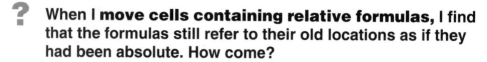

When I move cells containing relative formulas, I find that the formulas still refer to their old locations as if they had been absolute. How come?

What you want to do is *copy* the cells. Then the formulas will be adjusted relative to their new positions. Excel assumes that when you *move* a formula you want the formula to keep pointing to the original cells no matter where you move the formula. You'll find this very handy in many situations.

ADDING FORMATTING, PATTERNS, AND BORDERS

How do I format numbers with the English pound sign?

Use these steps:

1. Right-click on the number or range of numbers and choose Format Cells in the Context menu. The Format Cells dialog box will open.
2. Select Currency from the Category list in the Number tab.
3. Choose £ English (British) as the symbol.
4. Select the number of decimal places and how you want negative numbers to be displayed, as shown here:

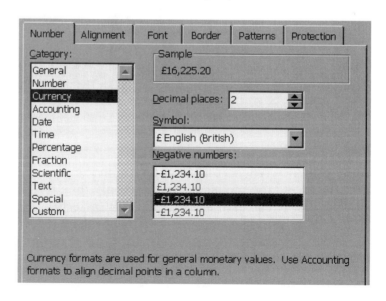

5. When the Format Cells dialog box is the way you want it, click OK.

? Why are some of my **numbers flush to the right edge of the cell** and others are moved to the left one space?

Some of your numbers are formatted so that when they are negative they have parentheses around them. That means the positive numbers must be moved to the left one space to accommodate the right parenthesis if the number becomes negative. You can see that in the last two numbers in this column:

3,456.82
-4,395.94
(5,194.23)
1,324.54
1,853.67

You can change this by reformatting the cells you want changed. Right-click the cells, choose Format Cells from the context menu, and change the negative-number style to either add or remove the parentheses, whichever you want.

? I want to apply **patterns and fancy formatting** to my worksheet in the easiest way possible. What is that way?

By using the AutoFormat option in the Format menu. This opens the AutoFormat dialog box shown here.

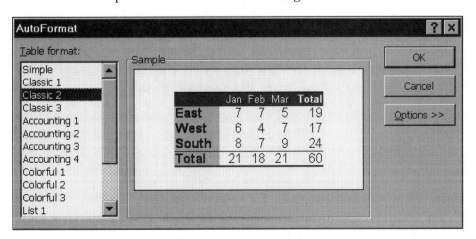

Microsoft Excel - Budget98.xls:4

File Edit View Insert Format Tools Data Window Help

Arial   11   B I U

A1   =   SUPERIOR OFFICE SUPPLIES

	A	B	C	D	E	F	G	H
1	SUPERIOR OFFICE SUPPLIES							
2	Main Street 1998 Budget							
3	ACCOUNT	'97 YEAR	1st QTR	2nd QTR	3rd QTR	4th QTR	'98 YEAR	% GRTH
4	REVENUE							
5	PAPER SUPPLIES	188,423	63,400	64,668	65,961	67,281	261,310	38.7%
6	WRITING INSTRUMENTS	123,164	27,800	28,356	28,923	29,502	114,581	-7.0%
7	CARDS AND BOOKS	68,914	18,300	18,666	19,039	19,420	75,425	9.4%
8	OTHER ITEMS	94,628	22,450	22,899	23,357	23,824	92,530	-2.2%
9	TOTAL REVENUE	475,129	131,950	134,589	137,281	140,026	543,846	14.5%
10								
11	COST OF SALES	152,041	44,863	47,106	45,303	44,808	182,080	19.8%
12								
13	GROSS INCOME	323,088	87,087	87,483	91,978	95,218	361,766	12.0%
14	GROSS MARGIN %	68.0%	34.0%	35.0%	33.0%	32.0%	33.5%	
15								
16	EXPENSE							
17	SALARIES AND WAGES	90,465	23,500	23,853	24,210	24,573	96,136	6.3%
18	EMPLOYEE BENEFITS	10,856	2,820	2,862	2,905	2,949	11,536	6.3%
19	FACILITY COSTS	40,709	10,330	10,485	10,642	10,802	42,259	3.8%
20	UTILITIES	25,330	6,428	6,524	6,622	6,721	26,294	3.8%

Main St. ╱ University ╱ West Mall ╱ Total Co. ╱

Ready

Figure 4-5:   Using AutoFormat on the worksheet in Figure 4-2

If you were to apply the Classic 2 Table Format to the
Budget98 worksheet shown in Figure 4-2, it would look like
it does in Figure 4-5.

? **I want to reuse a format that I just spent a whole lot
of time working on. I'd like to use it in several other
locations. Is there a way to do that without having to
reapply all the formats one at a time?**

Yes; there are two ways depending on how much
information you want to format. First and most simply
you can use the Format Painter tool in the Standard toolbar.
Do that by selecting the cell containing the formatting, and
click the Format Painter button:

Then click or drag across the cell or cells in which you want to reuse the formatting.

The second way is to create your own style. Do that like this:

1. Select the cell containing the formatting and choose Style from the Format menu.

2. Type the name of the new style, turning off or modifying any parts of the existing formatting you don't want included, click Add, and click OK.

You can now apply the style to selected cells by choosing Style from the Format menu, selecting the style name, and clicking OK, or you can attach the style to a toolbar button:

1. Open the Tools menu, choose Macro, and then click Record New Macro. Name the macro after your new style, give it a shortcut key if desired, select Personal Macro Workbook to store the macro in, and click OK.

2. Open the Format menu, choose Style, select your new style in the *Style name* drop-down list, click OK, and then click the Stop Recording button in the Stop Recording dialog box.

3. Right-click on any toolbar or the menu bar and choose Customize.

4. In the Customize dialog box Commands tab, select Format as the category, choose any command, like Comma Style (you're going to modify it).

5. Drag the command you choose to where you want it on the toolbar.

6. Click Modify Selection in the Customize dialog box. In the pop-up menu that opens, change the Name as desired, for example, change "&Comma Style" to "&Heading Style." This name is what you see when you place the mouse pointer over the tool.

7. Still in the Modify Selection pop-up menu, click Edit Button Image and create the image you want. Click OK when you are done.

8. Again click Modify Selection in the Customize dialog box, and click Assign Macro.

9. Select your new macro and click OK.

10. Click Close to close the Customize dialog box.

11. Select a cell or cells that you want to apply your formatting to and click your new toolbar button.

❓ Can I **rotate text** in a cell?

Yes. Right-click the cell to be rotated, choose Format Cells, click the Alignment tab, and drag the orientation to the angle you want, like this:

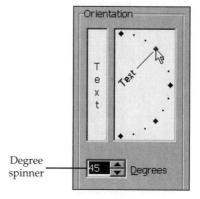

You can also use the degree spinner to accomplish a more precise position. When you are satisfied, click OK to return to the worksheet and see the results.

❓ Is there any way to **split a cell with a diagonal line?**

Yes. You can draw it with the Drawing tools or, more simply, you can apply a diagonal border. Here's how to add the diagonal line shown here:

	A	B	C	D	E
12					
13		City	Atlanta	Boston	Chicago
		Results			
14		Attendance	418	365	847
15		Revenue	188,100	164,250	381,150
16		Expenses	114,950	100,375	232,925
17		Net Receipts	73,150	63,875	148,225

1. Type the higher, rightmost text first, press ALT-ENTER, and type the lower, leftmost text. Press ENTER to complete the entry, and the row should automatically resize to fit two lines.

2. Left-align the cell with the new text, enter one less than the number of spaces in front of the top entry to right-align it, and then press ENTER.

3. Right-click the cell and select Format Cells from the Context menu.

4. In the Format Cells dialog box click the Border tab, select the line style you want, and click the right-hand diagonal line button, as shown here:

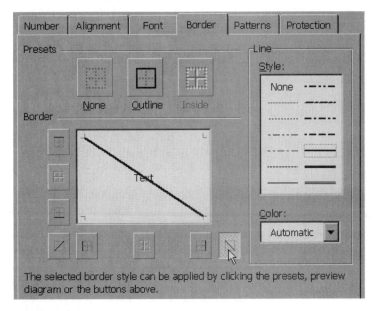

5. Click OK to close the dialog box.

I work a lot with English currency. How do I add a **toolbar button for English pound formatting?**

Add a button for English Pound formatting with the following steps:

1. Choose Macro from the Tools menu, select Record New Macro, type **EnglishPound** (no space) for the macro name, select Personal Macro Workbook to store the macro in, and click OK. A very small Stop Recording dialog box will appear on your screen. All keystrokes and many mouse movements will now be recorded.

2. Open the Format menu and choose Cells. From the Number tab, select Currency, choose £ *English (British)* as the symbol, select the number of decimal

places and the negative-number format you want, and click OK.

3. Click the small square in the Stop Recording dialog box.

4. Right-click on any toolbar or the menu bar and choose Customize.

5. In the Customize dialog box Commands tab, select Format as the category.

6. Drag the $ Currency Style command to where you want it on the toolbar.

7. Click Modify Selection, type **&English Pound** for the name, and click Assign Macro.

8. In the Assign Macro dialog box, select PERSONAL.XLS!EnglishPound and click OK.

9. Click Close to close the Customize dialog box.

10. Select a number and click your new toolbar button. The number will be formatted with the English pound symbol.

11. Reopen the Customize dialog box, click your new button, click Modify Selection in the dialog box, and then click Edit Button Image.

12. Click the pixels in the Picture box so that the image on the button is an English pound sign as shown here:

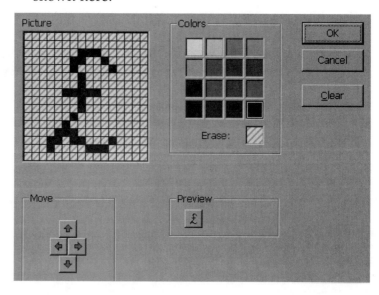

13. When you are satisfied with your image, click OK to close the Button Editor dialog box, and click Close in the Customize dialog box.

CREATING AND FORMATTING CHARTS

? I didn't add an axis title when I created a chart with the Wizard. How do I do that now?

You can change and add or delete just about anything on a chart you have previously created. Follow these steps to add an axis title:

1. Right-click on the chart and choose Chart Options. Notice the other options that are available on the Chart Context menu to change the chart type, source data, and location.

2. In the Chart Options dialog box click the Titles tab and then type the title in the appropriate axis text box. Click OK to close the dialog box.

3. To change the font and alignment of the axis title, right-click on the new title and choose Format Axis Title to open the dialog box of that name.

4. Click the Font tab to change the font or the font style or size.

5. Click the Alignment tab and adjust the alignment as desired.

6. When the axis title is the way you want it, click OK.

? I want to add a callout with some text to a chart. How can I do that?

You can create a callout using these steps:

1. Click the Drawing button in the Standard toolbar to open the Drawing toolbar.

2. Click the Oval drawing tool and use it to draw an oval where you want your callout.

3. Right-click in your new oval and choose Add Text. Type the text you want in the oval.

4. When you are done typing the text, resize either the text or the oval or both so they fit each other. You can resize the oval by dragging it, and you can change the

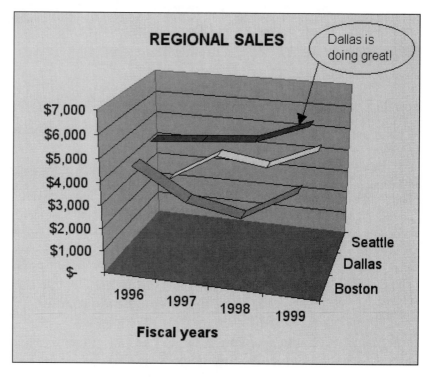

Figure 4-6:   Callout created with the Drawing tools

    font characteristics by right-clicking on the text, then
choosing Format AutoShape.

5. Click the Arrow tool and drag an arrow from the oval
to the object to which the callout applies. An example is
shown in Figure 4-6.

**? The Chart Wizard automatically assumes what data will be
plotted on which axis. How can I change the axis that
data is plotted on?**

    In Step 2 of the Chart Wizard you can choose whether the
series are in Rows or Columns, which are the only choices,
even with 3D charts. If you finish a chart in Chart Wizard
and then want to change the axis assignment, you can do
so using the By Row and By Column buttons in the Chart
toolbar.

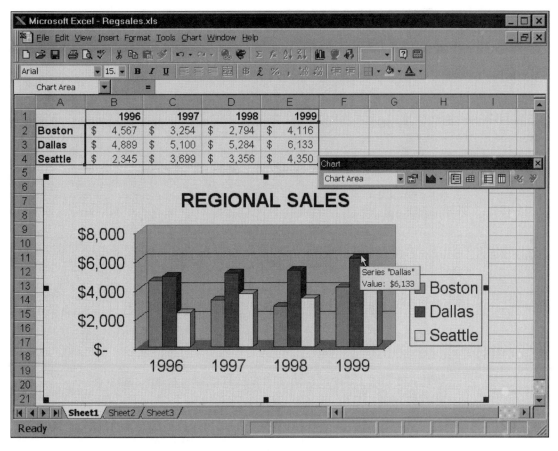

Figure 4-7:   An Excel chart and its data range

What is the best **chart type** to use with my data?

This is not an easy question to answer, and there are probably several substantially different opinions. For example, the data shown in the chart in Figure 4-7 might be more informative if it were a line chart, as you can see in Figure 4-8, but it is not as interesting. The best answer comes from asking yourself if the chart tells the story you are trying to tell. The sidebar "Chart Types" provides some quick guidelines for the more common chart types.

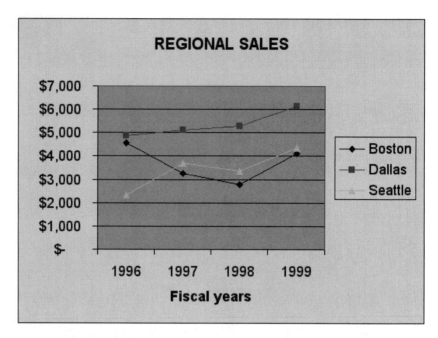

Figure 4-8:   The data from Figure 4-7 replotted as a line chart

? What's the difference between **data markers and data labels?**

A data marker distinguishes one series from another. In Figure 4-7 it is a bar on the chart. It is uniquely colored or patterned for each series. A data label is a piece of text representing a value plotted on the chart. The sidebar "Elements of an Excel Chart" describes all of the parts of an Excel chart.

? What are **data series and data ranges?**

A data range is the area on the worksheet that contains all of the data used to create a chart. A data series is a set of related numbers that produces one element of the chart, such as a set of bars or a line. In Figure 4-7, which shows a chart and the data that created it, the data range is A1:E4

● ● ● ● ● ● ● ● ● ● ●

Chart Types

Excel offers 14 standard chart types, each with a number of variations and combinations. The best way to see how these work with your data is to start up the Chart Wizard, click the different standard and custom chart types, and see how they look in the preview window. Here are some observations about the more common standard chart types:

Area charts   show the magnitude of change over time. They are particularly useful when several components are changing and you are interested in the sum of those components. Area charts let you see the change in the individual components, as well as the change in the total.

Bar charts   consist of a series of horizontal bars that allow comparison of the relative size of two or more items at one point in time. For example, a bar chart might compare the sales for each of three products in each of five years. Each bar in a bar chart is a single data point or number on the sheet. The set of numbers for a single set of bars is a data series.

Column charts   consist of series of vertical columns that allow comparison of the relative size of two or more items, often over time. For example, a column chart might compare annual sales by presenting a column for each year's sales. Each column in a column chart is a single data point or number on the sheet. The set of numbers for a single set of columns is a data series.

Line charts   are used to show trends over time. For example, the line chart in Figure 4-8 shows that Dallas has continuous upward growth while Boston is having a hard time. With line charts, the reader can make a projection into the future (maybe inappropriately). In a line chart, each of the data series is used to produce a line on the chart, with each number in the range producing a data point on the line.

High-low-close charts   are line charts with three data series used to display a stock's high, low, and closing prices for a given time period. High-low-close charts also work well for commodity prices, currency exchange rates, and temperature and pressure measurements. The vertical lines are formed by drawing a line between the high and the low data points, while the tick mark is the closing price.

Pie charts   are best used for comparing the percentages of a sum that several numbers represent. The full pie is the sum, and each number is represented by a wedge, or slice. An example is a pie chart where each slice represents the percentage of total sales contributed by different product categories. There is only one data series in a pie chart.

Radar charts   show how data changes in relation to a center point and to other data. The value axis of each category radiates from the center point. Data from the same series is connected by lines. You can use a radar chart to plot several interrelated series and easily make visual comparisons. For example, if you have three machines containing the same five parts, you can plot the wear index of each part on each machine on a radar chart.

Scatter, or XY, charts   show the relationship between pairs of numbers and the trends they present. For each pair, one of the numbers is plotted on the X axis and the other number is plotted on the Y axis. Where the two meet, a symbol is placed on the chart. When a number of such pairs are plotted, a pattern may emerge. Examples of scatter charts are temperature vs. time of day and years of production experience vs. number of parts produced.

Elements of an Excel Chart

Charts have a number of common elements, although there are differences between a 2D chart and a 3D one. Most of the chart elements can be changed or created apart from the creation of the chart itself.

Elements of a 2D chart

Figure 4-9 shows the elements of a 2D chart, which are described here:

▷ The **Y axis,** or value axis, is normally the vertical axis in a 2D chart, and it shows the value of the data points that are plotted, such as dollars in Figure 4-9.

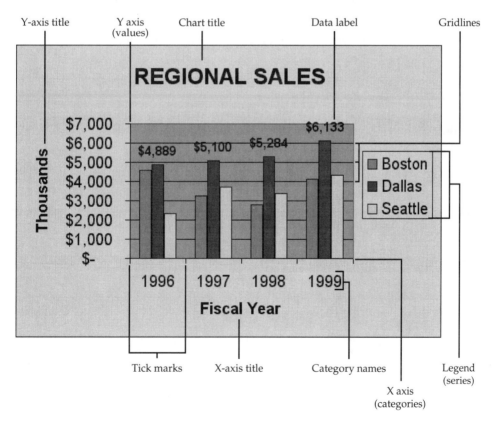

Figure 4-9:   Elements of a 2D chart

• • • • • • • • • • •

- ☞ The **X axis,** or category axis, is normally the horizontal axis, and shows the categories of the data points that are plotted, such as years in Figure 4-9.
- ☞ The **Chart title**, which can be taken from a cell on the sheet or added directly to the chart, is the primary descriptive text on the chart.
- ☞ The **Category names** identify the individual data points. They may be dates, locations, products, and so forth. The category names are taken from the topmost row or the leftmost column, depending on the orientation of the sheet.
- ☞ The **Legend** is a set of labels that describe each of the data series. These labels are attached to a symbol, a color, or a pattern that is associated with the series and placed on the chart (initially to the right, but you can move it). It is used to distinguish one data series from another. The text for a legend is taken from a text row or column depending on the orientation of the sheet.
- ☞ The **Data marker** is used to distinguish one data series from another and has a unique color, symbol, or pattern. It is the bar, line, column, or pie wedge on the chart.
- ☞ **Tick marks** are small lines used to divide the two axes and provide the scaling.
- ☞ **Gridlines** may be displayed for both axes to help read the value of individual data points. Gridlines are scaled according to the values on the axes and can be changed (only horizontal grid lines are shown in Figure 4-9).
- ☞ **Data labels** are sometimes displayed to show the value of single data points.
- ☞ The **Selected Border** indicates that a chart can be sized, moved, or deleted and contains nodes or handles for that purpose. The chart in Figure 4-7 has a selected border.

Elements of a 3D chart

3D charts have the following additional or changed elements, which are shown in Figure 4-10:

- ☞ The **Z axis,** or value axis, shows the value of the data points and is normally the vertical axis.

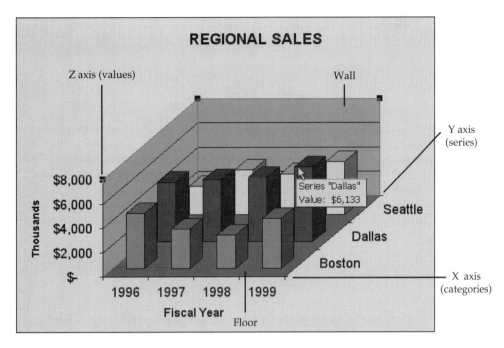

Figure 4-10:   Elements of a 3D chart

- ● ● ● ● ● ● ● ● ● ● ●

⊳ The **X axis,** or category axis, is the same as in 2D charts and is normally the horizontal axis.

⊳ The **Y axis,** or series axis, shows the individual series. It is normally the depth or inward axis.

⊳ The **Wall** is the background of the plotted area.

⊳ The **Corners,** which are shown with nodes in Figure 4-10, can be rotated to change the view.

⊳ The **Floor** is the base upon which the series are plotted.

Each chart element can be accessed and either changed or used to modify the chart in some way.

and one of the data series is A3:E3—the data for one city, Dallas. In this case the data series is said to be "by rows." It could just as easily be by columns—the data for one year, as shown next:

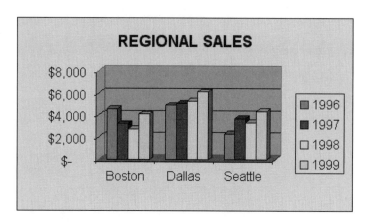

How data will be charted is an important consideration when you create the data. This is discussed in the sidebar "Guidelines for Charting Data."

Guidelines for Charting Data

The data that you intend to chart should be prepared with the following guidelines (use the data in Figure 4-7 as an example):

☞ The data must be in one or more rectangles or ranges (they don't have to be contiguous), with text labels in the topmost row and/or leftmost column. Otherwise, the range may contain numbers and text, but text is interpreted as zeros.

☞ Excel defines the first data series—a range of numbers that is composed of related data points to be plotted (points that would form, for example, a single line on a chart)—as beginning with the first cell in the upper-left corner of the highlighted range containing a number not formatted as a date and continuing across the rows and columns that are highlighted.

☞ Excel determines whether more rows or more columns are highlighted and, with the assumption that there will be more data points than data series, makes the larger of rows or columns the data points. So if you highlight six columns and three rows, each column will be a data point (a single number to be plotted) and each row a data series.

➤ Additional data series can be included in the range by highlighting additional rows or columns, depending on whether you are building a columnwise or rowwise chart. You can have ten or more data series, but the resulting chart may not be readable.

➤ If the first column or row of the highlighted range contains labels or date-formatted numbers and/or the cell in the upper-left corner is blank, the first column or row—depending on whether the data series are down columns (columnwise) or across rows (rowwise)—is used for the X, or category, axis.

➤ The numbers on the Y, or value, axis are formatted with the same format that was used with the data points on the sheet.

➤ The initial default is to produce a Column or Vertical Bar chart. This and other options can be easily changed.

Figure 4-7 contains a range of rowwise data series that fits the guidelines for a standard chart. The first row contains number-formatted dates that are used for the X axis; the next three rows are data series, each containing four numeric data points used to produce the Column chart shown in the lower part of the figure. The labels in the legend are taken from the first column.

SORTING, FILTERING, AND SUMMARIZING DATA

I have a lot of data to enter. What is the easiest way to do it?

First, look at your data and see if there is any repetitive information. If there is, you should split it into several tables so you enter only the unique information in each record. For example, if you are entering sales information that looks like the data shown at the top of the screen in

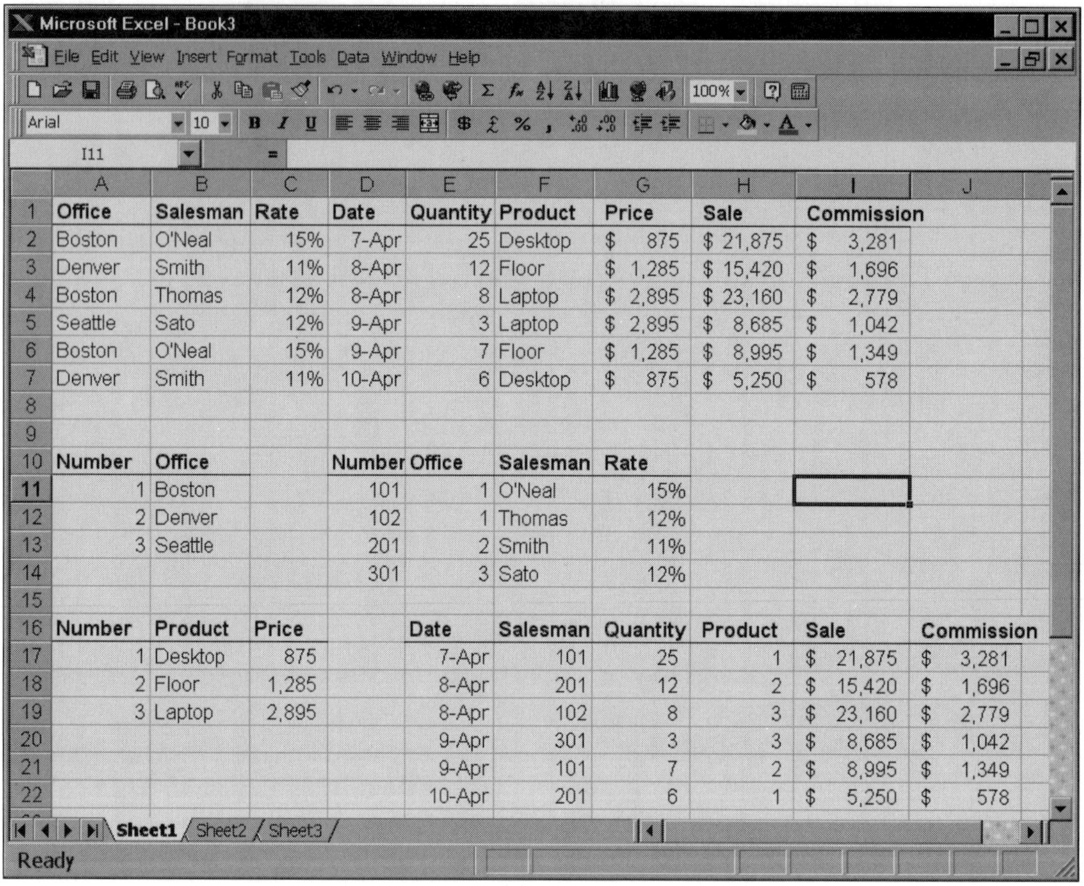

	A	B	C	D	E	F	G	H	I	J
1	Office	Salesman	Rate	Date	Quantity	Product	Price	Sale	Commission	
2	Boston	O'Neal	15%	7-Apr	25	Desktop	$ 875	$ 21,875	$ 3,281	
3	Denver	Smith	11%	8-Apr	12	Floor	$ 1,285	$ 15,420	$ 1,696	
4	Boston	Thomas	12%	8-Apr	8	Laptop	$ 2,895	$ 23,160	$ 2,779	
5	Seattle	Sato	12%	9-Apr	3	Laptop	$ 2,895	$ 8,685	$ 1,042	
6	Boston	O'Neal	15%	9-Apr	7	Floor	$ 1,285	$ 8,995	$ 1,349	
7	Denver	Smith	11%	10-Apr	6	Desktop	$ 875	$ 5,250	$ 578	
8										
9										
10	Number	Office		Number	Office	Salesman	Rate			
11	1	Boston		101	1	O'Neal	15%			
12	2	Denver		102	1	Thomas	12%			
13	3	Seattle		201	2	Smith	11%			
14				301	3	Sato	12%			
15										
16	Number	Product	Price		Date	Salesman	Quantity	Product	Sale	Commission
17	1	Desktop	875		7-Apr	101	25	1	$ 21,875	$ 3,281
18	2	Floor	1,285		8-Apr	201	12	2	$ 15,420	$ 1,696
19	3	Laptop	2,895		8-Apr	102	8	3	$ 23,160	$ 2,779
20					9-Apr	301	3	3	$ 8,685	$ 1,042
21					9-Apr	101	7	2	$ 8,995	$ 1,349
22					10-Apr	201	6	1	$ 5,250	$ 578

Figure 4-11: Breaking a database into related tables

Figure 4-11, then it should be split into four separate tables, as shown in the lower part of the figure. This way you enter the three small tables only once and enter the minimum information only once.

Excel also provides an automatic data entry form for any database table you create. Simply click any cell in the table, open the Data menu, and choose Form. A dialog box will open, displaying the first record in the table you selected. Click New. A blank form will open, like the one you see next:

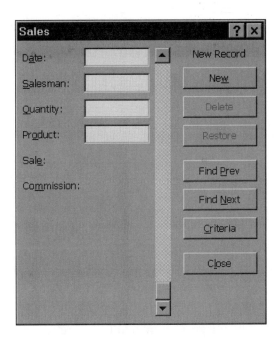

Notice that calculated fields are grayed out. You only have to type entries in blank fields, which speeds up data entry.

❓ How can I **import database files** into Excel?

The easiest way to get information into Excel is to export the information from its source as a comma- or tab-delimited text file. This means that each record is a single line of text with a carriage return at the end of it and a comma or a tab character separating each field. If you have a choice, tabs are better than commas, because your data may have commas in it but it is unlikely that it will have tabs. Once you have a comma- or tab-delimited text file, start Excel, choose File Open, select Text Files in the *Files of Type* drop-down list, identify the folder and file, and click Open. (The Text Import Wizard may open, showing you how the file will be imported and allowing you to make changes. Make any necessary changes, and click OK.) The file will come in as if it were an Excel file, with each record in a separate row and each field in a separate column.

How do I select certain records from my database?

Click any cell in the table and choose Filter, AutoFilter from the Data menu. Drop-down list buttons appear next to each of the field names, like this:

Date ▾	Salesm ▾	Quanti ▾	Produc ▾	Sale ▾	Commissi ▾
7-Apr	101	25	1	$ 21,875	$ 3,281
8-Apr	201	12	2	$ 15,420	$ 1,696
8-Apr	102	8	3	$ 23,160	$ 2,779
9-Apr	301	3	3	$ 8,685	$ 1,042
9-Apr	101	7	2	$ 8,995	$ 1,349
10-Apr	201	6	1	$ 5,250	$ 578

If you open a field name's drop-down list, you see a list of the unique entries in the column as well as several special entries. Select the column's entries and the data table will change to show only the records that reflect the chosen entry. For example, if you were to open the Salesm drop-down list in the table shown above and click "101," you would get a new table, as shown next. Chosen entries are called the criteria, and only the records that match that criteria are displayed.

Date ▾	Salesm ▾	Quanti ▾	Produc ▾	Sale ▾	Commissi ▾
7-Apr	101	25	1	$ 21,875	$ 3,281
9-Apr	101	7	2	$ 8,995	$ 1,349

 Note: When a criterion is applied, the table only displays the selected records—the entire rows containing the records not displayed are hidden.

You can return the table to its original view by again opening the drop-down list in the column where you selected the criteria and choosing All. You can select criteria in several columns and further refine your selection. Also, you can choose Custom in the drop-down list and specify multiple criteria for one column, like this:

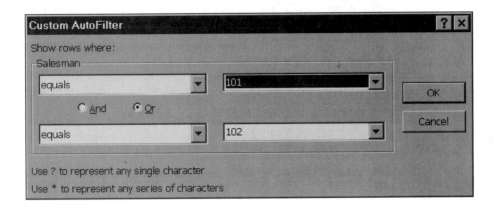

The Custom AutoFilter dialog box allows you to enter criteria other than exact matches, such as "is greater than" or "begins with," and to use the wildcard characters ? and *. The wildcard characters allow matches like 10? to select all numbers from 100 through 109.

❓ How do I **sort on more than three levels?** Three is the most the Sort dialog box offers as a choice.

For, say, a four-level sort you sort the second, third, and fourth levels first, and then sort a second time on just the primary sort criteria.

❓ How do I decide which application to use to **store data—** Excel or Access or another application?

The principal function of Excel is to analyze data. If you have a database with which analysis is important and with significantly less than the maximum 65,536 rows in Excel (each row is a database record and you normally do not want to build a database you can't add records to), then Excel is a possible choice. Also, if you have a very small database, up to a couple of thousand records, and it will have a short life and limited use, then Excel might be the easiest way to produce and use such a database. On the other hand, if you have a large database (over a couple of thousand records) that is liable to be around for a long time (over a year), and if fast searching, forms, and reports are major considerations, then Access is the application of choice. Access is also your best choice if you have a complex data set such as salespeople, products, and sales, where three related tables would be the way to handle the information.

Tip: If you are creating a database of names and addresses, such as a contacts list, then Outlook may be the best choice of application in which to use it.

? Is there an easy way to create **subtotals in a sorted list?**

Yes. Open the Data menu, choose Subtotals, and then select the appropriate options from the Subtotals dialog box shown here:

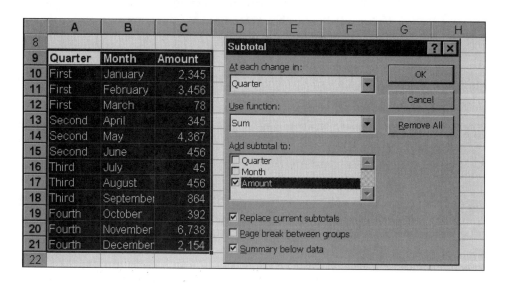

chapter

5 Answers!

Presenting with PowerPoint

Answer Topics!

PowerPoint
@ a Glance

PowerPoint provides Office 97 with tools and features to create stunning presentations. While the other Office products are capable of producing professional-looking reports, letters, spreadsheets, and other business and personal products, PowerPoint was created with the idea of showmanship as a primary design consideration.

A PowerPoint presentation is a file (with extension .ppt) that is composed of one or more slides. A slide is a single screen of text, graphics, background, and other objects that illustrate a topic. Similar to 35-millimeter photographic slides, PowerPoint slides can be just that, but they can also be much more: you can print slides to use as handouts, you can attach notes related to each slide for yourself or for distribution to your audience, and you can hide slides in your presentation with jumps to them if needed. Slide shows generated from a computer can include sound, video clips, and amazing transitional effects from one slide to the next; in short, you can do just about anything you want in electronic or printed presentations to deliver the impact you're after. The power of the personal computer offers an endless variety of special effects and multimedia features that you can use to enhance your presentation.

PowerPoint also realizes most of us are not professional graphic artists or designers and does a great job of providing professionally prepared presentations that you can modify for your own use. These include the following:

➤ **Presentation templates,** which are complete presentations with color schemes, graphics, and dummy text, as shown in Figure 5-1. There are 33 presentation templates that cover a broad range of corporate needs for printed, electronic (run from

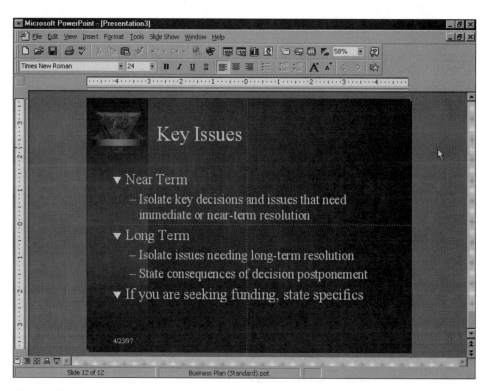

Figure 5-1:   Presentation templates provide everything needed for a professional appearance

a computer through a monitor or projection device), or online use over the Internet or an intranet.

☞ **AutoContent Wizard,** which walks you through the process of creating a presentation by getting feedback from you on what specific elements you want in your presentation.

☞ **Presentation designs,** which provide a single slide with a color scheme and graphics from which to build your presentation. You can either start with the design and then add your own text or other objects or you can apply one of the presentation designs to your existing presentation. PowerPoint includes 17 different presentation designs from which to choose.

☞ **Design assistance** to specific elements such as the slide layout, color scheme, and background. This method provides the best opportunity for you to use your creative ideas from the start. However, all of these methods allow you to modify the design elements to your liking.

Flexibility in creating a presentation and consistency in delivering it are key aspects of PowerPoint. Many presentations contain the same "look and feel" throughout their slides by incorporating design elements such as the company logo in the same location on each slide, locating each slide's title and bullets in exactly the same spot, and other consistent formatting techniques. PowerPoint uses masters to ensure you can lock in those design elements that you want to remain the same throughout your entire presentation. There are four masters that you can use:

☞ **Slide master** sets the basic elements of a slide, including placement of the slide title, main text layout and formatting, background, graphics, slide number, date, and other objects.

☞ **Title master** covers the design of the title slide, or first slide, as well as title and subtitle placement and formatting.

☞ **Handout master** sets up the arrangement of multiple slides on a page or the presentation outline for printing as audience handouts.

☞ **Notes master** determines the sizing and placement of the slide being described and its corresponding notes area.

The true beauty of PowerPoint's ease of use is centered around the five views available to you to create, edit, and show your presentations.

Understanding what each view does and how it can be used to accomplish your work will save you much time and effort. Table 5-1 describes the main function of each view.

Table 5-1:   Views Available in PowerPoint

	View	Function
	Slide	To display the slide in full-view, incorporate text and graphic elements, and modify its appearance
	Outline	To condense slide content to text-only for ease in organizing the slides in a presentation
	Slide sorter	To display thumbnails of each slide in a presentation for ease in rearranging slide order and adding transitions
	Notes page	To allow the speaker to include notes that correspond to each slide in the presentation
	Slide show	To preview a full-screen view of the presentation with any transitions or animation, and check timing and sequence

WORKING WITH POWERPOINT AND ITS VIEWS

 I e-mailed a copy of a presentation to one of my field reps, but he says he can't open the presentation. What's wrong?

Best guess is either he's using an earlier version of PowerPoint (the PowerPoint 97 file format is not recognizable by previous versions) or he doesn't have PowerPoint installed on his computer. You have several options:

➡ Save the presentation as the type corresponding to the version of PowerPoint he's using and resend the file (some features of your presentation may not display properly, since several newer features in PowerPoint 97 are not supported by earlier versions).

➪ Have your rep download PowerPoint Viewer 97 from the Microsoft Web site, http://www.microsoft.com/powerpoint. He'll be able view and print the presentation but won't be able to make changes.

➪ Create a package using the Pack and Go Wizard (Pack and Go in the File menu) that includes all the files and fonts used in the presentation, and in this case, you could also add PowerPoint Viewer 97. This is your best choice to ensure that your presentation appears on another computer as it was designed.

≡ *Note:*   The PowerPoint Viewer included on the Office 97 CD-ROM only supports PowerPoint 95 file format features. In order to view a presentation saved as a PowerPoint 97 file you will have to download PowerPoint Viewer 97 from the Microsoft Web site.

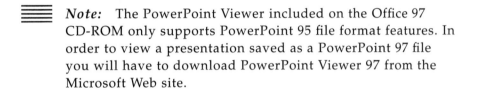

Can I easily change the layout of a slide once I've created and saved it?

Sure. In Slide, Outline, or Slide Sorter view (in Slide Sorter view first select the slide) choose Slide Layout from the Format menus. In the familiar Slide Layout dialog box, select a new layout and PowerPoint will try and match it.

I find it cumbersome to view bulleted text in my presentations by using the Slide Sorter view to locate the text I want to edit and then switching to Slide view to be able to edit it. Is there an easier way to view and edit my main points?

Sure—use Outline view to quickly see your text and immediately edit it. Figure 5-2 shows a portion of a presentation in Outline view.

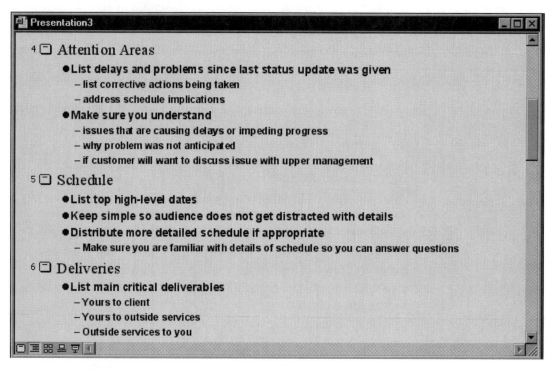

Figure 5-2:   Outline view works well for editing text

? What is the best way to **move text in Outline view**?

To move a single bullet, position the pointer to the left of the bulleted item until it turns into a four-headed arrow, as shown here.

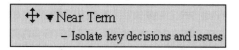

Drag the bullet to another location in the presentation. You can move the text of an entire slide by positioning the pointer over the slide icon to the left of the slide title and then dragging it to its new location; all subordinate text will follow.

? When I'm using Outline view I only see items that are titles or bullets. How can I tell if a slide contains other objects?

The slide icon that contains paragraph text or other objects changes from this...

to this...

CREATING PRESENTATIONS

? Every time I start PowerPoint the same dialog box appears with choices to open or create presentations. I just want PowerPoint to open so I can use the menu bar and toolbars to get to work. Is there a way to go right to PowerPoint?

Yes and no. The PowerPoint dialog box, shown here, is great for new users to help them get going, but after you acquire more familiarity with the program you might find it to be just an extra "layer" between you and your work.

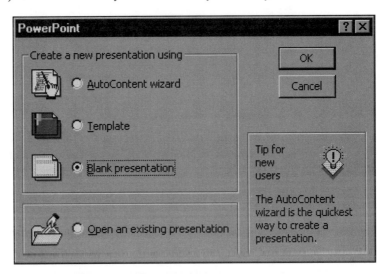

To prevent this dialog box from opening, choose Options from the Tools menu, click the View tab, and click *Startup dialog* to clear the check box.

The next time you open PowerPoint the Startup dialog box won't open *but* the New Slide dialog box will appear so you can select a slide layout. To also prevent this dialog box from opening return to the Options dialog box, View tab, and then click *New slide dialog.* Now, finally, when you restart PowerPoint you will open to a new presentation.

■■■■ *Caution:*   If you choose not to have the New Slide dialog box displayed, whenever you create a new slide you won't be offered the list of AutoLayouts from which to choose. PowerPoint will open a new slide with the default title box layout.

❓ I have many presentations saved on several drives and networked computers. How can I best **locate the presentation I need?**

Use keywords to uniquely identify each presentation when you create it. Open the Properties dialog box for a presentation by choosing Properties from the File menu. On the Summary tab, type one or more keywords that you'll remember for each presentation and then click OK. Find a file based on keywords with these steps:

1. Click the Open button.

2. Use the *Look in* box to select the drive where you think the file is stored.
3. Click the Advanced button and in the Advanced Find dialog box, open the Property drop-down list box and select Keywords, as shown next.

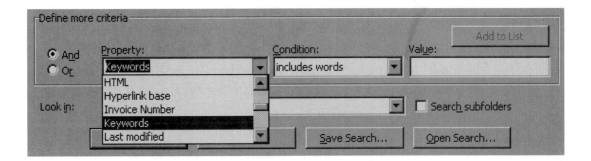

4. Ensure that the Condition box displays *includes words* and then type the keywords in the Value box.

5. Click Add to List and select the Search subfolders check box.

6. Click Find Now.

The Advanced Find dialog box closes and the Open dialog displays the filename you were looking for.

Tip: To remind yourself to add keywords to each presentation, you can automatically display the Properties dialog box when you first save a presentation. Choose Options from the Tools menu, click the Save tab, and then select Prompt for file properties.

? I think the built-in presentation templates and designs that PowerPoint provides are great time savers. Do you know where I can find **more templates and designs**?

Check the ValuPack folder on the Office 97 CD. There are two subfolders that contain additional presentations (\ Present) and designs (\ Designs).

? Can I **open more than one presentation at a time**?

Yes. Choose Open from the File menu and navigate to the folder where your presentations are located. Press CTRL as you click all the presentations you want opened. When you click Open, PowerPoint will display the first presentation and all others can be quickly displayed by choosing them from the Window menu or by cycling through the list by pressing CTRL-F6.

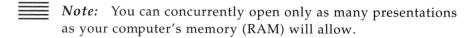 *Note:*   You can concurrently open only as many presentations as your computer's memory (RAM) will allow.

?   **I'd like to include a presentation in a Web site that I maintain. How can I run the presentation as a slide show on my home page?**

First, save the PowerPoint presentation as a PowerPoint show. Open the presentation, choose Save As from the File menu, and then select PowerPoint Show (file extension .pps) from the *Save as type* drop-down list box:

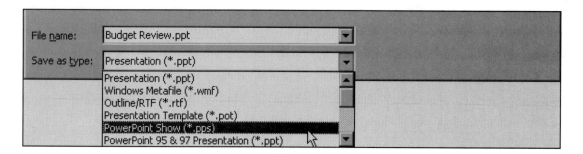

Next, open your home page in an HTML authoring tool such as Microsoft FrontPage 97 and insert the .pps file. When a user clicks the icon, the PowerPoint slide show will run.

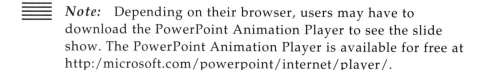 *Note:*   Depending on their browser, users may have to download the PowerPoint Animation Player to see the slide show. The PowerPoint Animation Player is available for free at http:/microsoft.com/powerpoint/internet/player/.

?   **I originally created a presentation for audience handouts using a built-in template, but now my boss wants to put the presentation on a corporate intranet. Do I have to start all over and choose the online version?**

No. You can use your current presentation and simply save it in HTML, the language of the Internet and intranets. Choose *Save as HTML* from the File menu and a wizard of the same name will open, offering you several choices to modify your existing presentation so that it better conforms to online conventions.

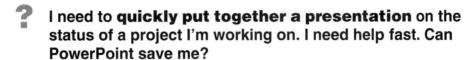

I need to quickly put together a presentation on the status of a project I'm working on. I need help fast. Can PowerPoint save me?

You bet. When PowerPoint is started you are presented with a dialog box that offers several "get started" options. Select *AutoContent wizard* and click OK. The wizard will walk you through four areas of presentation design, where you build a presentation to your requirements. The four areas are

➪ **Presentation type,** where you scan a list of built-in presentation topics to find one that most closely matches the subject of your own

➪ **Output options,** where you choose the underlying architecture for standard printed and electronic usage or online delivery (for example, on the Internet)

➪ **Presentation style,** which offers you a choice of output media for the presentation

➪ **Presentation options,** which allows you to add unique information such as your title, name, and company

PowerPoint will provide everything for your presentation except the specifics of your project and the coffee and doughnuts. The sidebar "PowerPoint's Presentation Templates Summary" provides the complete list of available templates for onscreen, printed, and online use.

Note: The online versions of presentation templates are identical to the standard versions except they may have additional buttons to facilitate hyperlink navigation, and they are saved in HTML format.

USING TEMPLATES AND MASTERS

I use the Project Status presentation design for weekly briefings and wind up customizing it each time with our same company logo, company profile, and other objects that don't change. Is there a way to create a custom template and avoid this repetitive work?

Sure. After you have added the text and objects that don't change from one week to another, you can save the Project

PowerPoint's Presentation Templates Summary

The following table lists the presentation templates available in PowerPoint.

Presentation Template	Standard (for printed and onscreen usage)	Online (for use on the Internet or a corporate intranet)
AutoContent	X	X
Business Plan	X	X
Company Meeting	X	X
Corporate Financial Overview	X	X
Corporate Home Page	X	X
Facilitating a Meeting	X	
Flyer	X	X
Generic	X	X
H.R. Information Kiosk	X	X
Introducing a Speaker	X	
Managing H.R. Changing Role	X	
Marketing Plan	X	X
Motivating a Team	X	
Organization Overview	X	X
Personal Home Page	X	X
Presentation Guidelines	X	
Presenting a Technical Report	X	
Product Overview	X	X
Project Status	X	X
Recommending a Strategy	X	X
Reporting Progress	X	X
Selling Your Ideas	X	
Thanking a Speaker	X	

Note that if you find you do not have all of the templates listed in the table available to you, run Office 97 Setup and, under Options in Microsoft PowerPoint, make sure the Content Templates component is fully selected. A grayed check box, shown here, indicates only one of the two subcomponents has been selected.

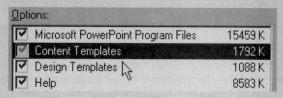

Status template as a new template such as Weekly Briefing. The Project Status template will remain intact and you will have created a custom template for your own use. To create a custom template follow these steps:

1. Click the Open toolbar button, choose the path to your presentation templates (the default is C:\Program Files\Microsoft Office\Templates\Presentation), select Presentation Templates in the *Files of type* drop-down list box, and double-click the PowerPoint template you want to start with.

2. Make the changes to the template that you want in your new template.

3. Choose Save As from the File menu to display the dialog box of the same name, and in the *Save as type* drop-down list box, choose Presentation Template (filename extension .pot).

Caution: Make sure you choose Save As and not Save—if you choose Save, the original PowerPoint template will be overwritten with any changes you make.

4. Type a name for the new template in the *File name* box and use the *Save in* box to select a folder where you want to store the template. See the sidebar "Templates Folder Locations" for help in storing templates.

5. Click Save.

● ● ● ● ● ● ● ● ● ●

Templates Folder Locations

You can store a template in any folder, on your computer, or on a network. If you want to store a new template where it will appear with PowerPoint's built-in presentations when you open the File New dialog box, use the folder locations described in the following table.

Note that the default Office 97 installation path is C:\ Program Files\ Microsoft Office.... If you changed from this default location, adjust the following paths accordingly.

Presentation Type	Folder location C:\ **Program Files**\ **Microsoft Office**\ ...
Blank presentation	... Templates
Presentation designs (schemes that can be applied to your existing material)	... Templates\ Presentation Designs
Presentation templates (fully contained presentations with suggested text)	... Templates\ Presentations

?

Most of the speaker notes in my presentation don't fit in the default notes area. I know I can reduce the size of each slide to gain more space for notes, but it seems quite tedious to do this for every slide. Is there an easy way to increase the notes area on speaker notes?

Yes there is. By using the Notes Master for a particular presentation you can customize the notes layout for all slides, saving time and ensuring that all slides are sized uniformly. In any of the five views, choose Master from the View menu and Notes Master from the submenu. Reduce the size of the slide image by clicking it to select it and then pressing SHIFT (to maintain the height-width ratio) while you drag a corner selection handle inward. Enlarge the size of the Notes Body Area by dragging the selection handles in the direction you want the increase to occur, as shown here:

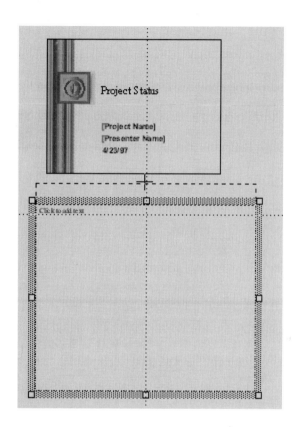

?   **I have a background of our corporate logo in my Slide Master that works great in all but a few slides in my presentation. How do I remove a master background from a slide?**

Open the slide whose background you want omitted. From the Format menu, choose Background and select the *Omit background graphics from master* check box.

Tip: You can manually override formatting set in the Master Slide for individual slides by changing the formatting in Slide view.

? **I don't want to show the page number on my opening slide. How do I remove the page number on the first slide and retain it in the remaining slides?**

With these steps:

1. Open the Slide Master by opening the View menu, pointing on Master, and choosing Slide Master.

2. Verify that you have a slide Number Area object on the master slide, as shown here.

(If it's not there you can see how to add it in the question on **restoring the date area to the master slide** in this section.)

3. Choose *Header and Footer* from the View menu.

4. Select the *Slide number* check box to place slide numbers on each slide in the presentation.

5. Select *Don't show on title slide* to prevent the slide number from appearing on the opening slide.

? **I inadvertently deleted the date area from the master slide. How do I restore the date area to the master?**

Open the Slide Master by opening the View menu, pointing on Master, and choosing Slide Master, and then right-click on an empty spot on the slide. Choose Master Layout from the pop-up menu, select the Date placeholder, and click OK.

⬚⬚⬚ *Tip:* If the Common Tasks floating toolbar is displayed, as shown here, the Master Layout dialog box is always readily available when using a master.

To display the Common Tasks toolbar select it from the View menu Toolbars options.

CUSTOMIZING PRESENTATIONS

 I'd like to annotate key points in my slides by adding a consistent set of onscreen remarks. Is there a way to do this?

Yes. Use callouts to amplify or emphasize elements in your slides. You can manually create callouts by using the Text Box tool (to contain the callout narrative) and the Line tool (to connect the callout with the point of interest), but to achieve fast, consistent results you can choose from one of several designs PowerPoint provides. On the Drawing toolbar (in Slide view), click AutoShapes, point to Callouts, and select one of the twenty designs. Click the crosshair pointer where you want the end of the connecting line or shape to begin and then drag. Figure 5-3 shows an example of a callout.

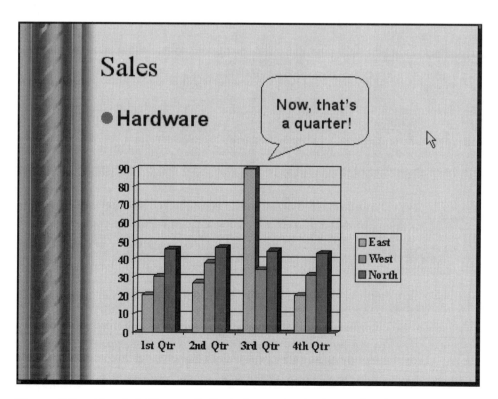

Figure 5-3:   Use AutoShapes Callouts to emphasize key points in a slide

Tip: Customize the size and appearance of AutoShapes by using the Format AutoShape option.

? I find it very difficult to **align and size boxes and lines** in an organization chart for my company. Is there an easy way?

Yes. With the slide where you want to put the chart open in PowerPoint, open the Insert menu, point on Picture, and then select Organization Chart. This will open Microsoft Organization Chart 2.0, a separate program that is included with Office 97, whose sole purpose is to create and format organization charts. The program opens with the skeleton of a simple chart that you can easily build upon:

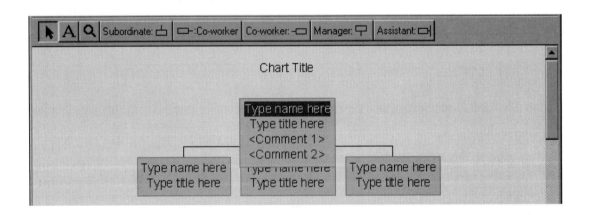

You can save an organization chart as a separate file or copy it to other material you are preparing, or it can be linked to your current presentation. See Chapter 8, "Integrating Office Documents," for a complete description of linking objects between Office 97 products.

Tip: If you get an error when you try to create an Organization Chart, you probably did not install it when you installed Office. You can install it by rerunning Office Setup and looking in the Office Tools options.

? **How can I quickly align multiple boxes in a column along their centers?**

Use PowerPoint's automatic aligning and distributing feature. You can try for hours to get several objects into a uniform position, or, with a few mouse clicks, you can have them all fall into line like good soldiers. Follow these next few steps to achieve perfect positioning:

1. In Slide view, hold SHIFT while selecting the objects you want to work on.

2. On the Drawing toolbar, click Draw, point to *Align or Distribute,* and select Align Center. The objects will align but their spacing is commonly haphazard.

3. Repeat step 2 but select Distribute Vertically.

? **I want to show data in the form of a chart but I'm a little confused about my charting options for data. What are they?**

One of the downsides of Office 97 is that you are often presented with too many choices. PowerPoint 97 accesses a small program called Microsoft Graph 97 (as do Word and Access) to provide charting functionality. But since you have Office 97 and not just the stand-alone PowerPoint program, you also have Excel, the charting master, available to you. Which should you use? See the sidebar "PowerPoint Charting" for help.

? **I know there are some neat effects that can be used when transitioning between slides in a slide show. Does PowerPoint have any effects for objects in a slide?**

Yes. PowerPoint offers a set of effects, called animations, similar to those available for slide transitions for text and other objects in a slide. For example, you can have the title materialize letter by letter from outside the boundary of the slide as if typed by a typewriter, complete with sound. You can preview the effects with the following steps:

● ● ● ● ● ● ● ● ● ●

PowerPoint Charting

Whether you the use Microsoft Graph 97 or Excel 97 mainly depends on two factors.

▷ Are you already an experienced Excel user?

▷ Is the supporting data already in a spreadsheet?

The answers to these questions will help you determine which method is better for you. Microsoft Excel is unquestionably one of the best full-service data manipulation and representation programs. If you have the data you will be displaying in PowerPoint already charted in Excel or contained in worksheets, why bother creating it twice? Use one of the methods described in Chapter 8, "Integrating Office Documents," to include the Excel chart in your presentation. If you are presenting data for the first time and don't expect to use it in a spreadsheet, then using PowerPoint's charting capability (Microsoft Graph) makes sense.

This is not to imply that Microsoft Graph is an inferior charting product. With few exceptions, such as the absence of a Charting Wizard and the ability to perform calculations on data, you will not find many significant functional differences between the two products. Perhaps the main attraction to using PowerPoint's integral charting capabilities is that you avoid any problems with pasting, embedding, or linking files that can arise when using Excel.

1. In Slide view, select the object to which you want to apply the animation.

2. Choose Custom Animation from the Slide Show menu to open the dialog box of the same name.

3. On the Effects tab, open the *Entry animation and sound* drop-down list boxes and select a sample, as shown on the following page.

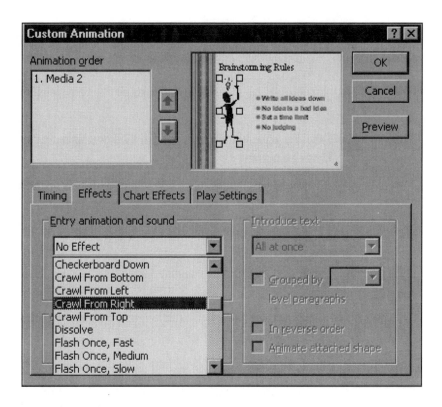

4. Click the Preview button and the effect you chose will run on the selected object in the preview box.

You can have several animated objects on a slide, change their appearance order, adjust timing, and control a host of other attributes to bring your animation to life.

? I've designed a rather complex slide where I want to lock together several drawing objects so I don't inadvertently change anything. How do I do this?

Use the Grouping feature to make a single object from several component objects. Select all of the objects that you want to be included as one by holding SHIFT while clicking each of the components, and then right-click on any of the selected objects. Point to Grouping in the pop-up menu and click Group in the submenu. The selection handles that surrounded each object will change to surround the perimeter of all the objects. Now you can move, size, change color, or otherwise change all the objects as one.

     Tip: When selecting multiple objects for a grouping it may be easier to select all objects on a slide and then deselect those that don't belong in the group. Choose Select All from the Edit menu and then press SHIFT and click those objects you want deselected.

I'd like to use **music on a CD as background** sound. Can I do that?

 You bet. In Slide view, from the Insert menu, point on Movies and Sounds and then choose Play CD Audio Track. In the Play Options dialog box, choose the tracks and timing you want and click OK. A CD icon is inserted on the open slide.

     Caution: Using sound from commercial sources can get you involved with copyright infringement. A safer approach is to use Music Tracks, an add-in program available from the Office 97 ValuPack folder, to make your own sound tracks.

     The sound file from the CD isn't copied to the presentation, so you have to make sure the CD is loaded in your CD-ROM player before you run the presentation. In Slide Show view, click the icon to start the music.

     Tip: Make sure your Windows 95 or other CD player program is *not* open when you try to play the sound track from PowerPoint. If any other CD player is open, the PowerPoint player won't work.

How do I use the Rectangle and Oval drawing tools to create **perfect circles and squares**?

Press SHIFT as you drag to create the circle or square; the object will be constrained to equal width and height.

Whenever I resize an object I always seem to "stretch" it too far in either its height or width. How can I **resize an object proportionally**?

Avoid trying to resize the object with the selection handles. Instead, right-click on the object, choose its format option (for example, *Format Picture for clip art and other pictures* or *Format AutoShape for drawing objects*), and click the Size tab. Ensure that the *Lock aspect ratio* check box is selected, as shown next, and then change the object's size by using actual values or percentages.

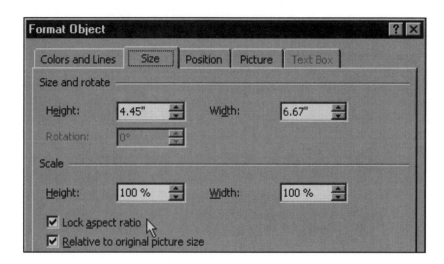

I want the **same background color in several boxes** I've drawn on a slide. What's the fastest way to do this?

First, in Slide view, select all of the objects you want to change as a unit by drawing a selection outline around them, as shown here,

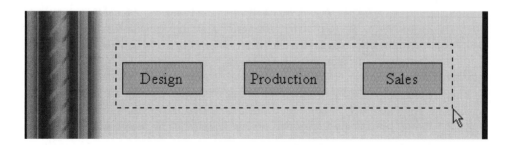

or by pressing SHIFT while clicking each object. Choose Color and Lines from the Format menu and select a new Fill color from the Color and Lines tab.

I've made several changes to the standard bar chart that I'd like to use in other presentations. Can I somehow save a chart's formatting so I don't have to re-create it every time I want to duplicate the chart's appearance?

Sure. What you're looking to do is create a user-defined chart type that you can select as you would any of the chart types that PowerPoint provides. Create a chart type with these steps:

1. Format your chart as you want it to be saved for future use.

2. Choose Chart Type from the Chart menu.

3. Click the Custom Types tab and choose User-defined below the list of chart types.

4. Click the Add button and in the Add Custom Chart Type dialog box, name and describe the new chart. Click OK twice.

The next time you want to format a chart with these attributes, just select it by name from the Custom Types tab.

Tip: If you find that the standard bar chart that appears by default every time you create a chart is not useful for most of your work, you can change the default to any other chart type provided by PowerPoint or created by you. Select the new chart type in the Chart Type dialog box and click the *Set as default chart* button at the bottom of the dialog box.

 I want to use some special effects for titles in slides, such as stretching, skewing, and vertical stacking, but I can't figure out how to accomplish these techniques from the standard drawing tools. Am I missing something?

Yes, but you're close. From the Drawing toolbar you can access WordArt, a separate program that ships with Office 97. It offers the features you want to use and many others. Click the WordArt button to open the WordArt Gallery. Choose a special effect, type your title text in the Editing dialog box, and click OK. The text appears on the slide along with the WordArt toolbar, where you can make further modifications to your title, as shown next.

The tools available on the WordArt toolbar are described in the sidebar "The WordArt Toolbar."

? I have a self-running presentation where I want to provide user ability to display background data if the user wants to. Is there an elegant way to do this?

Yes, you can create a button and hyperlink it to, for example, a Word document. When the button is clicked, Word will start and display the document. Open the slide that will contain the hyperlink, point on Action Buttons from the Slide Show menu, and choose the Document button. Drag the crosshair pointer to create the button and move it to where you want it. In the Action Settings dialog box, choose *Hyperlink to,* select Other File, and browse to the file location. Click OK and run the presentation in Slide Show. The following figure shows what the action button looks like in a slide show.

Click here for sample ideas ⟶

The WordArt Toolbar

The following table describes the functions of the
WordArt tools.

Tool	Description
Insert WordArt	Opens the WordArt Gallery and Edit WordArt Text dialog boxes to get you off and running
Edit Text	Opens the Edit WordArt Text dialog box where you enter text, change font and font size, and style with bold and italics
WordArt Gallery	Opens a dialog box where you can select from several predesigned formats
Format WordArt	Opens a dialog box where you change color, size, and positioning
WordArt Shape	Provides several shapes that WordArt "bends" your text to fit
Free Rotate	Allows you to rotate your WordArt text around a central axis
WordArt Same Letter Heights	Changes all letters to the same height
WordArt Vertical Text	Stacks text in a vertical orientation
WordArt Alignment	Provides standard alignment tools (left, center, right, and justify) and adds other special effects such as stretching
WordArt Character Spacing	Changes the amount of space between characters

? **I generally work with Snap to Grid turned on, but I can't see the gridlines. How can I view the grid?**

Sorry, but the grid is designed to be invisible. If the 12 gridlines per inch were displayed on screen, the Slide view workspace would be severely cluttered even before you started adding objects.

? **I'd like to add my own voice remarks to some of my slides. What do I need to do?**

Foremost, you need to have the required hardware: a sound card and a microphone to record, and a sound card and speakers to play back. Next, you will need plenty of hard disk space available. Sound files recorded in PowerPoint can consume disk space at up to 172 K per second of recording. Finally, you need to decide if want to record throughout the presentation or just for a single slide.

To record throughout a presentation,

1. Choose Record Narration from the Slide Show menu.
2. In the dialog box of the same name adjust recording settings if necessary and click OK.
3. The presentation will start in Slide Show view so you can record narrations on each slide you want.
4. Right-click on the screen to navigate through the show and pause narration.
5. End narration by ending the show. (Press ESC or right-click on the screen and choose End Show from the pop-up menu.)

Tip: For very long narrations you should link the sound file to the presentation; otherwise, the sound is embedded in the presentation file (.ppt), thereby possibly increasing its size dramatically. In the Record Narration dialog box select the *Link narrations in* check box and choose a file location. See Chapter 8, "Integrating Office Documents," for a complete description of object linking and embedding (OLE).

To record remarks on a single slide,

1. In Slide view, display the slide where you want the remarks.

2. Point on Movies and Sounds from the Insert menu and choose Record Sound.

3. In the Record Sound dialog box, click the Record button to start recording and the Stop button when finished.

4. Give the sound a name and click OK.

 Using either method to record sounds will add a sound icon to the slides that contain sound.

ORGANIZING PRESENTATIONS

 I've created a slide that contains too much information. Besides cutting and pasting data onto new slides, is there a better way to move data to a new slide?

Yes; by using the Expand Slide feature to take the original slide's data and break it up into additional slides, as shown in Figure 5-4. Display the slide in question in Slide, Outline, or Slide Sorter view and choose Expand Slide from the Tools menu. In Outline or Slide Sorter view you will see immediately how PowerPoint broke up the information; in Slide view you will be asked whether you want to view the new slides in Outline or Slide Sorter view. The number of additional slides you make depends on the complexity of your original data.

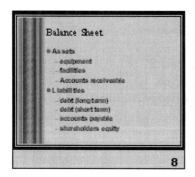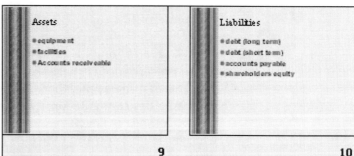

Figure 5-4:   Dividing one slide into two

❓ Is there an easy way to **move two or more slides**?

You bet. In Slide Sorter view select the first slide in the group by clicking it, and then press and hold down SHIFT while clicking any other slides. After all slides are selected drag any of the selected slides to the position where you want them, and when the vertical line appears indicating where the slides will be moved, release the mouse button. To copy slides, press CTRL while dragging the group.

Note: When selecting a group of slides for moving or copying, it doesn't matter in what order you select them; they will be arranged in their original numeric order at their new location.

❓ Does PowerPoint offer any editing resources that can provide **reviews of presentations**?

Yes it does. You can have PowerPoint scan for three key presentation style elements:

▷ Spelling

▷ Visual clarity

▷ Case and end punctuation

You start the review process by choosing Style Checker from the Tools menu. The Style Checker dialog box lets you choose which elements of style you want checked, as shown below.

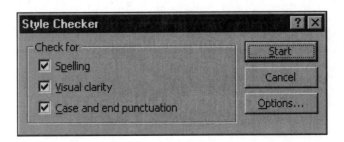

You can customize how each element is reviewed by setting options for PowerPoint to follow. Spelling options are provided in the Spelling tab of the Tools menu Options command. Visual clarity and punctuation options are contained on tabs in the Style Checker Options dialog box, opened by clicking the Options button in the Style Checker dialog box.

I've been asked to review a presentation developed by one of my co-workers. Are there **revision marks for onscreen edits**?

No, there isn't a formal revision-mark feature in PowerPoint. You can use onscreen comments to make your annotations a part of the presentation. (These can be hidden (click Comments on the View menu to toggle between viewing and hiding comments) so they won't inadvertently appear in a public viewing.) To attach onscreen notes, open the slide you want to comment on in Slide view, choose Insert Comment, and start typing. You can change some of the comment attributes such as its color by right-clicking the comment and choosing Format Comment from the pop-up menu. Figure 5-5 shows an example of a comment on a slide.

Figure 5-5:   Comments are like electronic Post-it Notes that can be saved with presentations

Tip: When you insert a comment the Comment toolbar is displayed to offer quick access to comment options and for sending them to other users by e-mail or Outlook.

? I'd like to use **slides from other presentations** in my current presentation. Does PowerPoint offer anything to make this task easier?

Yes it does—using a new feature for PowerPoint 97 called Slide Finder. First, open the presentation in which you want to insert the slides. Select in Slide Sorter view the slide *after* which you want the new slides inserted. Choose *Slides from Files* in the Insert menu to open the Slide Finder dialog box. Browse to the presentation that contains the slide you want and click the Display button. You can view the slides either as thumbnails, as shown below, or in a list, by clicking the buttons in the middle of the dialog box. Select the slides you want (hold down SHIFT to select more than one) and click Insert.

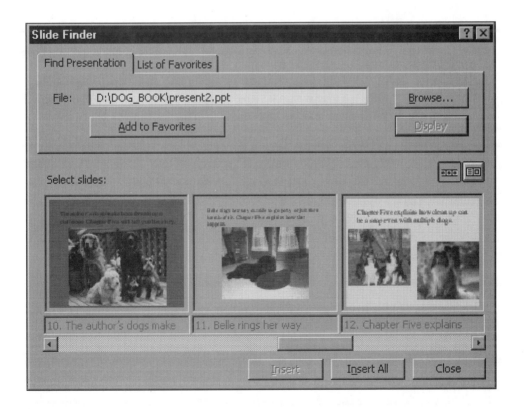

? **I have a very long presentation and find it difficult to organize my slides in Slide Sorter view, because I can only view a handful at a time. How can I view more slides in my presentation?**

The number of slides that you can view is determined by several factors including the video-related components of your computer. Assuming you have the horsepower to display dozens of slides you can view them all by adjusting the zoom percentage, as shown in Figures 5-6 and 5-7. Choose Zoom from the View menu, and then select a zoom percentage that fits your needs.

Tip: As you display more slides, the smaller slide titles become difficult or impossible to read. To quickly display a slide's title, press ALT and click a slide.

PRODUCING PRESENTATIONS ON PAPER AND ON SCREEN

? **My presentation handout has a slide I would like add some notes to. How can I create additional pages of notes?**

This is a good situation in which to use hidden slides. Create a slide consisting only of notes with these steps:

1. In Slide Sorter view, select the slide that needs the notes and choose Duplicate Slide from the Insert menu.

2. Right-click on the new slide and choose Hide Slide.

3. Switch to Notes Page view, select the slide image, and press DEL.

4. Type in your notes in the notes area.

You can increase the size of the notes area by dragging one of its upper three selection handles upward.

Now when you print out notes you will have a second page of notes for this one slide; however, if you choose to run the presentation as a slide show, you won't see the new slide since it's hidden.

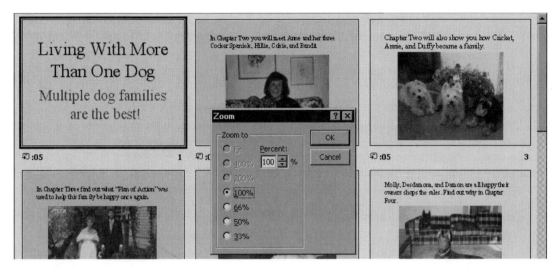

Figure 5-6: Slide Sorter view at 100% zoom

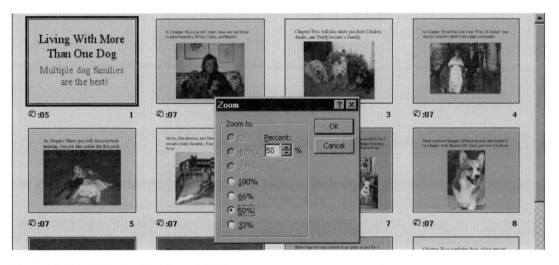

Figure 5-7: Slide Sorter view at 50% zoom

? **When I'm practicing to give a presentation, is there a way for me to compare narration time with the slide timings that I originally set?**

Yes. PowerPoint provides a neat feature to do just that, called the Slide Meter. During the running of a slide show, right-click on the screen and choose Slide Meter from the pop-up menu. The Slide Meter will provide a running counter of the individual slide and a visual representation of its progress, as well as a counter for the cumulative amount of time elapsed and a status meter that lets you know how fast or slow you are progressing overall. Here's an example of a Slide Meter in a running show:

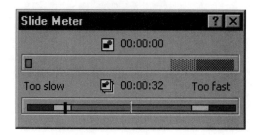

? I would like to provide a handout of a presentation to my audience so they can take notes. Is there a slick way in PowerPoint to do this?

Sure. Before you print your presentation, open the *Print what* drop-down list box in the lower section of the Print dialog box. Choose *Handouts (3 slides per page)* and then print your presentation. To the right of each slide will be space for several lines of note taking, as shown in Figure 5-8.

? I want to be prepared to show information on a topic if a question arises, but I don't want my audience to see the slide unless the topic is broached. What is the best way to prepare optional slides?

With a combination of PowerPoint features you can have a hidden slide waiting in the wings in case it's needed. First, create the slide, and then hide it by choosing Hide Slide from the Slide Show menu. The second set of actions will place a button on the slide where you think the question might arise. This button will open the hidden slide when clicked. Set that up with these steps:

1. In Slide view, open the slide that will contain the button, click Action Buttons from the Slide Show menu, and choose the Custom action button.

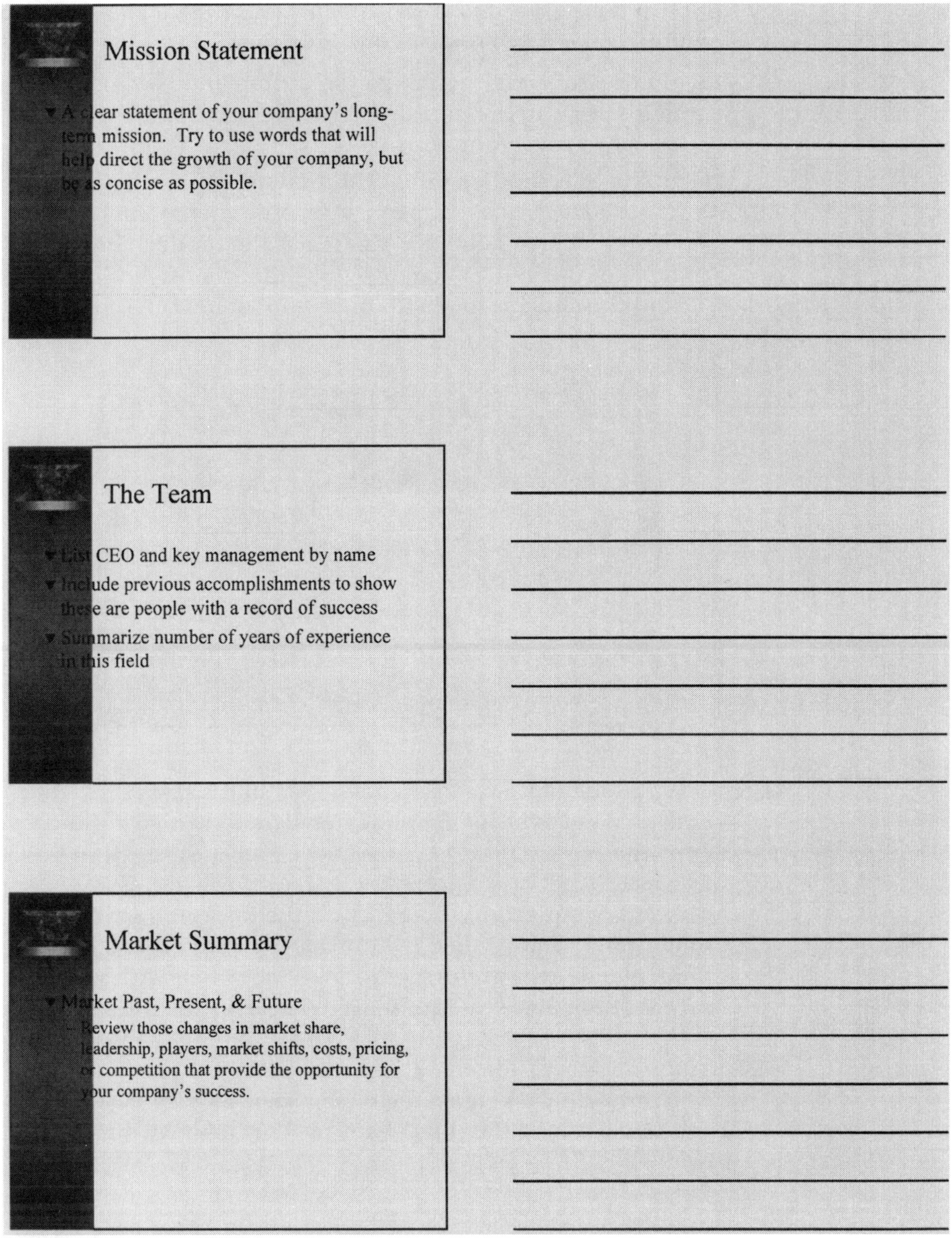

Mission Statement

▼ A clear statement of your company's long-term mission. Try to use words that will help direct the growth of your company, but be as concise as possible.

The Team

▼ List CEO and key management by name
▼ Include previous accomplishments to show these are people with a record of success
▼ Summarize number of years of experience in this field

Market Summary

▼ Market Past, Present, & Future
  Review those changes in market share, leadership, players, market shifts, costs, pricing, or competition that provide the opportunity for your company's success.

Figure 5-8:   Printing three slides per page for audience note taking

2. Use the crosshair pointer to click and drag a small button to an inconspicuous place on the slide.

3. If necessary, right-click on the button and choose Action Settings from the pop-up menu. Choose Yes if you are asked to save your work.

4. In the Mouse Click tab in the Action Settings dialog box, choose *Hyperlink to,* open its drop-down list box, and then click the value that describes the hidden slide. If none of the values matches the slide, choose Slide and find the slide in the list box, as shown next.

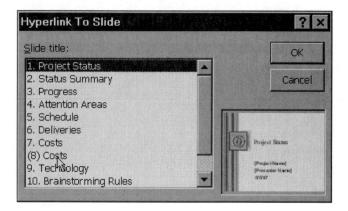

Tip: Hidden files are easily identified in the Hyperlink To Slide dialog box. Look for slide numbers contained within parentheses.

Now, if a question comes up on the information in the hidden file, simply click the button you created and the hidden slide will appear; otherwise, continue with your presentation and your audience will never see the slide.

Tip: During a slide show, you can quickly display another slide by right-clicking on the screen, choosing Go By Title, and then clicking the slide you want to display by number or title.

? **What is the quickest way to display a particular slide during a slide show?**

Press the number key corresponding to the number of the slide and then press ENTER; for example, 5 and ENTER. The sidebar "Slide Show Key Summary" provides the complete list of keys that can be used during a slide show.

? **I want to use the same presentation for several different purposes. For example, first I'll be delivering it to a live audience, but then I want it to be available for people to look at on their own. How can I quickly switch a presentation from one type to another?**

Open the Set Up Show dialog box found on the Slide Show menu. You are presented with several *Show type* options that let you control how your slide show will run:

? **The built-in presentations provided by PowerPoint look great on screen in full color, but I print out handouts on a black and white laser printer. Is there a way to view black and white slides before printing them?**

Yes. PowerPoint has a Black and White view that lets you see what several grayscale and black and white schemes look like, and allows you to print in those schemes without affecting the original colored objects and backgrounds. In Slide view, click the Black and White View button in the

Slide Show Key Summary

This table describes the keys that you can use to control a slide show.

Key	Action
B	Toggles between a black screen display and the slide show display
E	Removes any onscreen annotations
H	Advances to the next hidden slide in the show
M	When rehearsing, sets slide advancement to be a mouse click
N	Advances to the next slide
O	When rehearsing, uses original timings
P	Returns to the previous slide
T	When rehearsing, uses new timings
S	Stops or restarts an automatic show
W	Toggles between a white screen display and the slide show display
BACKSPACE	Same as the P key
ENTER	Same as the N key
Number key, ENTER	Advances to the slide whose number is pressed
ESC	Terminates a slide show
SPACEBAR	Same as the N key
CTRL-A	Changes the pen to the pointer
CTRL-H	Temporarily hides both the pointer and the Context Menu button
CTRL-L	Always hides both the pointer and the Context Menu button
CTRL-P	Changes the pointer to the pen
SHIFT-F10	Displays the Context menu

Tip: To return to the beginning of a slide show, press the left and right mouse buttons together and hold for a few seconds.

Standard toolbar. To select one of the grayscale or black and white options from a pop-up menu, right-click on an empty spot to affect the entire slide show, or right-click on an individual object to limit the effect to that object, and then choose Black and White from the context menu.

When you print, verify that the *Black & white* check box is selected in the Print dialog box. If you don't want any grayscale gradients, select the *Pure black & white* check box to print out just black and white.

Tip: You can see how your entire presentation looks in black and white by changing to Slide Sorter view before or after switching to Black and White view.

chapter

6 Answers!

Organizing
with Access

Answer Topics!

**IMPORTING, EXPORTING, AND
LINKING DATA**   236
   Exporting data to dBASE 5
   Hyperlinks from Access to Word

     **Importing data from other programs
     Viewing and editing another
       program's data**

Access
@ a Glance

Access brings a premier data manager to the Office suite. From storing a limited quantity of items in a home inventory to cataloging parts and tracking orders in larger companies, Access provides an easy-to-use but powerful way to enter, manipulate, and view information.

   Access takes a somewhat different approach in how it structures its database, the container that Access uses to hold its data and supporting objects. Typically, a database file is composed of data for a single table, with any supporting tables stored as separate files in a common folder or directory. Access, on the other hand, bundles everything that is related to a specific set of data into a single file. Within the confines of an Access database file (file extension .mdb) are six objects that handle all storage, retrieval, and manipulation of data. Figure 6-1 shows the Access window and, in it, a typical Database window with its associated objects. These objects are described below:

Tables   provide a matrix consisting of columns of data categories, or fields, and rows of information, or records, where each row uniquely defines a set of data. For example, a mailing list contains fields for each individual's name, street address, city, state, and postal code; each record defines a set of data for an individual on the list.

Queries   allow you to pose questions and extract just the information you want from one or more tables or from other queries.

Forms   provide a more graphical means to view or enter data in one record at a time.

Reports   present data on screen and on paper that can be formatted to achieve readable, attractive results, in contrast to the row and column appearance of tables and queries.

Macros   provide a quick means to automate relatively simple tasks.

Modules   provide the framework for designing very sophisticated custom applications using Visual Basic for Applications, the programming language used by several Office programs.

Databases can be daunting to users who think they are too complicated and too powerful for day-to-day tasks. Microsoft, though, has gone to great lengths to make Access a useful and easy-to-use program for the beginner, as well as for the application developer.

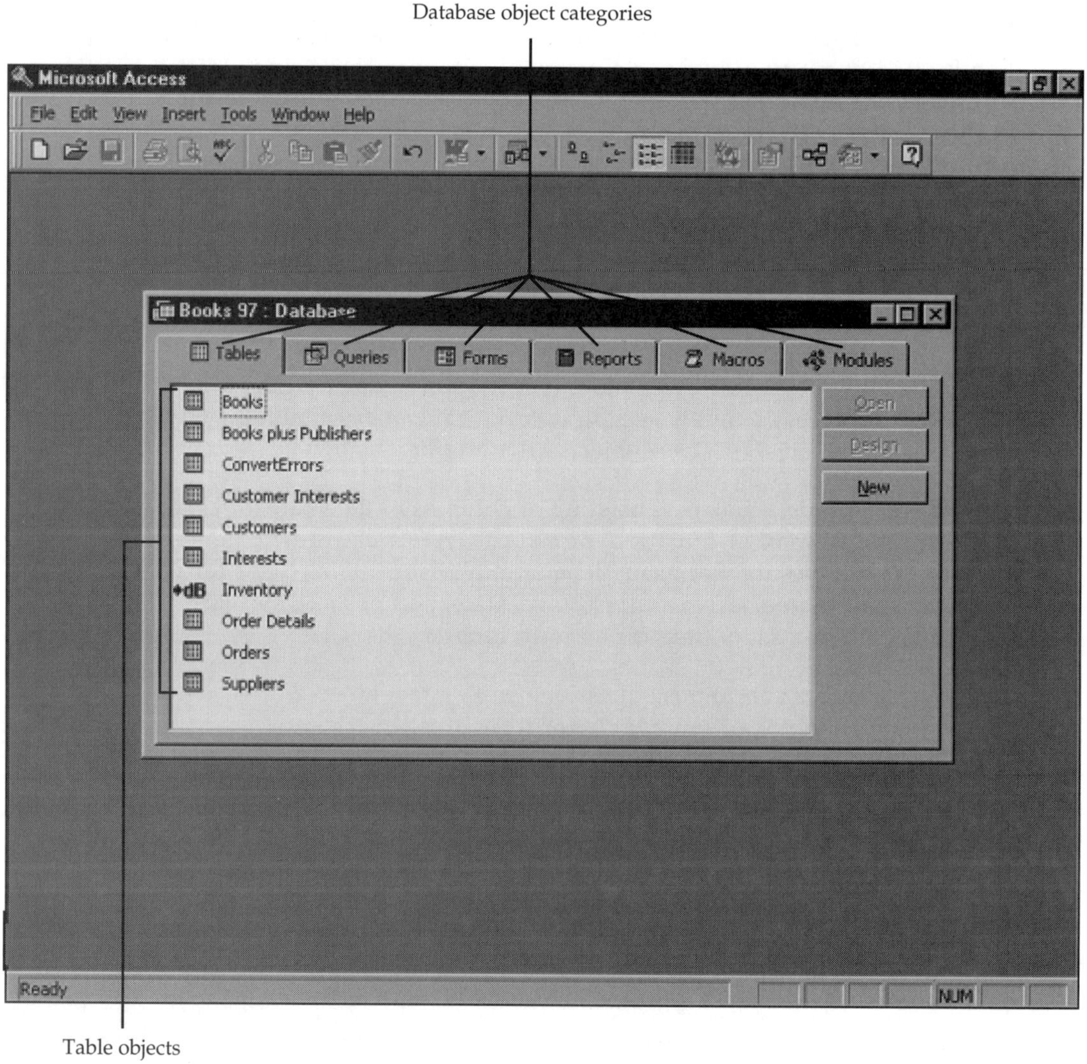

Database object categories

Figure 6-1:   The six objects that make up an Access database

Wizards are one powerful tool to make Access easier to use and can assist you in areas such as

▷ Creating a database

▷ Designing professional-appearing forms and reports

▷ Creating charts

▷ Importing and exporting data from and to non-Access sources

▷ Publishing data on the Internet or an intranet using built-in or custom templates

WORKING WITH ACCESS DATABASES

When I open the Northwind sample database I get an extra menu item called Show Me. I don't seem to get this in other databases. How do I add or remove menu items in my own databases?

What Microsoft has done is to create a custom menu bar that appears when you open the Northwind database, as shown here:

The only difference between the standard menu bar and this one is the addition of the Show Me menu. You can create your own custom menu bar (see Chapter 2, "Getting Started with Office 97," for a description of how to create a custom menu bar) and have it appear when your database opens. After you create the new menu, choose Startup from the Tools menu in the Database window and select the custom menu bar from the Menu Bar drop-down list, shown here:

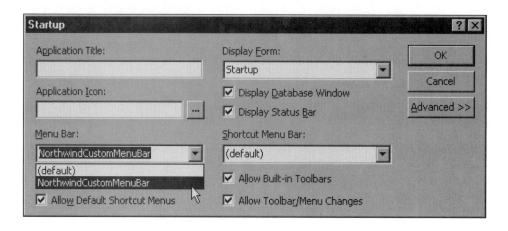

Click OK and the next time the database is opened, the new menu bar will appear. This is great way to "hide" certain Access features from those users of your database who like to "tinker." See the sidebar "Startup Options" for a complete rundown on the other attributes you can set at startup.

● ● ● ● ● ● ● ● ● ●

Startup Options

You can customize how Access presents your database (or application) when first opened. These are some of the reasons you might consider creating a custom startup:

▷ Display an opening form with your corporate logo

▷ Hide Access features and commands that you don't want available to other users

▷ Display a custom menu bar and toolbars that easily access specific forms and reports

▷ Accommodate users who are not familiar with the Access user interface by creating one that offers only a limited, but very specific, set of options

Note that the options you choose in the Startup dialog box set global database properties, but they do not override any property settings you may have set for specific forms or reports.

Table 6-1 describes the customization options that affect opening a database or starting an application. These options are set by opening the Tools menu and choosing Startup.

Table 6-1:   Startup Options

Attribute	Allows You To
Title	Display your own text in the title bar instead of *Microsoft Access*
Icon	Display an icon other than the yellow key to the left of the text in the title bar
Menu bar and Shortcut menu bar	Display custom menus in lieu of those provided by Access and permit or prevent changes to the menu bar
Display form	Display an opening form that introduces the user to the database or application
Display Database window	Display or hide the Database window that shows the contents of each object in the database
Display status bar	Display or hide the Status bar located at the bottom of the Access window
Toolbars	Permit or deny use of the toolbars provided by Access and any changes made to them
Code viewing after run-time errors	Permit or prevent display of the Debug window to view Visual Basic for Applications (VBA) code after an error has been detected while executing a module.
Keys	Permit or deny use of keys that affect several of the actions described above
ALT-F1 or F11	Display the Database window
CTRL-BREAK	Halt code execution and display the Module window
CTRL-F11	Switch display of the Access menu bar and a custom menu bar
CTRL-G	Display the Debug window

? **I find that I keep returning to the Database window several times while I'm working in Access. Is there an easier way to display the Database window besides minimizing open windows or forms?**

Sure, simply press F11 and the Database window will be brought to the front, as shown in Figure 6-2.

? **I have several field reps that are on the road taking orders. Is there a way for all of them to merge data into one master database and synchronize all their input?**

Yes, by using replication you can have as many copies, or replicas, of a database as you want. Then you can combine the data in one location and resolve any possible conflicts.

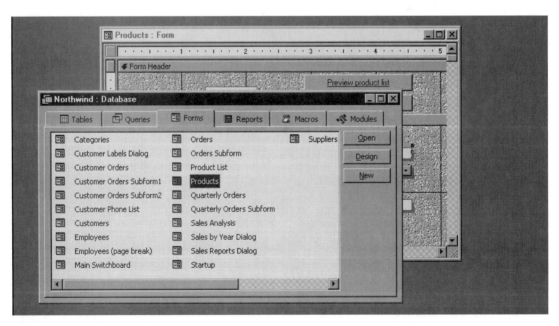

Figure 6-2:   Pressing F11 brings the Database window in front of other windows

Replication

The replication process takes an existing database and converts it into a Design Master and one replica (you can easily create more replicas to add to the replica set). The Design Master maintains the structure of the database. Users working with replicas cannot change fields or change the design of any of the database objects; they can only add, modify, or delete data.

Caution: Replicating a database is a one-way process; once you choose to replicate you cannot undo the changes made to the database. It's always a good idea to back up the original database when Access prompts you.

There are several changes in Office 97 that accommodate replication, including the following:

> Fields are added to each table to assist Access in tracking changes.

> Tables are added to the database to store conflicting information.

> AutoNumber data type fields are replaced by random numbers to avoid sequencing conflicts.

To replicate a database follow these steps:

1. With the database you want to replicate open, choose Replication from the Tools menu and click Create Replica.

2. Click Yes in the message box that asks if want you to close the current database and create a replica.

3. Click Yes when asked if you want to make a backup copy. In the *Location of New Replica* dialog box, shown here, a new database is created in the same folder as the original database and named *Replica of . . .* (your original database).

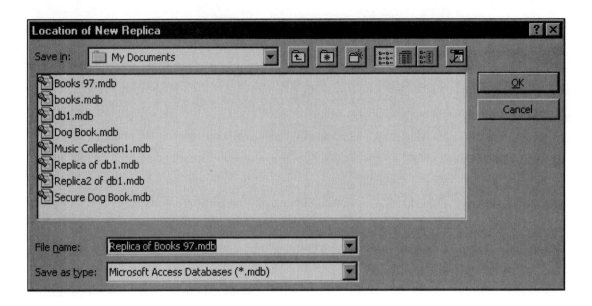

4. Click OK to accept the filename, or change the name and then click OK.

A final message box informs you that the original database has been converted into a Design Master and the replica has been created.

 Note: You can add objects to replicas for local computer use only; added objects are not copied to other replicas or the Design Master during synchronization.

Once replicas have been created and put into use, at some point you have to collect the information that has been added and check for conflicting data. Synchronization compares data between two files in the replica set (which can be two replicas or a replica and the Design Master) and incorporates any new or modified data in each file.
To synchronize files,

1. Open a file in the replica set.

2. Choose Replication from the Tools menu and click Synchronize Now. The Synchronize Database dialog box

opens, as shown below, where you can choose another file to synchronize with.

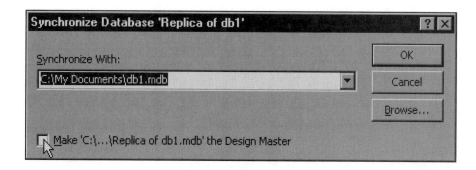

If you want to transfer control from the current Design Master to another replica, click the check box at the bottom of the dialog box.

3. Click OK to start the synchronization process.

4. Click Yes in the completion message box to reopen the database so you can see if there are any conflicts. Conflicts are resolved in the Resolve Replication Conflicts dialog box:

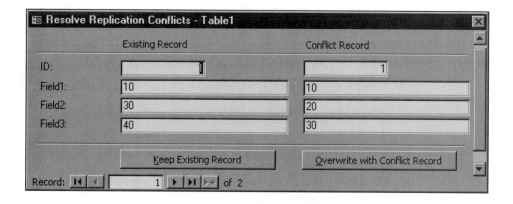

Tip: You can also synchronize members of a replica set by using the Briefcase feature included with Windows 95.

?   **I find it somewhat annoying that in Access I cannot open two databases at once. Is there a way to work around this limitation?**

Yes there is, providing you have the computer resources. Open one database in the currently running copy of Access and then start a second instance of Access (Start menu, Programs, Microsoft Access) and open the other database. Instead of switching between databases within Access you'll be switching between the two instances of Access. Use the Taskbar, as shown here, or ALT-TAB to switch back and forth.

?   **I'm working with databases that take up quite a bit of disk space. Is there a way to reduce a database's size?**

Sure. The best method to gain more disk space is to compact each database. Deleted tables in a database are notorious for leaving fragmented chunks of unused space throughout a file. Compacting recovers disk space that has been tied up with deleted objects. To compact a database, open it, choose Database Utilities from the Tools menu, and click Compact Database. The new compacted database will replace the original database.

Tip: Before you compact a database check its file size by choosing Database Properties from the File menu and clicking the General tab, as shown in Figure 6-3. Repeat after you compact to see how much free disk space you gained.

You can also compact a database that isn't open. Follow the same procedure as above, but when you click Compact Database, the *Database to Compact From* dialog box opens so you can select a database. Click Compact, and the Compact Database Into dialog box opens, where you can select the same file or create a new compacted database with a new filename or location.

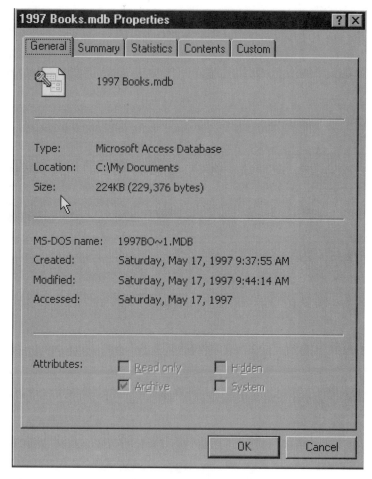

Figure 6-3:   Check a database's file size before and after
                   compacting to see how much disk space you
                   freed up

I just want to create a simple database to track my audio CD collection. Are there **sample databases** that I can use to get me going?

Yes, there are. Access, like the other Office 97 products,
provides several wizards that assist you in creating
databases for common home and business uses. When you
first start Access you are presented with the opportunity to
create a database or open an existing one. Select Database
Wizard, as shown next, and click OK.

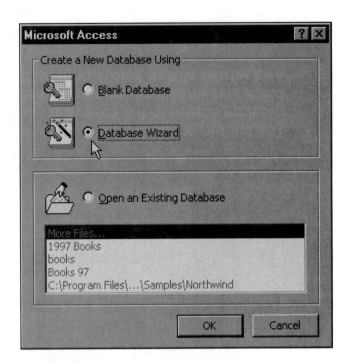

The New dialog box, shown in Figure 6-4, opens with the Databases tab displaying the selection of available database wizards.

Tip: Choosing New from the File menu or clicking the New button on the Database toolbar also opens the New dialog box.

Double-click the Music Collection wizard icon to open the File New Database dialog box, where you provide a name and location for the new database-to-be. Click Create to start the wizard. Follow the steps the wizard leads you through, adding or removing suggested fields, including or excluding sample data, choosing a style for forms and reports, and providing a title. Click Finish in the final wizard dialog box. The database is created and its startup form displays options for you to start entering data, as shown in Figure 6-5.

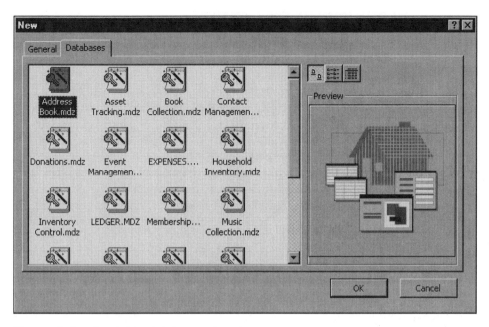

Figure 6-4: Available database wizards

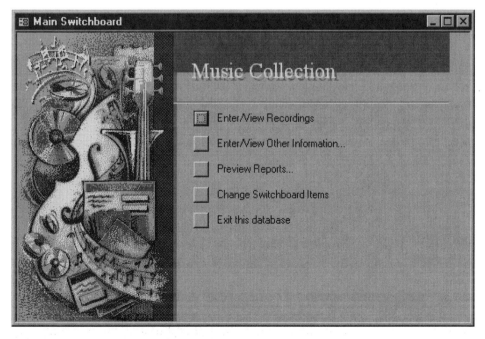

Figure 6-5: Sample startup form for an Access database

WORKING WITH TABLES

Table Views

Tables provide the best way to quickly view and navigate through your data, and they often provide the fastest way to enter new information or make changes. There are two views in Access:

Datasheet view   displays the common column and row arrangement you find in other data management programs.

Design view   displays and allows modifications to the table's field structure and is where you set properties on fields to control associated attributes.

Datasheet View

While forms let you view and edit data one record at a time, tables in Datasheet view give you access to the full breadth of your information. Datasheet view, shown in Figure 6-6, offers the benefit of seeing the whole picture while being able to quickly find just the record or records you want.

If you often find yourself entering or modifying information in Datasheet view, there are several keys that you will find handy. Table 6-2 describes the Navigation keys you can use.

A number of keys only work in Navigation mode; that is, when an entire field is selected and the insertion point is obscured. The following table lists the Navigation mode keys.

Key	Function
CTRL-DOWN ARROW	Selects the last record in the current field
CTRL-END	Selects the last record in the last field
CTRL-HOME	Selects the first record in the first field
CTRL-UP ARROW	Selects the first record in the current field
END	Selects the last field in the current record
HOME	Selects the first field in the current record

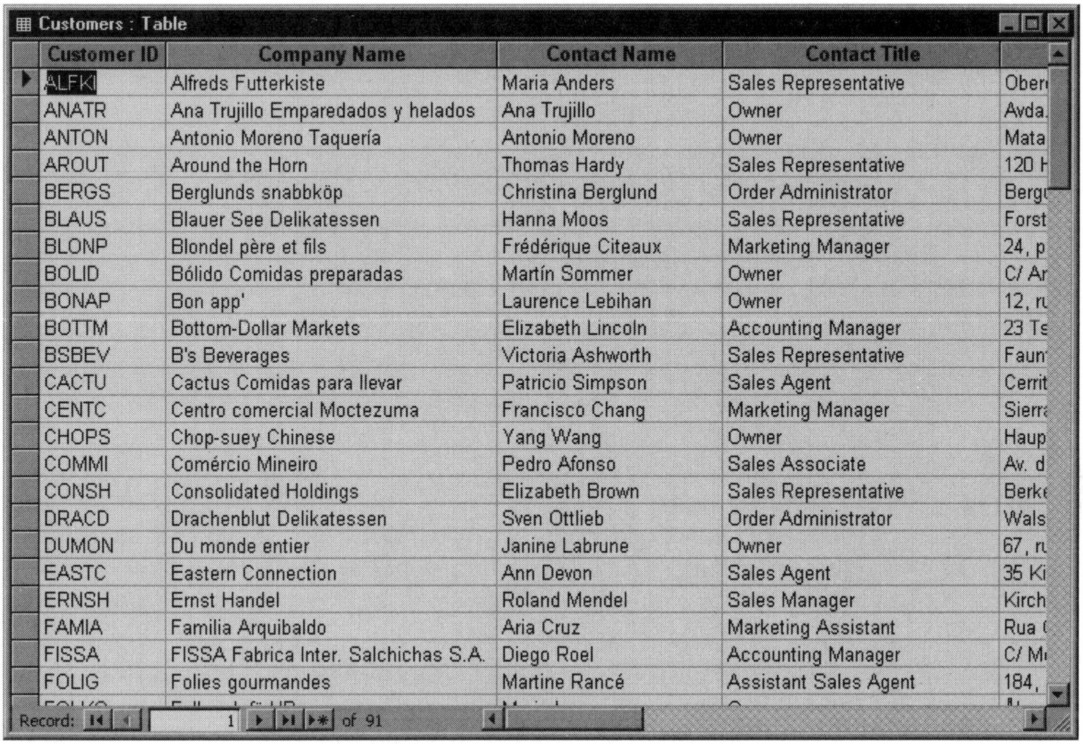

Customers : Table

Customer ID	Company Name	Contact Name	Contact Title	
ALFKI	Alfreds Futterkiste	Maria Anders	Sales Representative	Ober
ANATR	Ana Trujillo Emparedados y helados	Ana Trujillo	Owner	Avda.
ANTON	Antonio Moreno Taquería	Antonio Moreno	Owner	Mata
AROUT	Around the Horn	Thomas Hardy	Sales Representative	120 H
BERGS	Berglunds snabbköp	Christina Berglund	Order Administrator	Berg
BLAUS	Blauer See Delikatessen	Hanna Moos	Sales Representative	Forst
BLONP	Blondel père et fils	Frédérique Citeaux	Marketing Manager	24, p
BOLID	Bólido Comidas preparadas	Martín Sommer	Owner	C/ Ar
BONAP	Bon app'	Laurence Lebihan	Owner	12, ru
BOTTM	Bottom-Dollar Markets	Elizabeth Lincoln	Accounting Manager	23 Ts
BSBEV	B's Beverages	Victoria Ashworth	Sales Representative	Faun
CACTU	Cactus Comidas para llevar	Patricio Simpson	Sales Agent	Cerrit
CENTC	Centro comercial Moctezuma	Francisco Chang	Marketing Manager	Sierr
CHOPS	Chop-suey Chinese	Yang Wang	Owner	Haup
COMMI	Comércio Mineiro	Pedro Afonso	Sales Associate	Av. d
CONSH	Consolidated Holdings	Elizabeth Brown	Sales Representative	Berk
DRACD	Drachenblut Delikatessen	Sven Ottlieb	Order Administrator	Wals
DUMON	Du monde entier	Janine Labrune	Owner	67, ru
EASTC	Eastern Connection	Ann Devon	Sales Agent	35 Ki
ERNSH	Ernst Handel	Roland Mendel	Sales Manager	Kirch
FAMIA	Familia Arquibaldo	Aria Cruz	Marketing Assistant	Rua
FISSA	FISSA Fabrica Inter. Salchichas S.A.	Diego Roel	Accounting Manager	C/ M
FOLIG	Folies gourmandes	Martine Rancé	Assistant Sales Agent	184,

Record: 1 of 91

Figure 6-6: Table in Datasheet view

Table 6-2: Navigation Keys

Key	Function
CTRL-PG DN	Scrolls to the right one screen
CTRL-PG UP	Scrolls to the left one screen
DOWN ARROW	Selects the next record in the current field
ENTER	Selects the next record in the field to the right
F5	Selects the record number in the Record box at the bottom of the screen; type a new record number and press ENTER to move to that record
LEFT ARROW	Selects the record in the previous field
PG DN	Scrolls down one screen
PG UP	Scrolls up one screen
RIGHT ARROW	Same as ENTER
SHIFT-TAB	Same as LEFT ARROW
TAB	Same as ENTER
UP ARROW	Selects the previous record in the current field

Move mode keys are used to move selected columns. Turn on Move mode by pressing CTRL-F8 (MOV appears in the indicator section at the right end of the Status bar).

Datasheet View   MOV   NUM

The following table lists the Move mode keys.

Key	Function
CTRL-F8	Enables Move mode
ESC	Disables Move mode
LEFT ARROW	Moves the selected column(s) one column to the left
RIGHT ARROW	Moves the selected column(s) one column to the right

Design View

The structure of a table is created and maintained in Design view, shown in Figure 6-7. The upper portion of the table Design window contains three columns that are used to set up fields.

Field Name   lists current fields in the table and allows you to add new fields by simply typing them in the next blank cell.

Data Type   makes available a drop-down list of different field formats that you assign to fields when you create them.

Description   is an optional field where you can enter a narrative explanation of the field.

Tip: A field's description appears in the Status bar when the field is selected in either a table or a form. If you are working on a shared database it's best to choose your words carefully.

Data types are designed for specific uses and each comes with inherent limitations. Giving some forethought to what you might do with the data in any particular field will help you decide which data type to choose. For example, numbers are allowed in a Text data type, but you cannot

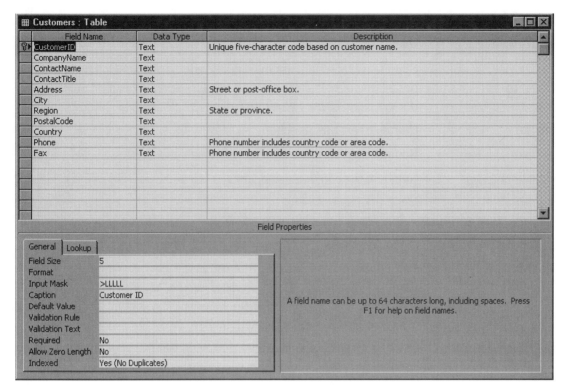

Figure 6-7:   Table in Design view

perform calculations on them (use the Number data type instead). The data types are described in Table 6-3.

The lower section of the Design view window lists additional properties that can be set for each field. The selection of properties depends on the data type assigned to the field, as you can see in Figure 6-8, where Date/Time properties are listed instead of the Text properties shown in Figure 6-7.

? My company's MIS guru told me I should **divide large tables into several smaller tables and relate them**. Does this make sense?

Yes it does. This creates a relational database, which is more efficient and easier to use. See the discussion of "Relationships" later in this section for a description of the features and benefits of a relational database scheme.

Table 6-3:   Data Types

Data Type	Used For
Text	Short text (255-character maximum), numbers that won't be calculated (for example, postal codes), and combinations of text and numbers (for example, street addresses)
Memo	Narrative text (65,535-character maximum)
Number	Nonmonetary numeric data used in calculations
Date/Time	Numbers used in dates and times
Currency	Monetary numeric data
AutoNumber	Automatic assignment of record numbers, either sequentially or randomly
Yes/No	Two-condition data such as True or False
OLE Object	Objects that are embedded or linked into an Access table. (See Chapter 8, "Integrating Office Documents," for more information on using the Office 97 products together.)
Hyperlink	Defining hyperlinks to access World Wide Web sites or HTML documents. (See Chapter 9, "Using Office with the Internet and Intranets," for more information on hyperlinking.)
Lookup Wizard	Assistance in creating a combo list box from which values can be chosen from a table or predefined list, eliminating user inputting errors

 I've come to rely on Office 97 providing me a template or other starting point from which I can then make changes to meet my unique needs. Does Access provide a quick and easy way to create tables?

Certainly. There is a very comprehensive wizard that offers suggested table structures. This at least gets you going and, in many cases, requires no further effort on your part to have a complete table. See how Access creates a table for you in these steps:

1. With an open database, click the Tables tab in the Database window and then click the New button. The New Table dialog box appears as shown next:

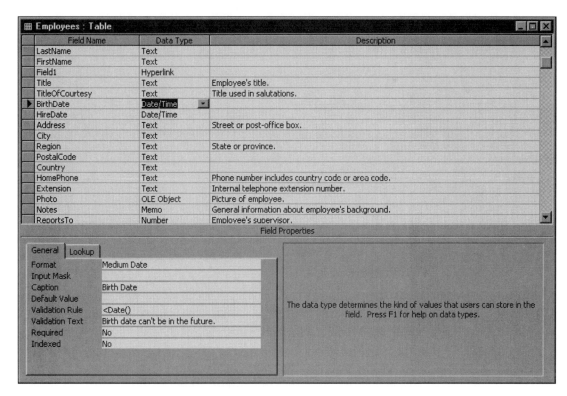

Figure 6-8: Date/Time data type properties

2. Double-click Table Wizard to start the wizard.

3. The first dialog box, shown in Figure 6-9, categorizes 45 sample tables as personal or business. Select a category and then choose a sample that most closely matches your needs.

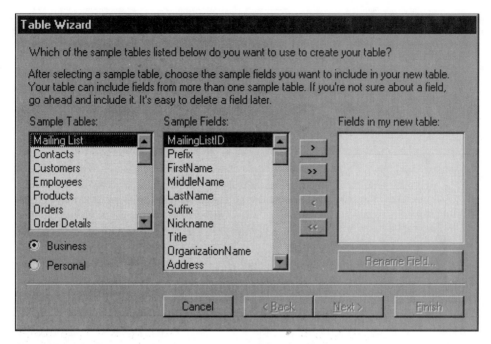

Figure 6-9:   Table Wizard lists sample tables and fields

4. Each sample table contains associated fields. It's usually easiest to click the rightward-pointing double-chevron (>>) button to move all of the sample fields to the *Fields in my new table* box. Then you can remove the few you don't need with the leftward-pointing single-chevron button. Select and rename fields as needed. Click Next.

5. Name the table and accept the default to have Access assign a primary key for you. You can change it later in Design view if needed. Click Next.

≡ *Note:*   If you decide to set the primary key yourself an additional dialog box will let you choose the primary key field and choose between automatic or manual sequencing of records.

6. The third dialog box provides the opportunity to relate the new table to existing tables in your database. (See "Relationships" next, for a further discussion of relational database structuring.) Click Next.

7. Click Finish in the final dialog box if you are comfortable with the Access-designed table and want to enter data

directly in Datasheet view. Otherwise, choose to make changes in the table in Design view or have Access create a simple form where you can enter data.

Relationships

Relationships are the key element that Access uses to efficiently store and access large volumes of data. In large, or flat-file, tables you need to add many repetitive fields of information for records that contain only a few fields that hold different information. For example, when you take an order from a customer you need to have his or her name, address, and other personal information along with the actual contents of what they are ordering from you. So every time that same customer places an order you have to enter the same fields of personal data—quite redundant. Multiply the amount of redundant data by thousands or even millions of entries and you can see why this might not be the most efficient way to handle this volume of data. Instead, why not keep all the personal data that doesn't change in one table and enter the data that does change, that is, each order, in another table. Tie the two tables together with a common field, or primary key, such as Customer Number, and you have a relational database.

There are three ways you can define relationships between tables in an Access database:

One-to-many   is the most common relationship, where a record in one table (for example, Customers) can have many matching records in another table (for example, Orders). There can be many records in the Orders table that have the same customer, but there is only one record for each customer in the Customer table.

One-to-one   relationships match one record in each table. These are not common since they can be easily handled in one table by adding the same fields that would have been created for the second table.

Many-to-many   relationships provide for a record in one table to have many matching records in another table, and one record in the second table to also have many matching records in the first table. These relationships employ a third table that contains the primary key from each table,

which is essentially the same as using two one-to-many
relationships with the third, or junction, table.

Relationships are best understood by looking at a visual
representation of the associations in the Relationships
window, an example of which is shown in Figure 6-10. In
the Relationships window you can do all of the following:

Create relationships   by dragging the related field names
from one table to another.

Edit relationships   by right-clicking the relationship
line between tables and choosing Edit Relationship. The
Relationships dialog box offers several options, as
shown here:

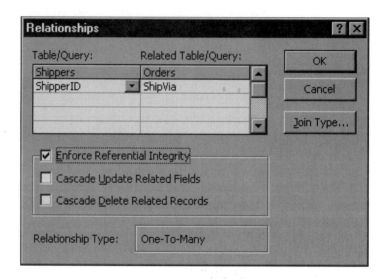

Delete relationships   by right-clicking the relationship line
between tables and choosing Delete from the pop-up menu.

   Add additional tables   by clicking the Show Table button
on the Relationship toolbar.

Save the layout   by closing the Relationships window and
answering Yes to save the changes. This doesn't affect the
actual relationships; it just saves how you view them.

To view the relationships for a database, open the
Database window and click the Relationships button on the
Database toolbar.

Junction table for a
many-to-many relationship

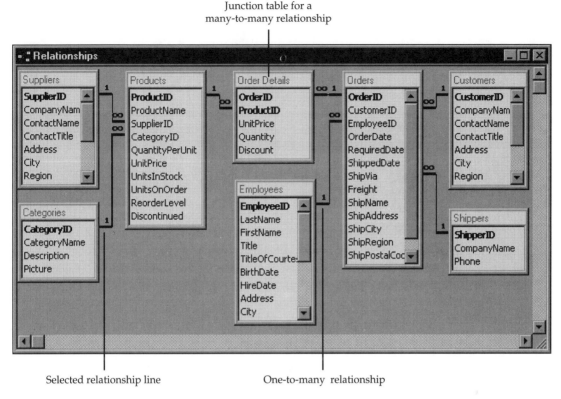

Selected relationship line   One-to-many relationship

Figure 6-10: Relationships window

? **I moved some fields in Datasheet view and saved the
layout, but when I ran AutoForm the order of the fields
didn't change. How do I permanently rearrange
field order?**

You need to rearrange the order of the fields in Design
view. Open the table in Design view by selecting it in
the Database window and clicking Design, or if you are
in Datasheet view, click the View button on the Table
Datasheet toolbar.

In Design view select a field to move by clicking the field
selection button on the left of the Field Name column. A
rightward-pointing arrow will appear in the field selection
button and the field will be highlighted, as shown next:

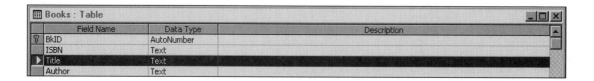

 Note: To select contiguous fields click somewhere in either the first or last of the fields outside of the field selection button, and the rightward-pointing arrow will appear in the field selection button without any highlighting. Drag up or down the field list to select the remaining fields.

Drag the field indicator button up or down the field list until the heavy border on the top edge of the field is where you want to place the field. Save changes to the table and the next time you use AutoForm the field order will be as you changed it.

I would like to add visual effects to the data presented in Datasheet view. For example, can I change the background color of the datasheet matrix?

Yes and a lot more. Choose Cells from the Format menu to open the Cell Effects dialog box shown here:

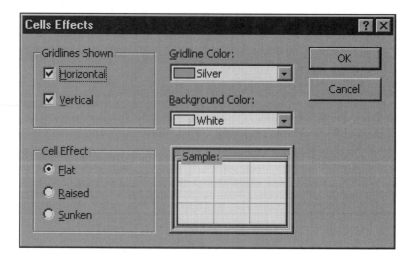

You have control over whether to display gridlines, background and gridline colors, and whether the cells appear flat or have a three-dimensional appearance. The Sample box shows how your changes will look as you make them.

 Note: Cell effects apply to all cells in a table; you cannot change the appearance of an individual cell.

FINDING DATA

Find Methods

Most database programs provide a strong mechanism to add data; however, the key to a good database program is the ease and speed with which you can extract only the data you want. If the number of records in a table is reasonably small, the only thing you need to do to find particular records is to scroll through the table. However, in tables with hundreds or thousands of records, scrolling is impractical. In this case, you need to rely more on automated features. Access offers several tools to help you find and organize (which makes it easier to find) data. The four methods discussed here are searching, sorting, filtering, and querying. The first three methods are on-the-fly techniques that you perform when viewing a table in Datasheet view (filtering can also be applied to forms and subforms).

Searching

The fastest method to search for individual records in a table is to use the Find dialog box, shown here:

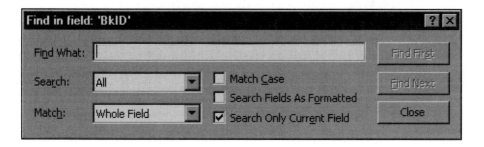

The Find What box provides a means for you to type text from a portion of the record you are looking for. As with the Find dialog boxes in the other Office 97 products, you don't have to type the entire word or phrase for Access to find the entry. However, the more specific your input, the fewer records you will have to look at. There are a number of parameters you can use to limit the search.

Search Only Current Field   searches one field. There is no need to search an entire address table of names, street addresses, cities, and states if you are looking for a ZIP code. Open the table in Datasheet view, position the insertion point anywhere in the field where you are searching, and then click the Find button. Select the Search Only Current Field check box.

Match Case   lets you search by case. Access will only find the words that match the case of the text entered in the Find What box.

Search Fields As Formatted   locates text, usually dates, that are formatted differently than they are stored in the table. For example, the fourth of July, 1997, could be entered in the table as 7/4/97, but you could type 04-Jul-97 and still find it.

Match   lets you broaden the search to words or phrases that are in any part of the field, not just the beginning of the field, or narrow it to cases where the text entered in the Find What box is all that is contained in the field. Select the degree of focus from the Match drop-down list.

Sorting

When sequential listing is an important aspect of trying to find information in a table, sorting provides a very quick way to accomplish that. If you want to sort on a single field you simply right-click the field you want to sort in

Datasheet view and choose an ascending or descending sort from the pop-up menu, as shown here:

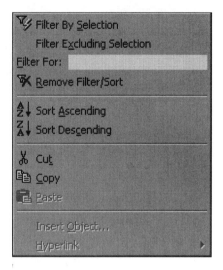

●●●●●● *Tip:*   You can also sort by using the Ascending and Descending Sort buttons on the toolbar or selecting the commands from the Records menu. Before you use either of these methods make sure the insertion point is in the field to be sorted.

More detailed sorts can be done on multiple fields. For example, suppose you wanted a quick look at all of your customers named Jones in Washington state. First, you would sort on the State field to focus on Washington and then on the Last Name field to display all the Joneses. See how to sort on multiple fields in the following steps:

1. Open the table to be sorted in Datasheet view.

2. Choose Filter from the Records menu and then click Advanced Filter/Sort. The Filter window appears as shown next:

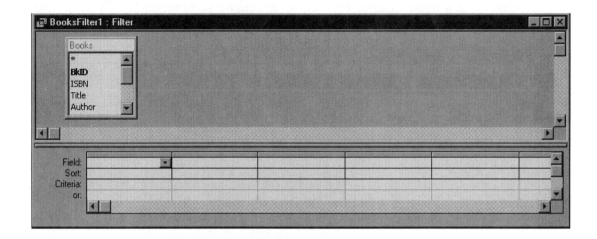

The upper pane of the window displays the table and its field list; the lower pane contains the design grid where the fields to sort on are assigned.

3. In the design grid, click in the leftmost cell in the Field row. Click the down arrow to display the fields in the table and choose the first-level field to sort (the State field in the earlier example).

Tip: You can also double-click the field name in the upper pane and it will appear in the first blank column in the design grid, or you can drag a field name from the field list to a Field cell in the design grid.

4. Click in the leftmost cell in the Sort row. Click the down arrow and choose Ascending or Descending.

5. Repeat steps 3 and 4 in the next column to the right for the second-level sort (the Last Name field in our example).

 6. Click the Apply Filter button on the Filter/Sort toolbar.

Tip: To return the table to its original unsorted state click again on the Apply Filter button or choose Remove Filter/Sort from the Records menu.

Filtering

Filtering is a process that creates a subtable of records (called a dynaset) that adhere to criteria that you establish. You can perform filtering on its own or as part of a query. There are six types of filters you can employ.

Filter by selection is the simplest form of filtering a table and is based on the occurrences of a selected value in a field, one field at a time. Simply click a cell that contains the value you want to filter on and click the Filter By Selection button in the Table Datasheet toolbar. A new table appears with the filtered records. The following example shows all the books in a table that are of the Mystery category.

	BkID	ISBN	Title	Author	PublD	Price	OnHan	Order	Category
▶	1	042511872X	Stolen Blessing	Sanders	6	$4.95	5	2	Mystery
	3	0446360074	Rage of Angels	Sheldon	7	$3.50	4	1	Mystery
	5	0553281798	Trevayne	Ludlum	4	$5.95	4	1	Mystery
	9	0451146425	Lie Down with L	Follett	11	$4.95	2	1	Mystery
	11	0671742760	Dragon	Cussler	14	$5.95	3	1	Mystery
	18	0061000043	A Thief of Time	Hillerman	8	$4.95	1	1	Mystery
*	nber)				0	$0.00	0	0	

Books : Table

Record: 1 of 6 (Filtered)

Filter by form allows you to choose values in one or more fields or directly enter an expression. In Datasheet view, click the Filter By Form button on the Table Datasheet toolbar. The table window shrinks to just the header row and one blank row. Click in the blank cell in the field you want to first filter and choose a value from the list of values for that field or enter an expression. To filter on more than one field the procedure varies depending on the criteria you want the records to satisfy:

> *Both criteria (And operator)* Select or enter a value in a different field.

> *Either criteria (Or operator)* Click the Or tab in the lower-left corner of the window and enter or select a second value. Each time you select an Or value, another Or tab is added, so you can string together as many values as you want. Click the Filter button on the Table Datasheet toolbar to filter the data; click it a second time to remove the filter.

Filter by input   This filter doesn't offer a selection option, but it provides a fast gateway into the filtering process. In Datasheet view, right-click the field you want to filter, type the field value or expression in the Filter For box, as shown here, and press ENTER.

Click the Apply Filter button to remove the filter.

 Note: For complex criteria involving more than one field in an expression, you can click anywhere on the datasheet and enter the expression in the Filter For text box. For example, to find records that have a ratio of *On order* fields to *On hand* fields greater than 50 percent, you would enter [On order]/[On hand]>**.5** (assuming there are no records with zero *On hand* fields).

Advanced filtering   uses the same filter window as sorting; however, you can establish criteria in addition to sorting. This method provides the most flexibility in setting up complex filters. Choose the fields to filter on by either double-clicking in the field list in the upper pane or selecting from the Field drop-down lists in the design grid. Then enter a field value or an expression in the Criteria row. You can filter using the Or and And operators on one or more fields. Click the Apply Filter button to perform the filtering.

Queries

There are several queries available in Access to achieve similar, yet different, results. A sampling of what you can do with queries includes the following:

Action queries   perform tasks on data, such as removing a group of records.

Append queries   add records to a table or another query.

AutoLookup queries   automatically add data to a record.

Crosstab queries   summarize data in a spreadsheet format.

Make-table queries   create tables using criteria against either the current or another database.

Pass-through queries   send commands to an ODBC-(Open Database Connectivity)-compliant database.

Select queries   find data in one or more tables or other queries using criteria you establish, and then display the data in a logical order. Select queries are the most commonly used type of query.

Queries are Access objects, which means they can be named, saved, and called by VBA modules in custom applications, just like tables, forms, and reports. In fact, the output from a query (called a dynaset) resembles a table, as shown here:

Sales by Book per month - 1993 : Crosstab Query					
Title	January	February	March	April	May
A Brief History			$15.26	$30.52	
Dragon				$9.52	
Hackers			$16.16		
Hard Drive				$20.66	
Making of Micro			$11.66		
Patriot Games			$4.21	$8.92	
The Power of W				$44.92	
Whirlwind				$20.66	

Record: |◄| |◄| | 1 |►| |►I| |►*| of 8

The dynaset appears to be a table, but any modifications to data performed in the dynaset are ultimately stored in the underlying table.

Designing a query from scratch can be a large undertaking, but Access relieves most of the effort by providing wizards to walk you through the steps. Use the Simple Query Wizard to create a basic select query with the following steps:

1. In the Database window, click the Queries tab and then click the New button. The New Query dialog box appears as shown here:

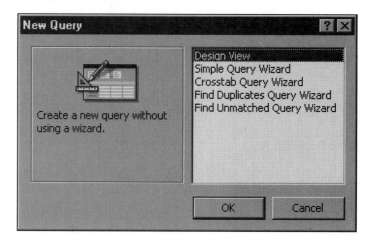

2. Double-click Simple Query Wizard to start the wizard.

3. In the first query wizard dialog box, choose the fields from the tables or queries in the database that are pertinent to extracting the data you want. You can add fields from multiple objects. Click Next.

4. Provide a name for the query and click Finish to view the query. You can easily switch to Design view after the query opens (click the View button on the Query Datasheet toolbar) to add criteria, add and remove fields, and rearrange the order of the fields in the dynaset.

 **I'm trying to build an expression in the Criteria cell of a query, but I'm having trouble putting it together. Can Access help me out?**

Sure. Access provides a feature called Expression Builder to assist users in building expressions in several objects including query Design view. To open Expression Builder, shown in Figure 6-11, right-click in the Criteria cell

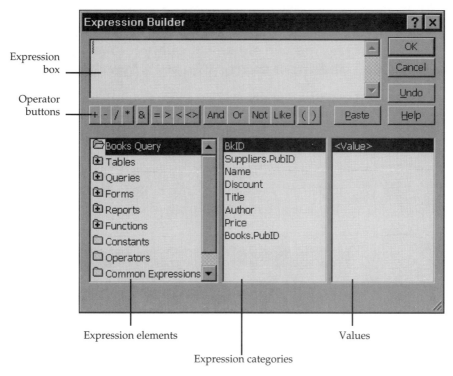

Expression box

Operator buttons

Expression elements

Expression categories

Values

Figure 6-11:   Expression Builder

where you want the expression, and choose Build from the pop-up menu. You can type directly in the Expression box, or you can paste operators from the row of buttons and expression elements from the three list boxes.

Tip: The operator button bar contains several of the most commonly used operators. For a complete list of operators, double-click the Operators folder in the leftmost list box.

The leftmost list box contains folders of expression elements. Double-clicking a folder displays its contents by categories of expression elements in the middle list box; values for each category are displayed in the rightmost list box.

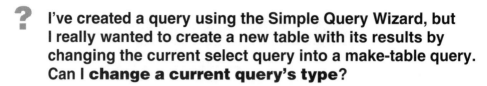 **I've created a query using the Simple Query Wizard, but I really wanted to create a new table with its results by changing the current select query into a make-table query. Can I change a current query's type?**

Yes, with these steps:

 1. Open the query you've created in Design view and choose Make-Table Query from either the Query menu or the Query Type button drop-down list.

2. In the Make Table dialog box, shown next, name the new table (or select an existing table to replace), choose the database in which to locate the table, and click OK.

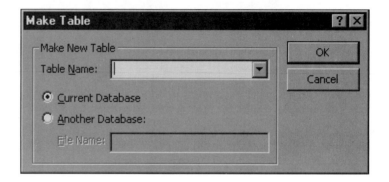

3. Modify the fields that appear in the Design view grid and their criteria as necessary.

4. Switch to Datasheet view to preview the new table. When satisfied, return to Design view and click the Run button on the Query Design toolbar.

5. Click Yes in the message box that tells you that you are about to paste new rows into a new table.

I'm reworking a rather large query with several fields and associated criteria in the Design view grid. Is there a way to quickly remove all the entries in the grid so I can start fresh?

Sure. Choose Clear Grid from the Edit menu when in query Design view.

Tip: The query Design view grid is also called the "query by example," or QBE, grid.

? I've gone through a great deal of work to create a filter. Isn't there some way I can **save a filter for repeated use?**

Yes there is; in one of two ways.

▷ Access will save the filter for you when you exit the table and choose to save changes. The next time you open the table you can click the Apply Filter button and the filter will run. However, if you have since created another filter in this table the original filter is overwritten.

▷ For a truly permanent save you need to save the filter as a query. Set up the filter either as Filter By Form or by using the Advanced Filter window. Choose Save As Query from the File menu and name the query. The next time you want to use the filter, open the new query from the Queries tab in the Database window and run it.

? How can I **verify that there are no blank fields** after data entry?

Simple. Create a query based on the table that contains the field you want to check. Drag the field from the field list to the grid and, in its Criteria cell, type Null. Access will change the cell entry to Is Null when you move out of the cell. Run the query by clicking the Run button and Access will display any records that are blank in the chosen field.

Note: The opposite of Is Null is Is Not Null, which returns records where there is a value in the chosen field.

CREATING AND MODIFYING FORMS

Form Design View

AutoForm and the Form Wizard are great for putting together simple forms, but sooner or later you will need to venture beyond their capabilities. Form Design view offers complete flexibility for what controls are placed on a form, how they are arranged, and how the form's overall appearance can be enhanced. Figure 6-12 shows a form in Design view.

Controls

Controls (objects in the Toolbox) are placed in the three main sections of a form to provide labeling and gateways to the underlying data. The Header and Footer controls provide consistency from record to record, such as the form title or special instructions to the user of the form.

●●●●● *Tip:*   If you don't see the Header and Footer sections, choose Form Header/Footer from the View menu.

The Detail section takes up the bulk of the form, with controls that show the field data in the underlying table or query, one record at a time.

Controls can be placed in any section by dragging them from the Toolbox to the location on the grid where you want them placed. Move and size the controls as needed and use the horizontal and vertical rulers to assist you in organizing the layout.

There are two types of controls:

Unbound controls   provide visual information, but no data is directly displayed or edited from an underlying data source. Examples are labels, line separators, command buttons, and images such as logos.

Bound controls   are directly linked with the data in the underlying table or query and display data and allow it to be edited. Examples are combo boxes, list boxes, and options buttons.

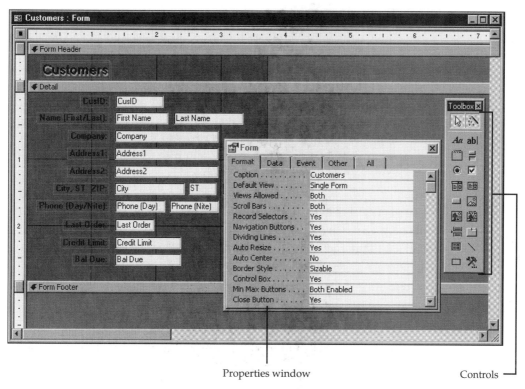

Properties window   Controls

Figure 6-12: Form Design view

Many controls have wizards associated with them that start when you place a control on the grid. This is what the Combo Box Wizard looks like:

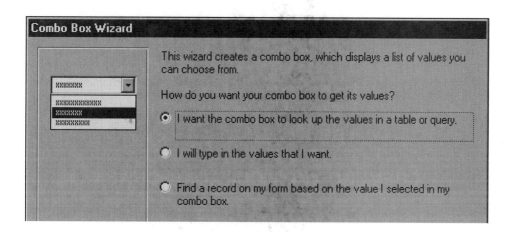

Properties

Each control in Access has several attributes, or properties, that can be modified to change its appearance, how it interacts with the data, and what actions occur on user input. To see the properties for any control, right-click the control and choose Properties from the pop-up menu.

Tip: Any time in the design process you want to see how the form will look in "real life," switch to Form view by choosing Form View from the View menu.

I find myself constantly having to look up other ordering information from an Orders Detail table when I'm entering data in the Orders form. Is there a better way for me to access supplemental information related to the data in a form?

You bet. This is a perfect application for the use of a subform, which is essentially a form within a form, as shown in Figure 6-13. Through the subform you can see

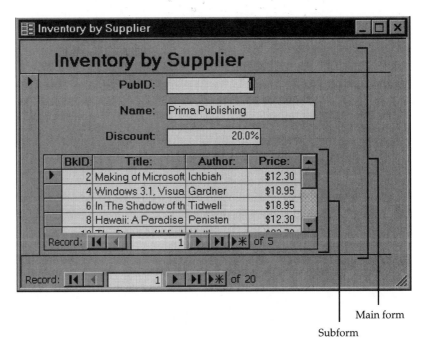

Main form

Subform

Figure 6-13:   A subform is a form within a form

data in a second, related table (See the discussion of "Relationships" in the "Working with Tables" section of this chapter for more information on related tables.) To create a subform follow these steps:

1. Open the form that will contain the subform in Design view.

2. Open the Toolbox, if necessary, click the Subform/Subreport button, and drag it to size on the grid. The Subform/Subreport Wizard opens, as shown here:

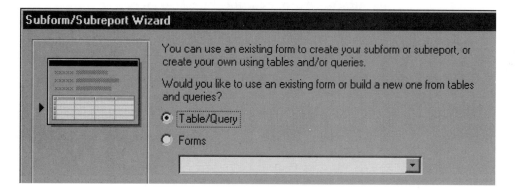

3. Accept the default option to build the subform from a table or query and click Next.

4. In the second wizard dialog box, select fields from tables and queries that you want to appear in the subform. Click Next.

5. Select or define your own links between the main form and the subform. Click Next.

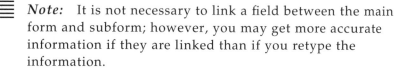 *Note:*   It is not necessary to link a field between the main form and subform; however, you may get more accurate information if they are linked than if you retype the information.

6. Provide a name for the subform and click Finish.

7. The subform doesn't look particularly impressive in Design view, so switch to Form view to see the complete subform and the data from the fields you chose.

I like using the AutoForm Wizards to create quick data entry forms, but I'm getting a little tired of the same background that appears for every form I create. Is there an easy way to change the layout for forms created by the AutoForm Wizards?

Yes there is. The layout you are currently using is actually one of 10 AutoFormats that are available. The layout that appears in the AutoForm Wizard is the default layout, or the last AutoFormat chosen. To select one of the other nine layouts for AutoForm follow these steps:

1. Open a form created by AutoForm, click the View button down arrow on the Form View toolbar, and click Design View (or you can simply click the View button directly if the Design View icon is displayed).

2. Choose AutoFormat from the Format menu to open the AutoFormat dialog box.

3. Click each of the Form AutoFormats and see how they appear in the sample box. There are two buttons that offer other features:

   ▷ *Options* increases the size of the dialog box and adds three check boxes that allow you to control the format's attributes.

   ▷ *Customize* opens the Customize AutoFormat dialog box, where you can create a new AutoFormat based on the current form, modify an existing AutoFormat, or delete one.

Tip: In Design view, you can further modify the form and save these changes to be incorporated in the new AutoFormat.

4. Select an AutoFormat that you want to use for future AutoForm Wizards and click OK.

5. Click the View button to return to Form view and close the form. You don't have to save the form to change the future layout.

After I rearranged the controls on my form, I found that in Form view when I press TAB to move from control to control, the focus doesn't move in sequential order. How can I change the order of tabbing so it follows the logical pattern of the form?

What you need to do is change the tab order for the form. When you initially create a form the tab order is set in one of three ways:

AutoForm and the AutoForm Wizards set the tab order the same as the field order in the data source.

Form Wizard sets the tab order according to the order of the fields you choose for the form.

Design view sets the tab order according to the order in which the controls are created.

To change the tab order, open the form in Design view and choose Tab Order from the View menu. Select which section of the form to change the tab order for, click the selection box next to a control name to select it, and then drag the selection box up or down the list into a new position, as shown here:

Tip: To move a single control, first click the selection box
to select and then drag. To move contiguous control names,
drag across their selection boxes to select them and then drag a
second time to move the selection.

Click OK and then switch to Form view to verify your
expectations.

Tip: In the Tab Order dialog box, click the AutoOrder button
if your form has a typical left-to-right and top-to-bottom logic
to its controls. Access automatically changes the tab order to
reflect that layout.

? I've been entering data in a table using Datasheet view, but I think I'd like to try using a form to guide me through the fields. Do I have to design and create a full-blown form to **quickly add data to a table**?

No. If all you're looking for is a simple data entry form
without any customization such as special formatting or
added controls, you can have Access make one for you.
Select the table or query that the form will be based on in
the Database window, and click the New Object/AutoForm
button in the Database toolbar. If only the New Object
button is available, click the down arrow to open it and
click AutoForm. If the AutoForm button is not visible, open
the table or query and you should see it.

Tip: You can also choose AutoForm from the Insert menu
when either the Tables or Queries tab is displayed.

A data entry form will be created that includes an entry
box for each field. Enter data for one record at a time. Start
a new record by pressing TAB in the last field, clicking the
New Record button on the Status bar, or clicking the New
Record button on the Form View toolbar. Close the form
when you're through and provide a name to save it.

The next time you want to add records in this table,
choose the form from the Forms tab in the Database
window. See the sidebar "AutoForm Wizards" for other
uses of AutoForm.

• • • • • • • • • • •
AutoForm Wizards

Creating a form by selecting a table or query in the Tables or Queries tab of the Database window is the simplest way to create a form, but the result is pretty spartan. Without much more effort you can have a form with a layout that is closer to what you want and a more appealing background. To create a form with AutoForm, select the Forms tab in the Database window and click New. The New Form dialog box displays the three AutoForm options:

Columnar,   a formatted form with all fields shown in a single column and only one record shown at a time

Tabular,   a formatted form with all fields laid out horizontally across the window, showing multiple records

Datasheet,   a form that looks just like a table in Datasheet view, showing multiple records with no special formatting

   Select an AutoForm and choose a data source by typing the name of a table or query, or by choosing one from the drop-down list box. Click OK to create the form. When you close the form you can choose to save it so it will be available in the Forms tab for future use.

? **I've changed the formatting of a label that I want to apply to all the labels in my form. Is there a way I can transfer formatting from one control to another?**

Sure—use the Format Painter to apply formatting from one control to another. Select the control that has the formatting to be copied and *double-click* the Format Painter button on the Form Design toolbar (to display the Form Design toolbar, choose it from the View menu Toolbars option). The mouse pointer changes to an arrow and paint brush that you can click on other labels to replicate the original formatting. Click the Format Painter button to turn this feature off.

••••• *Tip:* If you are applying formatting to only one other control, click the Format Painter button once (instead of double-clicking). The Format Painter will turn off after you apply it.

PRESENTING INFORMATION WITH REPORTS

 In the mailing labels I'm creating I need to include the abbreviation for "care of" before the company name, but I don't see any options in the Label Wizard's *Available fields* list for commonly used address terms. How do I add text that isn't offered in the *Available fields* list?

Although it isn't particularly evident how to do this, it's actually very easy. Many users that haven't upgraded since the earlier versions of Access are also taken aback by the lack of punctuation buttons. To add free text or punctuation marks simply type them in the Prototype Label box in the Label Wizard, as shown here:

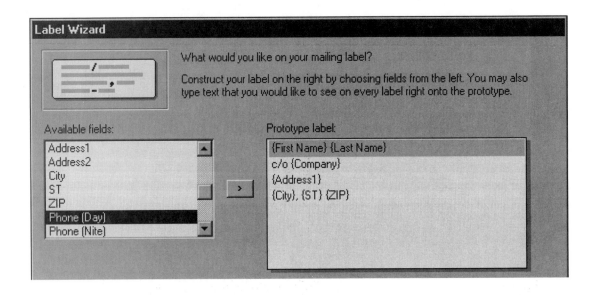

To do this, move the First Name field to the box, press SPACEBAR, and then move the Last Name field to complete the first line. Press ENTER to begin a new line, type **c/o**, press SPACEBAR, and move the Company field over to complete the second line. Use the same procedure to set up the address lines with spaces and commas.

❓ Is there a better method to align controls in report Design view than by trying to drag them into position with the mouse?

Yes, there are a number of ways Access can provide assistance with placement of controls; however, the first thing you need to do is select the controls that you want to change. Once the controls are selected, right-click one of them and choose Align from the pop-up menu. You can align the objects according to the most extreme edge (left, right, top, or bottom) of any of the selected controls. Choose the side on which to align them from the submenu to have Access reposition the controls. You also can have Access align a control or controls to the grid by choosing Align as above and then selecting To Grid in the submenu.

Tip: For the Align feature to work as designed, select only controls that are in the same column or row.

❓ I like to use the grid to help me position controls, but I find the dots distracting. Is there a way to remove the dots from the grid?

Sure. Open a report in Design view, right-click the report selector in the upper-left corner, as shown next, and choose Properties from the pop-up menu.

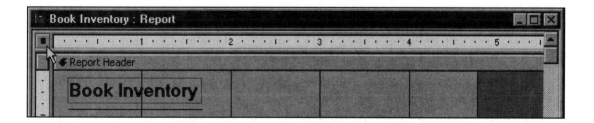

In the Report property window, click the Format tab and change the Grid X and Grid Y dot values to be greater than 24 dots per inch. This will make them impossible for your monitor to display.

▪▪▪▪▪▪   *Tip:*   If you are using centimeters as your measurement scale, change the Grid X and Grid Y values to be greater than 9 dots per centimeter to make the dots invisible.

❓ I'm a little confused by the different types of headers and footers in a report. What's the difference between the Report Header (and Footer) and the Page Header/Footer?

The Report Header and Footer define the beginning and end of a report. The Report Header displays and prints at the top of the report's first page; the Report Footer displays and prints at the bottom of the report's last page. The Page Header and Footer appear on every page and are useful for page numbering and report identification.

❓ My report takes what seems to be an inordinately long time to display in Print Preview. Can I do something to speed up display in Print Preview?

Probably. In reports that have to process a large amount of data you can get an idea of how it looks by using Layout Preview instead of Print Preview. You compromise viewing all your data since only a sampling is used to display the layout, but for purposes of checking the layout that's all you need.

≡   *Note:*   Do not rely on, or be alarmed by, the data presented in Layout Preview, as it is commonly incorrect.

To view your report in Layout Preview, open the report in Design view and choose Layout Preview from the View button drop-down list.

❓ I've gone to a great deal of work to create a good-looking form that would also make a fine report. Is there any way to use a form layout to create a report?

You bet. You can save the form as a report, but first, you have to make available the toolbar button that executes the save. Add a new button to a toolbar with these steps:

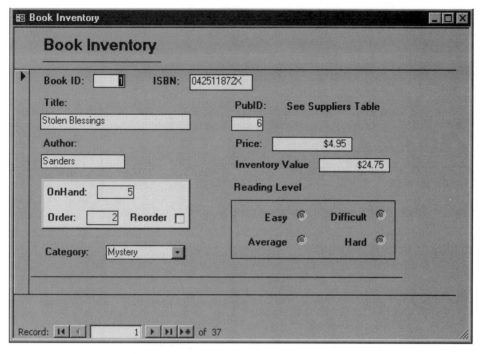

Figure 6-14:   A form to be saved as a report

1. Open a form, as shown in Figure 6-14, that you want to save as a report in Design view.

2. Choose Toolbars from the View menu and click Customize. The Customize dialog box opens.

3. In the Commands tab, select the Form/Report Design category. Scroll down the Commands list (if necessary) until Save As Report is visible, and then drag the command to a convenient location on the Form Design toolbar, as shown here:

4. Close the Customize dialog box, click the Save As Report button, and provide a name for the report.

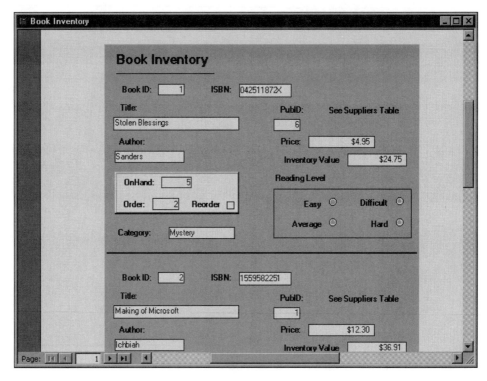

Figure 6-15: A report created from the form in Figure 6-14

5. In the Database window, open the Reports tab and double-click the new report name. Compare Figure 6-14 with Figure 6-15 to see how a typical transformation appears.

IMPORTING, EXPORTING, AND LINKING DATA

 I want to export data from an Access 97 table to a dBASE 5 database, but I cannot find a dBASE 5 file type available in the Save Table dialog box. Am I looking in the right spot?

You're right where you should be (File menu Save As/Export option), but you don't seem to have the converter for dBASE 5 installed. You need to re-run Office 97 Setup and add the dBASE converters to your current list of available file types. To add other program converters follow these steps:

1. Start the Office 97 CD by inserting it in its drive and double-clicking Setup.exe or by running Setup from its network location.

2. In the Microsoft Office 97 Setup dialog box, click the Add/Remove button.

3. In the Maintenance dialog box, select Data Access in the Options list box, and then click the Change Option button.

4. In the Data Access dialog box, select Database Drivers and click Change Option. Select the *dBASE and Microsoft FoxPro Drivers* option. Click OK twice and then click Continue to install the converter.

Note: Converters for other programs, such as Paradox, that are not listed in Setup are available in the Office 97 CD Value Pack folder. Open the Dataacc folder and run Dataacc.exe to install the Microsoft Data Access Pack.

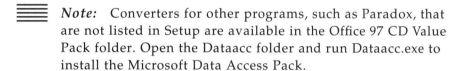

I'd like the users of my database to be able to quickly jump to amplifying information that's stored in Word documents. Can I use **hyperlinks from Access to Word?**

Yes you can, but if we told you how in this chapter we would have written Chapter 9, "Using Office with the Internet and Intranets," for nothing. See Chapter 9 for the answer to this question and others on hyperlinking.

I have data in a Paradox 4 file that I want to add to an existing Access 97 table. Can I **import data from other programs to a table?**

No, sorry; you can't do it in one easy step. Only data in Access tables, text files, and spreadsheet files can be directly added (or appended) to an existing Access table. The first thing to do is import the Paradox file into a new table with these steps:

1. Create a new table in the database that includes the table to which you want to append the Paradox file.

2. Choose Get External Data from the File menu and click Import.

3. In the Import dialog box, select *Paradox (*.db)* from the *Files of type* list box and locate your data file, as shown in Figure 6-16. Click Import.

4. Click OK in the message box that indicates a successful import, and close the Import dialog box.

The new table is displayed with its original filename in the Tables tab of the Database window along with your existing tables.

The second part of the procedure appends the data in the new table to the existing table. For this you need to create an Append query. Use the Simple Query wizard to create the query with the pertinent fields from the new table, and then in query Design view, choose Append Query from the

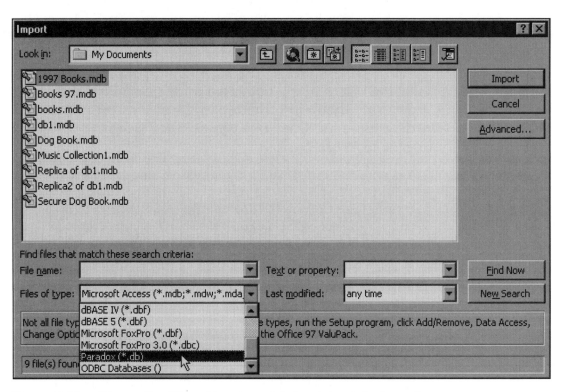

Figure 6-16: Change the *Files of type* to match the data you're importing

Query menu. You will be asked to name the table that is to be appended. Back in Design view be sure the fields to be appended in the new table have the same field names as in the original table. When you are satisfied with your design, run the query to add the new data.

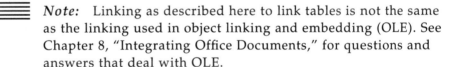

Our inventory control department maintains their records in a dBASE IV database, but there are occasions when I'd like to view and possibly add data to the master inventory. Can I view and edit another program's data from within Access?

Yes you can. By creating a link to the dBASE file you can view and edit data; create your own forms, queries, and reports in Access; and still allow the inventory control department full use through their dBASE program. The major limitation to using linked tables is that you cannot change the structure of the linked file; for example, you can't delete fields or change data types.

Note: Linking as described here to link tables is not the same as the linking used in object linking and embedding (OLE). See Chapter 8, "Integrating Office Documents," for questions and answers that deal with OLE.

To link data, follow these steps:

1. Choose Get External Data from the File menu and click Link Tables.
2. In the Link dialog box, select *dBASE IV (*.dbf)* in the *Files of type* drop-down list and locate the file to link to. Click Link.
3. In the Select Index Files dialog box, select the associated index file and click Select. If there is no index file, click Cancel.

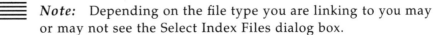

Note: Depending on the file type you are linking to you may or may not see the Select Index Files dialog box.

4. Click OK in the message box that informs you the table was successfully linked and close the Link dialog box.

The linked table appears in the Tables tab, as shown here:

Note: You can also link to a table in another Access database.

Communicating with Outlook

Answer Topics!

Outlook
@ a Glance

Outlook is in a new class of information management programs that combine information from

➤ **Electronic mail** sources such as Internet mail, Microsoft Mail, the Microsoft Exchange, CC-Mail, CompuServe mail, and other sources

➤ **Personal information** such as scheduling, contact lists, task lists, journals, and notes

➤ **Group information** including meetings, events, group contacts, task assignments, and the sharing of journals and notes

➤ **Traditional computer information** contained in disk files and folders, both personal and public

Outlook provides a fully integrated and easily used means of locating, controlling, using, and storing all of this information. To do this, Outlook replaces

➤ Your mail client, including the Windows 95 Exchange client (the Inbox) or any other mail program you might be using

➤ Microsoft Schedule+ or any other personal or group scheduling program

➤ Personal information management programs (PIMs) such as ECCO, ACT!, SideKick, and Lotus Organizer

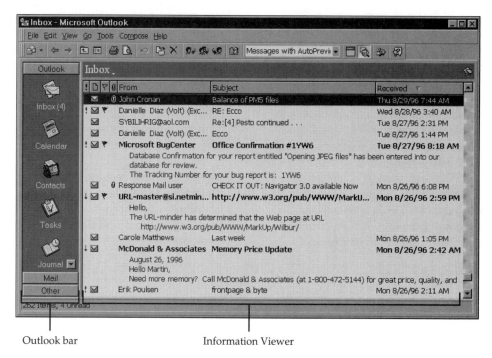

Outlook bar   Information Viewer

Figure 7-1: The Microsoft Outlook window

Microsoft Outlook includes seven components that perform the following functions:

▷ **Inbox** and the **Mail Group** for all e-mail-related functions

▷ **Calendar** for personal and group scheduling

▷ **Contacts** for maintaining business and personal contact information, including e-mail and Web page addresses

▷ **Tasks** for maintaining personal and group to-do lists or assignments

▷ **Journal** for recording or automatically collecting information tied to a time line

▷ **Notes** for creating, collecting, and categorizing extraneous information

▷ **Other** for accessing, viewing, and sharing all other disk files

When you open Microsoft Outlook for the first time after installing it, you will see a window similar to the one shown in Figure 7-1. In addition to the normal menu bar, toolbar, and status bar, the Outlook window has two major areas:

➡️ **The Outlook bar** on the left, which contains shortcuts that open corresponding folders. The shortcuts in the Outlook bar are divided into groups that include the Outlook components, Mail components, and Other. You can create additional groups, add and remove shortcuts, and change where and how the shortcuts appear.

➡️ **The Information Viewer** on the right, which displays the information selected in the Outlook bar. In the Information Viewer you can select one of several views, add and delete columns, and group, sort, or filter the information being displayed.

An optional area that is not initially displayed in the Outlook window is the folder list, shown here:

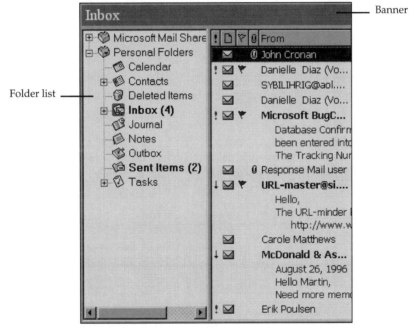

Banner

Folder list

The folder list shows the folders that are available in the current Outlook group. It is most valuable for viewing general disk files in the Other group. You can display the folder list by clicking the left end of the banner above the Information Viewer, clicking the Folder List button in the toolbar, or by choosing Folder List in the View menu. The number of unread items in a folder is shown in parentheses next to the folder.

The Outlook bar provides the primary way of selecting the Outlook component or folder that you want displayed in the Information Viewer. Whatever is displayed takes control of the Outlook window, is said to be "active," and determines some of the menu options and toolbar buttons.

CREATING AND SENDING E-MAIL

Outlook Mail Window

The Outlook mail window provides a list of mail you have sent (Sent Items) or mail you have received (Inbox). There are several ways to view the list of mail, but the most common is the tablelike list of messages shown in Figure 7-2.

If the added screen space does not bother you, then AutoPreview is a handy way to see a bit of a message's contents to determine if it is worth reading the rest of the message. On the toolbar, click AutoPreview to see the first three lines of all messages, or select Messages with AutoPreview as the current view to see the first three lines of unread messages only. The other views in the Current View drop-down list, shown next, allow you to focus on one element of the message, such as the sender or the subject.

```
Messages
Messages with AutoPreview
By Message Flag
Last Seven Days
Flagged for Next Seven Days
By Conversation Topic
By Sender
Unread Messages
Sent To
Message Timeline
```

The views are further described in the following table.

View	Description of Default Features
Messages	A list of messages in date and time order that displays the sender, the subject, and the date/time sent fields
Messages with AutoPreview	A list of messages as in Messages view, with the first three lines of the message displayed if the message is unread

View	Description of Default Features
By Message Flag	A list of messages as in Messages view, with the messages grouped by type of message flag (Open Item or Completed Item) and showing the follow-up due date
Last Seven Days	A list of messages as in Messages view, but displaying only those received in the last seven days
Flagged for Next Seven Days	A list of messages whose follow-up due dates fall within the next seven days, in ascending order of due dates (earliest first) and including sender, subject, message flag, and due By Fields
By Conversation Topic	A list of messages as in Messages view, with the messages grouped by conversation topic (the default is by subject)
By Sender	A list of messages grouped by sender and displaying the subject and the date and time received
Unread Messages	A list of messages as in Messages view, but displaying only those that are unread
Sent To	A list of messages in order of date and time sent and showing the recipient, the subject, and the date and time sent
Message Timeline	Messages shown as icons along an hourly time line based on the time they were sent

In the Message Timeline view, messages are represented by icons along an hourly time line, as shown in Figure 7-3. Any of the views can be changed, and new views can be added.

Low Importance marker

Message Read icon

Open Item flag

Attachments

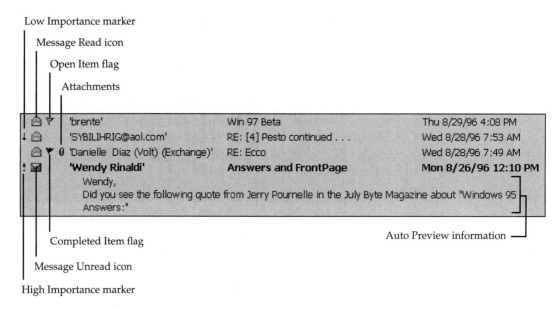

Completed Item flag

Auto Preview information

Message Unread icon

High Importance marker

Figure 7-2:   Outlook messages displayed in a table format

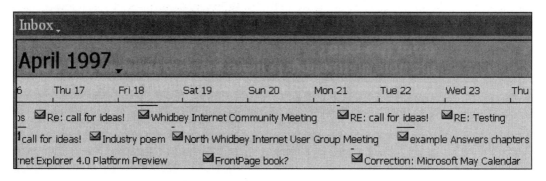

Figure 7-3:   Message Timeline view

Can I **attach or include another document in my e-mail message**? If so, how?

There are a number of things you can include in e-mail messages, such as files, other e-mail messages, bitmapped images, audio clips, and hyperlinks to intranet and Internet Web sites. The following steps show you how to do this:

1. Attach an ordinary file, such as a Word file by positioning the insertion point in the body of the message where

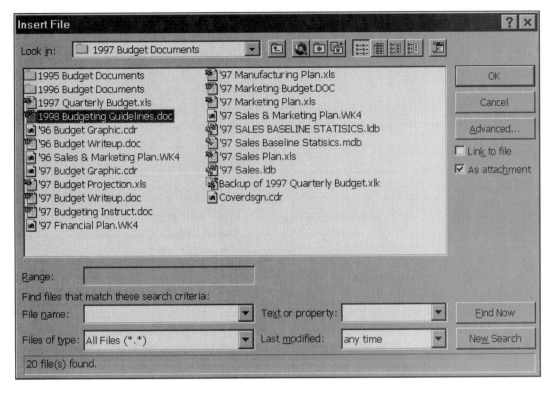

Figure 7-4: Selecting a file for insertion into a message

you want the icon for the message to appear, then clicking the Insert File toolbar button. The Insert File dialog box opens, as shown in Figure 7-4.

2. Make sure the *As attachment* check box is selected on the right of the dialog box, then double-click the file you want to attach. The icon for the file appears in your message at the insertion point.

Tip: If the recipient of your message has access to the disk on which the file you want to send is located, instead of *attaching* the file, you can choose *Link to file* in the Insert File dialog box, thus reducing the size of the actual file you send.

3. Attach another e-mail message to your message by choosing Item from the Insert menu and selecting the item from the Insert Item dialog box that opens. Make sure Insert as Attachment is selected and click OK. The icon appears on your message; for example:

4. Add a hyperlink or link to your message by simply typing or pasting a URL (Universal Resource Locator, or World Wide Web address) in the message. Outlook automatically changes the color (blue is the default) and underlines it to indicate a hyperlink, as shown next.

> http://www.cnn.com   http://www.microsoft.com|
>
> http://interactive5.wsj.com/edition/current/summaries/front.htm

If you click a link, your default browser opens and displays the linked Web page (assuming that you are connected to the Internet or an intranet through which you can reach the URL).

? **I understand that Outlook has some way to automatically process incoming mail, but I can't find anything like that. What am I missing?**

Microsoft has two very powerful tools for use with Outlook that automatically process your mail so it is easier for you to handle. These two tools are the Inbox Assistant and the Rules Wizard. The Inbox Assistant is built into Outlook, but it works only if you are connected to an Exchange Server. The Rules Wizard performs the same functions plus some additional ones. You can download it from http://www.microsoft.com/OfficeFreeStuff/Outlook.

Tip: There are a number of files to augment Outlook that you can download from http://www.microsoft.com/OfficeFreeStuff/Outlook.

The Inbox Assistant and the Rules Wizard

Both the Inbox Assistant and the Rules Wizard walk you through the construction of rules that, when they are applied, will select messages that fit your criteria and then handle the selected messages in the way that you specify. A rule has two components: selection criteria and actions to be performed on selected messages. For example, if you want to search your incoming mail for a particular sender and a particular subject, you would establish a rule that all mail from that sender with that particular subject would automatically be moved to a separate folder after it is read (the action). Some things you can do with the Inbox Assistant and Rules Wizard include the following:

- Assign categories to messages (Rules Wizard only)
- Move selected messages to a folder
- Delete selected messages
- Flag selected messages (Rules Wizard only)
- Forward selected messages
- Mark the importance of selected messages
- Mark the sensitivity of selected messages
- Perform a custom action on selected records
- Produce a special sound or message when selected messages arrive
- Reply to selected messages using a template

After you have acquired and installed the Rules Wizard or choose to use the Inbox Assistant, look at how to implement a rule that selects mail with a particular sender and subject and places that mail in a separate folder with these steps:

1. With the Inbox open in the Outlook window, open the Tools menu and choose Inbox Assistant or Rules Wizard. The blank Inbox Assistant or Rules Wizard dialog box will open. Click New to start a new rule. The next Inbox Assistant or Rules Wizard dialog box opens, as you can see in Figure 7-5 for the Rules Wizard.

2. Open the *Which type of rule do you want to create?* drop-down list and look at the options. The choice is between

a general-purpose rule (*Build as I go*) and a number of special-purpose rules.

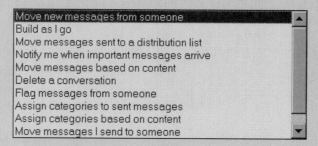

3. Choose the *Build as I go* rule and also keep the default of *Apply this rule when I receive a message in my Inbox* (the second option lets you apply a rule to messages being sent out), and click Next.

4. In the list of conditions or criteria for selecting a message, click *From people or distribution list*. In the lower part of the Inbox Assistant or Rules Wizard dialog box, *people or distribution list* appears. Click this underlined value. Your address book opens.

5. Double-click the person or distribution list that you want to use, and then click OK. That person or distribution list replaces the words *people or distribution list*.

Tip: If you want a rule to apply to several people, create a distribution list containing those people, as described in the question on **creating a mailing list** later in this section.

6. In the upper part of the dialog box, select *with specific words in the subject or body*. In the lower part, click *specific words*, type the words you want to use for the selection, and click OK. The words appear in the lower part of the dialog box, as you can see in Figure 7-6, where *Office 97* was typed as the specific selection.

7. Click Next, and in the *What do you want to do to the message?* list, click *Move it to the specified folder*. Click Specified and choose the folder you want to use or click New and enter a new one. When you are done, click OK.

8. Click Next and identify any exceptions that you want. Click Next again.

9. Type the name of the rule you have just created, make sure the *Turn on this rule* check box is checked, and click Finish. You are returned to the original Inbox Assistant or Rules Wizard dialog box, where your new rule now appears. This dialog box allows you to turn on or off specific rules and perform other rule-management functions. For now, click OK.

The Inbox Assistant and Rules Wizard are extremely powerful tools for managing your e-mail, and the Rules Wizard is definitely worth downloading from Microsoft if you don't have it.

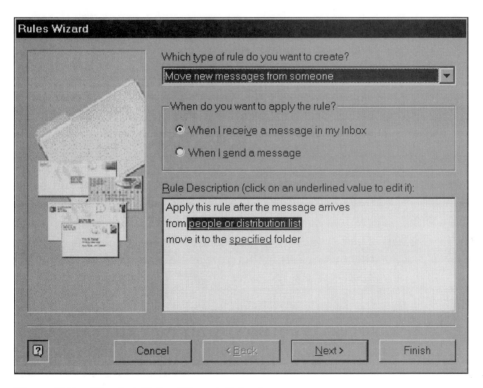

Figure 7-5:   The first Rules Wizard dialog box

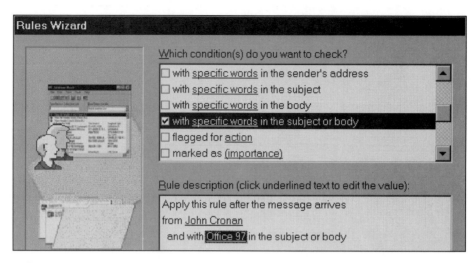

Figure 7-6:   The Rules Wizard dialog box

? **I know I can just type it in, but is there an easier way to capture an e-mail address on a message I received?**

You bet! Right-click on the name in the From field and choose Add to Personal Address Book from the context menu. The e-mail address will automatically be added to your address book. When you do this, the display name is the same as the e-mail address. If you want a different display name, open your address book from either the Outlook window or a new message window, right-click on the address, and choose Properties.

▓▓▓▓▓ *Tip:*   A message's subject is used in several ways to identify the message. It is therefore important to make the subject as descriptive as possible while still keeping it short.

? **I would like to categorize my mail so I can sort it into topics that can be more easily dealt with as a group. How is that done?**

The easiest way to add categories to an Inbox message is to right-click on the message and select Categories from the context menu that opens. This opens up the

Categories dialog box, from which you can choose one or more categories:

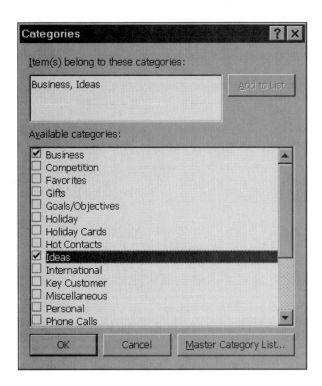

If you want additional categories or if you want to add your own categories, click the Master Category List button in the Categories dialog box. The Master Category List opens, where you can type a new category name in the text box at the top and click Add, or you can select one of the additional categories in the list. Click OK to close the Master Category List. To add the new or additional category to your message, you'll need to select it in the Categories dialog box. For more information, see the sidebar "Handling Incoming Mail."

● ● ● ● ● ● ● ● ● ● ●

Handling Incoming Mail

Handling your incoming mail may or may not be a problem. If you only get a few pieces of mail a day, it is easy to handle. If you get hundreds of pieces a day, you have a real task ahead of you. Outlook provides a large number of features and tools to help you work through the task, however large it is. The following table describes those tools.

Feature or Tool	Description
AutoPreview	Lets you see the first three lines of either unread messages (using the Messages with AutoPreview view) or all messages (with the AutoPreview toolbar button).
Message icons	Identifies whether a message is read or unread.
Message flag	Indicates that a flag has been set or cleared on a message.
Importance markers	Indicates that a message is of high or low importance, using the Importance setting in the Message window's Options tab or in the Properties dialog box opened from the File menu.
Categorizing	Allows you to add categories to messages so they can be grouped or filtered, using the Categories option on the Edit or Context menu (the Context menu is opened when you right-click on a message).
Replying and forwarding	Allows you to quickly reply to or forward a message, using the Reply, Reply to All, and Forward toolbar buttons.
Sorting	Allows you to sort on any field in either ascending or descending order by clicking the field name in the Information Viewer or by choosing Sort from the View menu.

Feature or Tool	Description
Searching	Allows you to search your message files in many different ways, using the Find Items option on the Tools menu.
Grouping	Allows you to group all messages that have the same contents in a given field, by using the Group By option on the View menu or the Group By toolbar button or by dragging the column heading by which you wish to group and dropping it in the Group By box.
Filtering	Allows you to select a set of messages based on complex criteria using the Filter option in the View menu.
Adding reply annotation	Allows you to identify changes you've made to a message by opening the Tools menu, choosing Options and the Reading tab, and then clicking *Mark my comments.*
Dragging and dropping	Allows you drag information from one part of Outlook to another, to the desktop, or to other applications or folders. (You can't drag onto your desktop if you're using WinNT 3.51.)
Adding folders	Allows you to store messages in subfolders under the Inbox, Sent Items, or even under Personal Folders, to more quickly find what you are looking for.
Setting rules	Allows you to describe how the messages you receive should be handled.

❓ An associate has a different-looking window for creating and reading mail messages. How can I change the message window?

Outlook actually has two similar but different e-mail message windows: the normal message window, shown first here, and the WordMail message window, shown second, which uses Microsoft Word for e-mail.

Normal message window

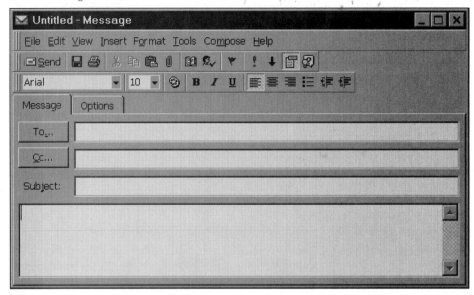

WordMail message window

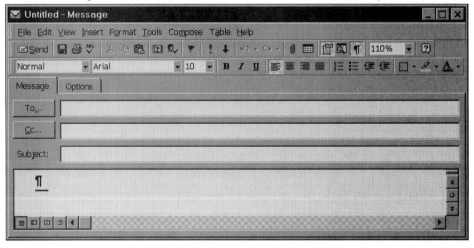

If you want to change your message window, open the Tools menu, choose Options, select the E-mail tab, and check or uncheck *Use Microsoft Word as the e-mail editor.*

❓ I frequently send e-mail to the same group of people. Is there away to create a mailing list so I don't have to re-enter or select all these names each time?

Sure—you can create a distribution list containing the names of the people in your group, and then you only have to enter the distribution list name when you address a message. Use these steps to create a distribution list:

1. Click the Address Book button in the toolbar or choose the Address Book option in the Tools menu of either the Outlook or Message window to open your address book.

2. Click the New button in the Select Names dialog box, which is opened from the Message window, or click the New Entry toolbar button in the Address Book window, which is opened from the Outlook window. In either case, the New Entry dialog box will open.

3. Select Personal Distribution List, as shown next, and then click OK.

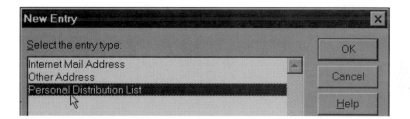

The New Personal Distribution List Properties dialog box opens (see Figure 7-7).

4. Enter the name you want to use to identify this particular list (this is the name you'll type in the To and Cc boxes), click Add/Remove Members, and double-click as many names in your address book as you want on the list or enter one or more new names and addresses and click OK. When all the members have been added, click OK again to return to the Message or Outlook window. In the message address box, only the distribution list name appears (in bold), but the message will be sent to all the names on the list.

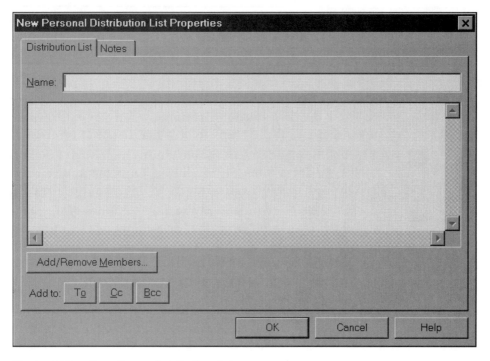

Figure 7-7: Creating a distribution list

5. Edit the distribution list by right-clicking the name, selecting Properties from the context menu, and adding and removing members as necessary. When you are done, click OK to return to the Message window.

? I have built up several hundred mail messages and am having a hard time finding particular messages. What are the best ways to find messages?

There are two approaches that you can use: searching and filtering. Searching and filtering are very similar, except that filtering gives you the results as a list of messages in the Outlook Inbox window and searching gives you the results in the Find window. There are advantages to both. To filter, use the following steps:

1. With the Inbox open (or you could use Sent Items if you wish), open the View menu and choose Filter. The Filter dialog box opens as shown next.

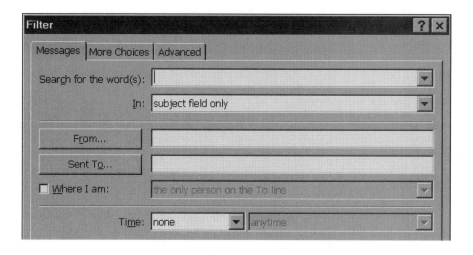

2. In the *Search for the word(s)* text box, enter the word or words that you want to search for. Choose whether you want to search in the subject field only, in the subject field and message body, or in frequently used text fields to search the majority of the text fields in the message.

3. Look at the many additional fields you can use to create your filter in the three tabs. At the bottom of the Messages tab, you can select one of several different time fields in which to look for a time span. In the More Choices tab, note the Categories option, which is one of the principal ways that categories can be used. The Advanced tab allows you to build more complex, free-form criteria to search on.

4. When you have established the filter criteria you want to use, click OK. The Outlook window with the Inbox displayed reappears with the words *(Filter Applied)* in the Inbox banner above the Information Viewer, showing only those messages that satisfy the filter criteria.

5. After you have looked at your filtered messages, again open the View menu and choose the Filter option, click the Clear All button to remove the filter, and then click OK. When you return to the Inbox, you'll see that the filter has been removed.

   If you wish to search instead of filter,

1. Open the Tools menu and choose Find Items to open the Find window shown next.

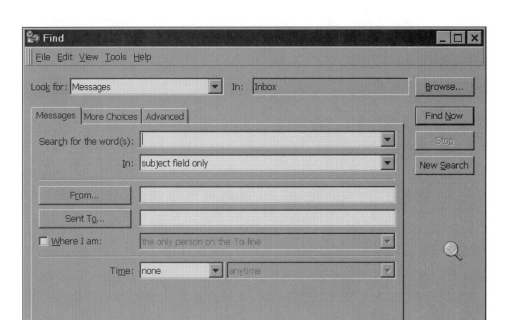

Notice that it is almost exactly the same as the Filter dialog box, except that Find can search for any Outlook item (appointments, contacts, files, journal entries, notes, and tasks, as well as messages), while Filter can search only the currently open folder, such as messages.

2. Enter the same criteria you used in the filter example above, look at the other options in the Find window (they are exactly the same as in the Filter dialog box), and then click Find Now. The found items are displayed at the bottom of the Find window (similar to the Windows 95 Find function).

3. Double-click a message in the bottom of the Find window to open it in the familiar Message window, which allows you to do anything you could otherwise do in that window.

? How many names can be in the To or Cc box of the message window?

You can have a large number (over 70) names in the To and Cc address blocks. As you enter additional names, put a comma between them. Then as they are checked against the address book, a semicolon will automatically replace the comma between the names.

I have a friend who has both **Inbox Assistant and Out of Office Assistant** in his Outlook Tools menu, but I can't find them in mine. How come?

Inbox Assistant and Out of Office Assistant are only available if you are connected to an Exchange server. If you are not connected to an Exchange server, you can download the Outlook Rules Wizard, which will perform all of the functions of the Inbox Assistant and then some. The Outlook Rules Wizard is available from the Microsoft Web site at http://www.microsoft.com/OfficeFreeStuff/Outlook. See the discussion of "The Inbox Assistant and the Rules Wizard" earlier in this section for more information.

How can I get automatically **numbered lists** in the e-mail messages I create?

If you want additional formatting such as numbered lists, more exotic paragraph styles, or (my favorite) spell checking as you type, you should create your e-mail with Microsoft Word's WordMail. You can use Microsoft Word as your e-mail message creator and reader with the following steps.

≣ *Note:* Many of WordMail's formatting features are not observable by recipients of a message unless they are connected to you through an Exchange Server and are using Microsoft Word 97 as their e-mail editor.

1. From the Outlook window with the Inbox open, open the Tools menu, choose Options, and click the E-mail tab, which is shown in Figure 7-8.
2. Click the *Use Microsoft Word as the e-mail editor* check box and then click the Template button to look at the many options you can use as the basic template for your e-mail. You can also create your own.

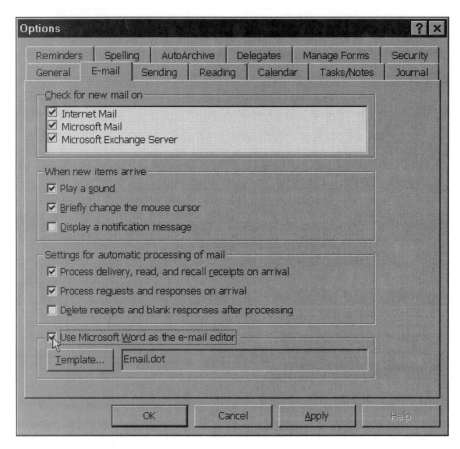

Figure 7-8: Setting up Microsoft Word as your e-mail editor

3. Click Cancel to close the WordMail Template dialog box, leaving the Email.dot default template, then click OK to close the Options dialog box.

4. Click the New Mail Message toolbar button to open a Microsoft Word window with the e-mail template, which was shown earlier in the question on **changing the message window.**

   It probably took longer to come up, but other than that, at first sight it is hard to see the difference between this window and the normal message window you have been working with. Notice the Table menu and the additional buttons on the toolbars. If you open the menus, you see additional differences; for example, if you open the Help menu, you see Microsoft Word Help.

Note: WordMail takes longer to load the first time it's used in a session, but if you use it again, it appears instantly and you will not have the added load time.

5. Use the To, Cc, Subject, and message fields as you would in the normal Message window. While typing the body of the message, try special formatting, see the Spelling and Grammar Checker operate as you type, and use AutoText and other Word features.

? I send out almost the same message quite frequently. I tried storing it in Word and copying and pasting it into my e-mail, but that is a pain. Is there a better way to repeatedly send the same message?

You bet. Outlook allows you to create and use both custom forms and templates for this purpose. The default Message window is an existing form that you can customize. A template is a standard blank message form with custom text in the body of the message. A custom form differs from a template in that the field structure (such as To, Cc, and Subject) can be changed from a normal message. There may be more or fewer fields and they may be in a different order or position, or the fields may have different labels or sizes. You may also add validation criteria to check what is entered into a field, add a calculation to a field, and even include some Visual Basic Script programming to determine how fields, and the form in general, behave. An example of a custom form is the While You Were Out message shown in Figure 7-9.

You can create a template by opening the standard Outlook blank message, adding the text you want to repeat, and then saving it as a template. Do that with the following steps, which create a template.

1. From the Outlook window, with the Inbox open, click the New Mail Message toolbar button to open a new message window.

2. Leave To and Cc blank, type what you want for the Subject, and enter the message text.

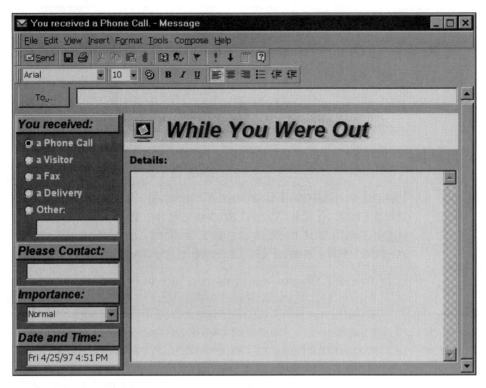

Figure 7-9: A While You Were Out custom message form

3. Save your template by opening the File menu, choosing Save As, and selecting the C:\ProgramFiles\Microsoft Office\Templates\Outlook folder (assuming that you used the default folder scheme); under *Save as type,* select Outlook Template (file extension .oft), then click Save. The new template will be saved under the name you used for the subject.

4. Close your message window (by clicking the X in the upper right of the window) and answer No when asked if you want to save the file (this is asking if you want to save it in your Inbox, which you don't—you've already saved it as a template).

5. To use your template, click the arrow in the New Mail Message toolbar button, then select Choose Template from the New Message menu. The Choose Template dialog box opens and your .oft file should be visible to you.

6. Double-click your file, and it opens as a new message window with the subject and body filled in as you left them. All you need to do is fill in the To information and click Send.

⬛⬛⬛ *Tip:* Any of the built-in templates can be customized by you and then saved under either the existing template or name a new one.

Using Custom Forms

If you want a custom form that simply repeats the text in the subject and body of a message, then you can use a template rather than creating a custom form. However, if you want to change the field structure of a message to add or delete fields or to rearrange fields, then you need to create a custom form and use that form to apply the new structure to your messages. Forms, of course, can also have special text in the subject and body of the message.

Several custom forms are included as part of the Value Pack on the Office 97 CD. To access the forms, open the \Valupack\Template\Outlook folder and double-click Outlfrms.exe. The forms will be placed in your \Program Files\Microsoft Office\Office folder unless you direct otherwise. To view these forms, open the Outlook File menu, choose Open Special Folder, click Personal Folder, and double-click Forms.pst. Then open the Folder List and click the plus sign beside Sample Forms. Here, you will see forms for handling the following:

Classified Ads to collect information to be placed in ads

Sales Tracking to manage sales activity; synchronized with the Calendar, Tasks, Contacts, and Journal

Training Management for course sign-up and scheduling; synchronized with the Calendar

Vacation Request for identifying time absent from work; synchronized with the Calendar

While You Were Out for notifying people of events while they are away

Note: Many of the best features of using a form rather than a template, such as adding fields, changing field positions or labels, and resizing or deleting fields, are transmitted to the message recipient *only* if you are using a Microsoft Exchange server on a LAN. If you transmit a message with those features over the Internet, an intranet, or while using a different mail server over a LAN, you'll lose the features and the message will revert to a standard e-mail format and field set. A customized form may still help you create the message and be worthwhile for that reason, but don't expect your Internet recipient to see your fancy formatting.

Outlook has three features that are used to work with forms:

▷ To create a form, use the Design Outlook Form in the message window's Tools menu.

▷ To save a form, use Publish Form As in the message window's File menu or on the design toolbar.

▷ To manage forms, use the Forms Manager, which you can open from the Outlook window's Tools menu by selecting Options and the Manage Forms tab.

Look at the design view of the message window by opening a new message. Then, from the Tools menu, choose Design Outlook Form. The message window changes to design view and the Field Chooser opens, as you can see in Figure 7-10. Some of the highlights of the form design window are discussed in later sections of this chapter.

Note: The Outlook form design tools are very comprehensive and are fully described in *The Microsoft Outlook Handbook*, written by Martin S. Matthews and published by Osborne/McGraw-Hill.

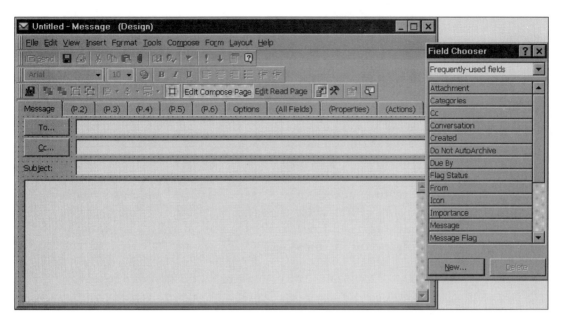

Figure 7-10: The message window in design view

? **Some of my e-mail correspondents use the same signature block on all their messages. Is there an automatic way of doing that?**

Yes, you can automatically add a closing and signature with Outlook's AutoSignature feature. To use AutoSignature with a normal (not WordMail) message, you must set it up by opening the Tools menu in the Outlook window and choosing AutoSignature. The AutoSignature dialog box opens:

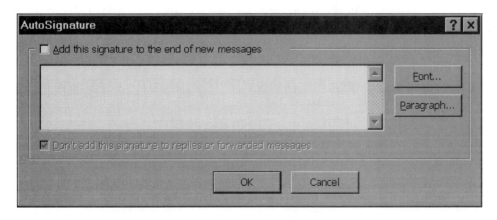

In the text box of the AutoSignature dialog box, you can place anything you want: your signature alone, a closing and a signature, or a statement of some type. To give your signature some further uniqueness, you can use the Font and Paragraph buttons to set the font and font size, color, style, and so on. When you have your signature the way you want it, click *Add this signature to the end of new messages* to have it placed on all new messages. Decide if you also want the signature placed on replies and forwarded messages. If you do want it on those documents, leave the lower check box unchecked; otherwise, click *Don't add this signature to replies or forwarded messages.* When you next open a new message window, you'll see your signature automatically placed on the message.

Tip: To use an AutoSignature with WordMail, enter and format your signature block the way you want it from within a WordMail message window, then select it and choose AutoSignature from the Tools menu.

? Is there a way I can **secure my messages** so they cannot be read by anyone except the recipient?

If you are connected to an Exchange server you can add two types of security to local messages that you send within the limits of your server. These are a digital signature to prevent the message from being altered and encryption to prevent someone other than the recipients from reading the message. These security procedures are controlled by your network administrator, who must give you a security file and a token or keyword to open it. The security file, which can be kept on either a floppy disk or on your hard disk, has the information necessary to encrypt or digitally sign a message.

When you have your security file and token,

1. Open the Outlook Tools menu, choose Options, and click the Security tab.

2. Identify the location of your security file and click Advanced Security.

3. Enter your token, and then enter and confirm a password of at least six characters. It is case sensitive.

4. Close the dialog boxes to return to the Outlook window.
You are now set up to use the security features.

If you wish to send either an encrypted or signed message
(or both), click the appropriate tool on the right of the
standard toolbar, click Send, and enter your password when
requested. Your recipients must also have set up security
and use their own passwords to either open your encrypted
message or verify your digital signature.

If you are not connected to an Exchange server or want
to send secure messages outside your local network, you'll
have to obtain a third-party product such as Pretty Good
Privacy's PGPmail, available from http://www.pgp.com.

What's the meaning of the underline in the To and Cc boxes of the message window?

When a name in the address box is underlined, it indicates
that it has been checked against and is in agreement with
the address book.

USING THE CALENDAR

The Outlook Calendar

The Outlook Calendar is the successor to Schedule+. The
Calendar provides both individual and group scheduling
and allows you to enter and maintain tasks that are kept in
Outlook Tasks. The Calendar lets you do the following:

- ▷ Schedule appointments, meetings, track events, and holidays
- ▷ Look at what you've scheduled for one day, one week, or one month, in two time zones
- ▷ Quickly move from one date to another, both for observation and to reschedule an activity

> ➤ Plan meetings by looking at times when others can attend and send out meeting requests
>
> ➤ Establish activities that recur every day, week, month, or year for a fixed or open-ended time
>
> ➤ Publish your free/busy schedule, be alerted when you receive a meeting request, and be notified when you have an overlap
>
> ➤ Show national and religious holidays and control the work hours in a day, what days are work days, and when the year starts
>
> The default Outlook Calendar window, shown in Figure 7-11, has three major areas:
>
> ➤ The daily schedule on the left, with the times listed
>
> ➤ The Date Navigator in the upper right
>
> ➤ The TaskPad in the lower right
>
> The default is the Day/Week/Month view, which shows the current day, one day at a time. The daily schedule shows events like birthdays and holidays at the top and appointments, meetings, and other activities in minimum half-hour increments down the schedule. The Date Navigator gives you one or two months (depending on the width of the daily schedule) in which you can open any date by clicking it. The TaskPad lists currently open, late, and past-due tasks of your own or that someone else has given or owes you. Outlook provides many alternatives to this view.

How can I accept meeting requests automatically if they don't conflict with other things in my schedule?

To set up automatic acceptance of nonconflicting meeting requests, you need to open the Outlook Tools menu and select Options to open the Options dialog box. Then, in the Calendar tab, click Advanced Scheduling to open the Advanced Scheduling dialog box.

Daily schedule   Event   Date Navigator

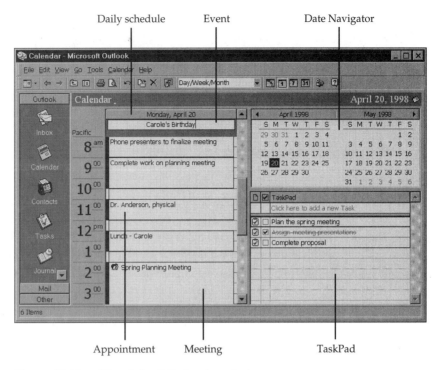

Appointment   Meeting   TaskPad

Figure 7-11:   The default Calendar window

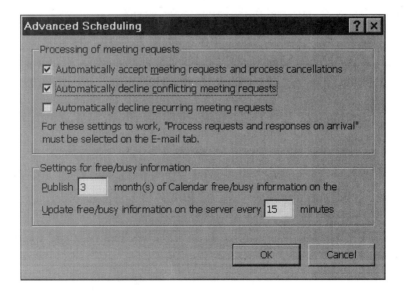

In this dialog box, the first three check boxes control the automatic response to meeting requests, as follows:

▷ The first check box causes all meeting requests and cancellations to be automatically accepted, unless you have checked either of the other two check boxes.

▷ The second check box causes all meeting requests that conflict with currently scheduled activities to be automatically declined.

▷ The third check box causes all meeting requests that are recurring to be automatically declined.

⬛⬛⬛⬛⬛   *Tip:*   Make sure that *Process requests and responses on arrival* is selected (checked) in the Options E-mail tab; otherwise the automatic response to meeting requests cannot work.

With the first two boxes checked, all requests that don't conflict with scheduled activities will be automatically accepted and will appear on your calendar. This can save you considerable time responding to requests, and all the meetings appear on your calendar, where you will be reminded of them.

❓ What is the difference between **appointments, meetings, and events?**

In the Outlook calendar you can enter three types of activities:

Appointments, which take time on your calendar, are less than 24 hours in length, and do not require inviting others to attend. Examples include a sales call, lunch with a buyer, and time you want to set aside to write a report.

Meetings, which are appointments that require that others be invited or that resources be reserved. Meetings are set up using the Meeting Planner to identify participants, send meeting requests to them, and track the responses.

Events, which are 24 hours or more in length and do not occupy time on your calendar. Each event appears as a banner on that day's calendar. Examples include birthdays, anniversaries, trade shows, and your vacation.

I work in a small office where all of our computer files are completely shared. In that environment is there any way I can directly change an associate's calendar?

If you have been given permission by the person, you can literally open their calendar and make an appointment. See how with these steps:

1. Open the File menu, choose Open Special Folder, and select either Exchange Server Folder or Personal Folder (depending on whether you are using the Exchange Server).

2. If you choose to open a Personal Folder, you immediately go to the *Connect to* dialog box, where you can select the path and .pst file in which you want to make an appointment (this may be C:\Exchange\Mailbox.pst or C:\Windows\Outlook.pst). A second Outlook window opens, although the same information is available in either the original or the new window.

3. Click the Folder List button in the toolbar to open the folder list. You now see two complete folder lists—one for you and one for your associate (you may have to open them). For example, Figure 7-12 shows two sets of personal folders (the names of your parent folders will be different, but the Calendar, Contacts, Inbox, and so on will be the same).

 Note: If you open an Exchange Server folder, you will see the *Open Exchange server folder* dialog box. There, you can enter the name of the owner (you can use the Exchange Global Address list by clicking the Name button) and, in the Folder drop-down list, you can choose the folder you want to go to. Upon clicking OK, you'll go straight to the folder you chose. (To open someone's folder in the Exchange Server, you must have been given permission, which the owner can do by opening the Tools menu, selecting Options, then selecting Delegates.)

4. Open the two Calendars in the two different windows to see them side by side and to prove that they are different, as shown in Figure 7-13.

5. Given that you have already set up the meeting in your calendar, right-drag it to the other calendar and click Copy in the context menu that appears.

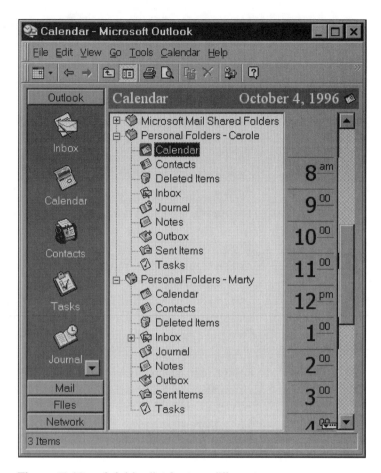

Figure 7-12:   A folder list for two different users

≡ *Note:*   You can also directly enter, move, or delete
appointments, events, or meetings in an associate's calendar;
you can do anything you can do in your own calendar, so long
as your associate has shared the folder, a parent folder, or
drive containing the file.

6. When you are done working with your associate's
   calendar, right-click on the parent folder (Personal
   Folders—Carole, in this example), choose Disconnect
   from the context menu, and close the extra window.

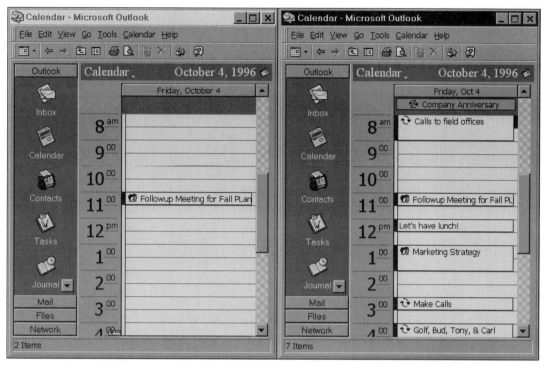

Figure 7-13: Comparing two calendars

? **I inadvertently entered an abbreviated and misspelled date and Outlook corrected it. What are all the date and time abbreviations that can be used?**

The Outlook Calendar has a feature called AutoDate, which allows you to enter dates and times as text and convert that text to numeric dates and times. For example, you can enter **next tue** and be given next Tuesday's date, or you can enter **sep ninth** and see that date. You can enter this in any date or time field in Outlook, such as the Go To Date dialog box reached from the Go menu or the Start and End date and time fields in the appointment and event forms and the Plan a Meeting dialog box. Following are some of the things you can do:

▷ Abbreviate months and days (for example, Dec or fri).

▷ Ignore capitalization and other punctuation (for example, wednesday, april, and lincolns birthday).

▷ Use words that indicate dates and times (for example, tomorrow, yesterday, today, now, next week, last month, five days ago, in three months, this Saturday, and two weeks from now). Words you can use include after, ago, before, beforehand, beginning, end, ending, following, for, from, last, next, now, previous, start, that, this, through, till, tomorrow, and until.

▷ Spell out specific dates and times (for example, August ninth, first of December, April 19th, midnight, noon, two twenty pm, and five o'clock a.m.).

▷ Indicate holidays that fall on the same date every year (for example, New Year's Eve, New Year's Day, Lincoln's Birthday, Valentine's Day, Washington's Birthday, St. Patrick's Day, Cinco de Mayo, Independence Day, Halloween, Veterans Day, Christmas Eve, Christmas Day, and Boxing Day).

 My calendar doesn't display holidays. Do I have to manually add them?

You don't have to type each holiday into your calendar, but you do have to select which holidays you want and tell Outlook to add them.

Note: When you start Outlook for the first time, the Office Assistant's *Welcome to MS Outlook* "helper" dialog box has an option to *Add holidays to your Calendar.*

If you have already run Outlook, then set up the holidays you want displayed with the following steps:

1. From the Outlook window, open the Tools menu, choose Options, and click the Calendar tab. The Calendar Options dialog box will open, as shown in Figure 7-14.

2. Click Add Holidays, select your country and, if desired, one of the religious sets of holidays (Christian, Jewish, or Islamic), and then click OK. You'll see a message that the holidays are being imported.

3. Click OK to close the Options dialog box. Open your calendar and you'll see that the holidays you chose have been added to your calendar as events.

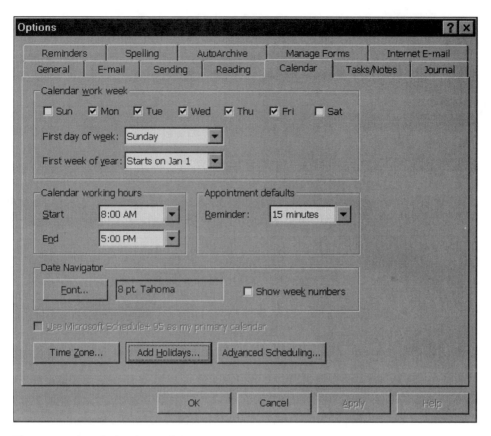

Figure 7-14:   Calendar options

≡ *Note:*   Once you have added holidays to your calendar, they
can be edited, moved, and deleted like any other event.

?   When I am **entering appointments directly in the
Outlook window** instead of in an appointment form, it
seems like sometimes I can enter text and sometimes
drag the appointment, but I am not sure when. How
does this work?

> When directly working on the calendar, there are two
> modes: text mode and object mode. In text mode, you
> can enter and edit the description. In object mode, you
> can change the time span and the start time and move
> the activity by dragging, plus change some of the options
> through the context menu. When you click in a time slot

you are placed in text mode. To get out of that mode you must press ENTER or click in another time slot. To use object mode to size or move an appointment (or meeting or event), drag the time slot or its border without first clicking in the time slot.

•••••• *Tip:* Combine direct entry and form entry to get the benefits of both.

? I am currently using ACT! as my personal information manager, or PIM. I would like to import ACT! data into Outlook but can't find a way to do that. Is there a way?

Some of the import/export options including Schedule+ 1.0 and 7.0, Tab and Comma Separated values (DOS and Windows), dBase, FoxPro, Access, Excel, and Personal Address Book are installed as part of the normal Setup. The rest—ACT!, ECCO, Lotus Organizer, and SideKick—are part of a Value Pack that comes with the CD version of Office 97 or can be downloaded from Microsoft at

http:/www.microsoft.com/OfficeFreeStuff/Outlook

If you have loaded the ValuPack files, choose *Import and Export* from the File menu, select *Import from Schedule+ or another program or file* in the first Import and Export Wizard dialog box, and then click ACT! in the second dialog box.

•••••• *Tip:* From ACT! (or other PIMs) you can export a comma- or tab-separated values file that can be read into Outlook without the Value Pack.

? I like using the Outlook Calendar, but I am used to carrying a Day-Timer™ for reference and making notes. Is there a way to print the Calendar in a pocket format?

Yes. Outlook includes a number of printed formats that fit the various sizes of binders made by several companies for such a purpose. Look at the printing options with the following steps:

1. With the Outlook Calendar open, select the day, week, or month that you want to print. (You don't have to do this first, since you can select the period in the Print dialog

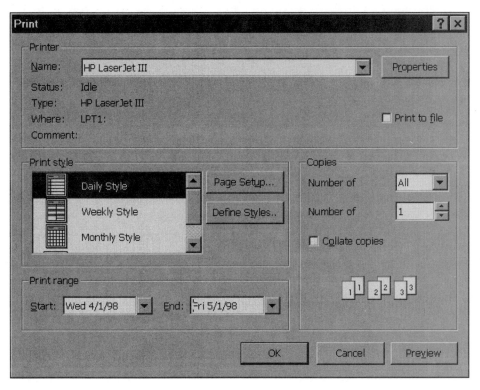

Figure 7-15:   The Calendar Print dialog box

box, but selecting it prior to printing allows you to see on screen what will print.)

2. Open the File menu and choose Print. The Print dialog box opens, as you can see in Figure 7-15.

3. The first decision is choosing which print style you want to use. Click the one you want (but try the others to see what they are like).

4. Click Page Setup to open the dialog box for the style you chose. Click Print Preview to see the default of all the options. Click the Page Setup button to return to Page Setup.

5. Make the changes that you want in Options and Fonts and then click the Paper tab. This tab, as you can see in Figure 7-16, allows you to select the type of paper or form you are using in your printer, as well as the size and type of the page you want printed on the paper.

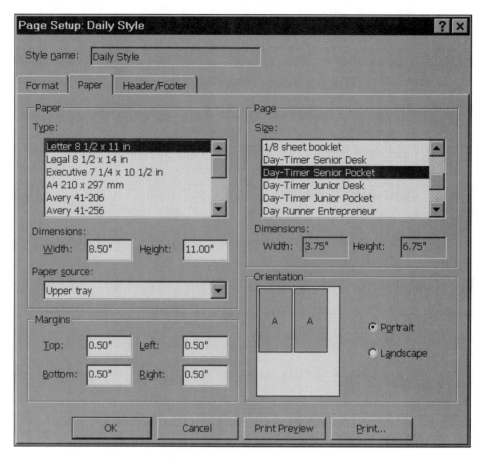

Figure 7-16: The Paper tab in the Page Setup dialog box

6. Make the choices that are correct for you and then click the Header/Footer tab to see its defaults. Make any necessary changes.

7. Click Print Preview to see your results. If they are acceptable, click Print to return to the Print dialog box, and click OK to print.

? **I have several regularly scheduled appointments and meetings that repeat every week or month. Is there a way around retyping or cutting and pasting these each time?**

You bet. You can make any appointment, meeting, or event be recurring either when you create the calendar item or when you edit it by clicking the Recurrence toolbar button

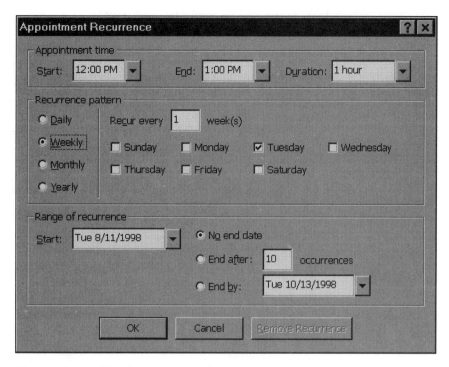

Figure 7-17:   The Recurrence dialog box

or by choosing Recurrence in the Appointment menu. This opens the Recurrence dialog box, which you can see in Figure 7-17. Here you can set the recurrence pattern and the length of time you want it to recur.

Note: Setting up appointments and events as recurring can save you a lot of time re-entering activities, but it can also generate a lot of entries, which may unnecessarily fill your calendar.

I know about recurring appointments, but how can I repeat an appointment just a few times?

You can copy an activity by right-dragging it to where you want the copy and selecting Copy from the context menu that appears when you release the right mouse button.

? **How can I view a date other than today's in the calendar?**

This is the function of the Date Navigator in the upper right of the Outlook Calendar. You can click a date to see that date, you can click a week to see it, or you can drag across several days to see them. There are also ways to scroll the months in the Navigator to display different ones. See the sidebar "Using the Date Navigator" for the details on this.

• • • • • • • • • • •

Using the Date Navigator

The Date Navigator, in the upper-right corner of the Calendar window and shown next, allows you to pick any date from April 1, 1601, to August 31, 4500 (Microsoft wanted to make sure that Outlook had staying power!).

◄	April 1998							May 1998					►
S	M	T	W	T	F	S	S	M	T	W	T	F	S
29	30	31	1	2	3	4						1	2
5	6	7	8	9	10	11	3	4	5	6	7	8	9
12	13	14	15	16	17	18	10	11	12	13	14	15	16
19	**20**	21	22	23	24	25	17	18	19	20	21	22	23
26	27	28	29	30			24	25	26	27	28	29	30
							31	1	2	3	4	5	6

To cover this span of over 2,800 years, Outlook provides a number of tools using the Date Navigator to perform the following functions:

▷ Show details for a day in one of the months displayed in the Navigator, by clicking the day.

▷ Show details for an active day in one of the months displayed in the Navigator, by clicking a day that appears in boldface.

▷ Show details for several days in the months displayed in the Navigator, by holding down CTRL while clicking the days or by dragging across the days if they are contiguous.

▷ Show details for a week in one of the months displayed in the Navigator, by clicking to the left of the first day of the week.

▷ Show details for several weeks in the months displayed in the Navigator, by holding down CTRL while clicking the weeks, as shown next, or by dragging across the weeks if they are contiguous.

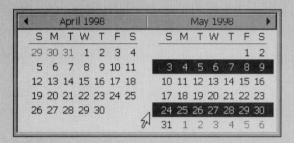

▷ Show details for one of the months displayed in the Navigator, by dragging across all the weeks in the month.

▷ Move an activity currently displayed to another date, by dragging the activity to that date in the Navigator.

▷ Make a small change in which months are displayed in the Navigator, by clicking the left and right arrows in the month bar.

▷ Make a large change in which months are displayed in the Navigator, by dragging the month bar up or down, as you can see next.

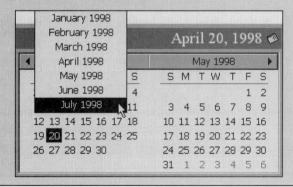

> ▷ If you drag the mouse either above or below the list, the list will scroll.
>
> ▷ Make direct and possibly large changes in the date displayed, by choosing Go to Date from the Go menu or by pressing CTRL-G.

? I do a lot of business in Japan and would like to see their time zone, as well. Is there a way to view different time zones?

Sure. To look at two times zones at the same time, use the following steps:

1. Open the Outlook Tools menu, choose Options, and click Time Zone in the Calendar tab. The Time Zone dialog box will open.

2. Select and label both your time zone and the additional one, as shown next.

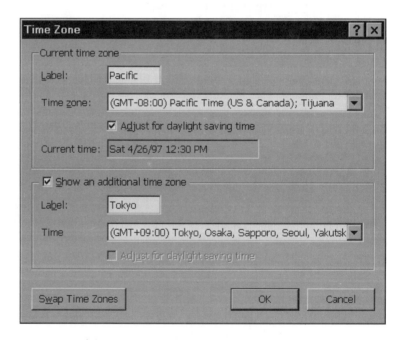

3. Click OK twice to close both the Time Zone and Options dialog boxes. The two time zones will appear in your daily schedule:

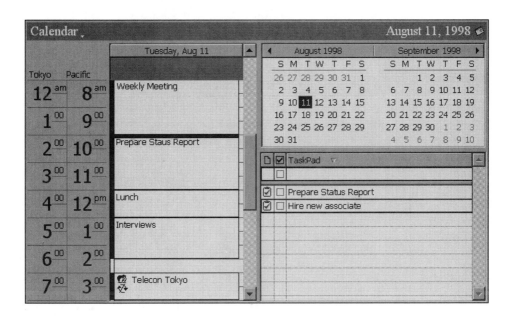

ENTERING AND MAINTAINING CONTACTS

Outlook Contacts

Outlook Contacts provides an easy means to enter, access, and maintain a comprehensive list of names, addresses, and phone numbers. It also provides many other features. With Contacts you can accomplish the following:

➤ Enter a full name and have Outlook divide or parse it into first name, middle name, and last name

➤ Enter a full address and have Outlook parse it into street, city, state, postal code, and country

➤ Enter a phone number and have Outlook format it into area code, phone number, and extension (in the United States) or other formats (for other countries)

➤ File contacts under their names, their company names, or separate entries that make them easy to find

> ▷ Maintain 15 or more phone numbers and up to three addresses and three e-mail addresses for each contact
> ▷ Quickly dial a contact's phone number, send a letter to a contact's address, or view a contact's World Wide Web site
> ▷ Send e-mail to, set up an appointment with, assign a task to, or maintain a journal of activities with a contact
> ▷ Use your contact list as your e-mail address book
> ▷ Create a custom form to gather your own contact information
> ▷ Print your contact list in many different formats that can fit the binders of different time management systems

The initial Contacts view is one of address "cards," as shown in Figure 7-18, similar to what you might see if you spread out address cards on a table. Each card contains a single address, the business and home phone numbers, fax numbers, and e-mail addresses. On the right side of the window is a set of alphabetical buttons; if you click one, you'll be shown the part of the contact list starting with the letter you clicked. You can scroll through the list by using the horizontal scroll bar at the bottom of the window. You can directly edit the information being displayed by double-clicking an entry (this opens the more detailed Contact form). You can also directly use an entry to make a phone call, send e-mail or regular mail, set up meetings, and assign tasks.

Tip: Take particular care in making entries to the File As field. In the built-in views it is the basis of how the cards are arranged (the sort field). It also allows you to identify an entry any way that makes sense to you, not just by name or company.

? ## Outlook **Address Book vs. Contacts**—What's the difference? Aren't they one and the same?

If you open the Outlook Address Book, you see the message *No entries in this Address Book.* The reason is that the Outlook Address Book is a parent folder for Contacts, so

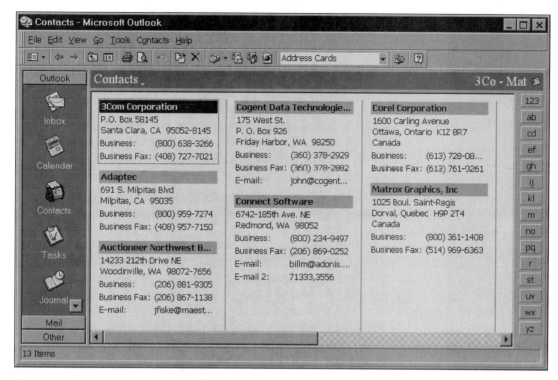

Figure 7-18: Default Contacts window

Contacts is where you have to look for the addresses in the Outlook Address Book. This allows you to get addresses from additional folders of contacts, if you wish to divide your contacts into several folders to make them easier to find.

? I know I can look up an e-mail address in my Contacts address book, but isn't there a more direct way to address e-mail from Contacts?

Yes, you can use the New Message button in the toolbar with these steps:

1. From the Contacts folder, select the person to whom you want to send e-mail.

2. Click the *New Message to Contact* toolbar button or select New Message from the Contacts menu. A new message opens with your contact's e-mail address in the To text box.

3. Fill in the remainder of the message form and send it.

Note: If your contact has more than one e-mail address, all the e-mail addresses will be placed in the new message; you can then remove the ones you don't want to use.

Now that I have all my e-mail addresses in Contacts, how do I use **Contacts as the default address book**?

You can make Contacts your default address book by choosing Services from the Tools menu, clicking the Addressing tab, and selecting Contacts in the *Show this address list first* box, as shown here:

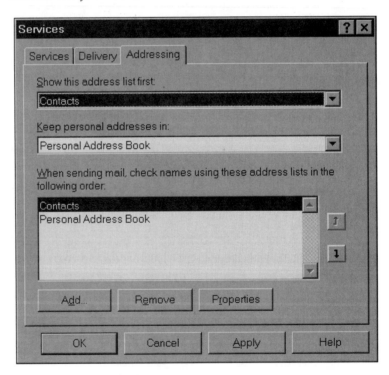

? Many of the Contact fields are not displayed in a Contact form. How can I see and **edit all the fields in a Contact record**?

By selecting *All Contact fields* in the All Fields tab of the Contact window, as shown in Figure 7-19, you can see all of the Contact fields. You can enter and edit all but the following fields: Attachment, Modified, Outlook Internal Version, Outlook Version, Read, and Size (which are all automatically set); and Business Address, Business Address Street, Home Address, Home Address Street, Mailing Address, Notes, Other Address, Other Address Street, and Street Address (which are set and edited only in the Detail tab).

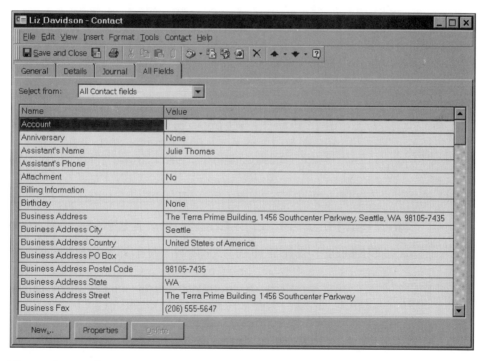

Figure 7-19: Displaying all Contact fields

I use both the Personal Address Book and Contacts for my e-mail and don't see any reason for it. Can I import my Personal Address Book into Contacts so I need only one address book?

Yes, you can. Here's how:

1. From the Outlook window, open the File menu and choose Import and Export. Accept the default *Import from Schedule+ or another program or file,* and click Next.

2. Select Personal Address Book from the file type list and click Next.

3. Select Contacts as the destination folder, as you see next, and click Next.

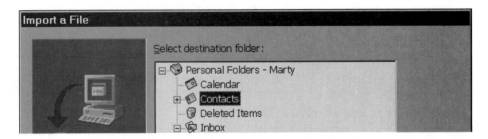

4. Confirm that the action to be taken is to import your Personal Address Book to Contacts and click Finish. You see a message showing the import/export progress. When it is completed, you'll see your Personal Address Book entries in your Contacts folder.

 How can I use names in Contacts in a Word mail merge?

Since you probably want to send letters to only some of your contacts, you need to create a Contacts folder that contains only the contacts you want to use (unfortunately, you can't just filter your contacts). You need to create a subfolder to Contacts, select the records you want, copy them to that subfolder, and have Word merge a letter to your subfolder. Here are the steps to do that:

1. With the Contacts folder open, click the Folder List toolbar button. Right-click Contacts in the folder list, choose Create Subfolder from the context menu, enter a name for the folder, and click OK.

2. With Contacts still open, open the View menu, choose Filter, and enter the criteria that select only the entries you want. For example, if you want only contacts that have Realtor in the File As field, then enter Realtor in the *Search for the words* text box and make sure that the File As field is the only one in the In text box. Then click OK. Only the contacts that you want are displayed.

3. From the Edit menu, choose Select All. Right-drag the contacts to your new folder and click Copy in the context menu that appears (to keep the contacts in the Contacts folder, as well as in the new folder). If you open the new folder, the selected contacts are there.

4. Open Microsoft Word and open the letter (or create a new one) that you want to send to your selected contacts. Leave blank the areas that will contain each recipient's name and address.

5. When the body of the letter is the way you want it, open the Tools menu and choose Mail Merge. The Mail Merge Helper opens.

6. Click *Main document Create,* choose Form Letters, and click Active Window to select the document you have just typed as the form letter.

7. Click *Data source Get Data,* choose Use Address Book, double-click Outlook Address Book, and choose your new folder, like this:

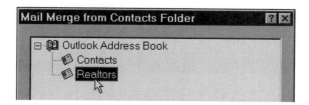

8. Click OK. You get a message that Word has found no merge fields (since you haven't entered them yet). Click Edit Main Document.

9. Back in the form letter, position the insertion point where you want the contact name to go, click the Insert Merge

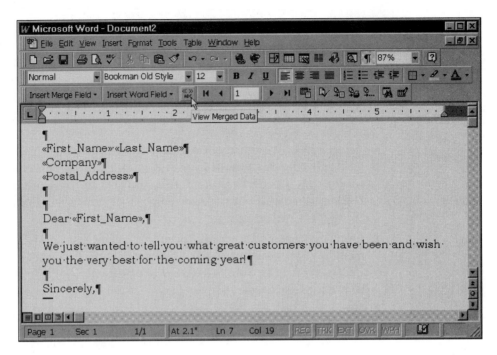

Figure 7-20: Mail merge form letter

Field button in the Mail Merge toolbar, choose First_Name, enter a space, click the Insert Merge Field button again, choose Last_Name, and so on to enter all the fields that you want to use in your letter. When you are done, your letter should look something like Figure 7-20.

Tip: Choosing Postal_Address as a merge field gives you the street address, city, state, and postal code all at one time.

10. Click View Merged Data in the Mail Merge toolbar to see your actual Contacts data in the letter. Click the left and right arrows in the Mail Merge toolbar to look at the various contacts to which you will merge the letter. Notice that only your selected contacts are merge candidates.

11. When you are ready to print your merged letters, click the Merge to Printer button in the Mail Merge toolbar.

ESTABLISHING AND USING TASKS LISTS

Outlook Tasks

Outlook Tasks allows you to create and maintain to-do lists to accomplish the following:

➤ Establish and track one-time and recurring tasks for yourself

➤ Send task requests to other individuals and to groups, and track their progress

➤ Reorder and reassign tasks

➤ Categorize and prioritize tasks

➤ Schedule tasks and look at them in the Calendar

➤ Track percent complete and prepare status reports

The default view of Tasks, and the view that you saw in the Calendar's TaskPad, is the Simple List shown in Figure 7-21. It shows you two columns for icons, a subject, and a due date. The first column shows you the type of task; these are described further in Table 7-1. The second column has a completion box to show if the task has been completed or not (a check mark indicates completion). The subject is displayed in one of four styles:

➤ Normal type indicates current tasks with a future due date.

➤ Bold type indicates tasks about which you have unread messages.

➤ Colored type (typically red) indicates past-due tasks.

➤ Strike-through type indicates tasks that are completed.

You can arrange or sort the task list by clicking a field in the heading, clicking once to sort the field one way (descending for dates and times; ascending for all other fields), and clicking again to sort the same field in the opposite direction. You can directly edit the information displayed in the list and you can open the more detailed Task form by double-clicking an entry. You can also prioritize and categorize this list and use it with the Calendar.

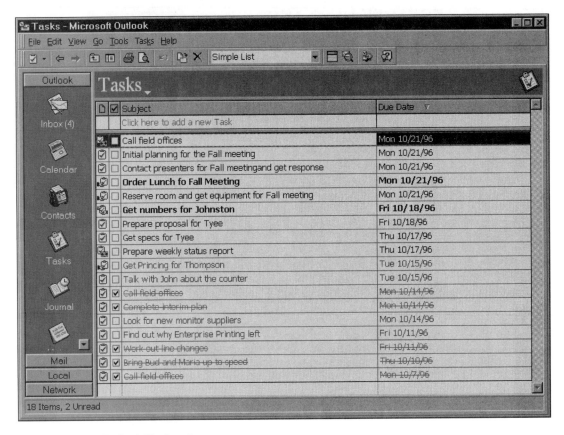

Figure 7-21:   Default Tasks view

Table 7-1:   Types of Tasks

Icon	Description
	Your own normal task
	Your own recurring task
	A task you've assigned to someone else
	A task you've assigned that's been accepted
	A task you've assigned that's been declined
	A task someone has assigned to you

? Can I add a field to Tasks and sort on it?

Yes, here are the steps to create a new field called Order:

1. From the View menu, choose Define Views. In the Define Views dialog box that opens, click Modify and click Fields in the View Summary dialog box.

2. Click New Field, type **Order**, and click OK three times; then click Close to create the new field.

3. Type numbers into the new Order field to represent the priority in which you want your tasks arranged. When you are done, click the column heading to arrange tasks in your priority order, as shown here:

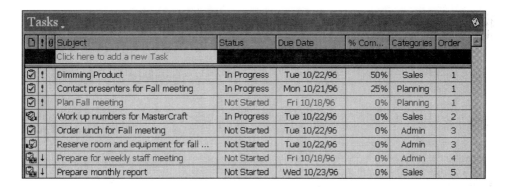

	!	0	Subject	Status	Due Date	% Com...	Categories	Order	
			Click here to add a new Task						
☑	!		Dimming Product	In Progress	Tue 10/22/96	50%	Sales	1	
☑	!		Contact presenters for Fall meeting	In Progress	Mon 10/21/96	25%	Planning	1	
☑	!		Plan Fall meeting	Not Started	Fri 10/18/96	0%	Planning	1	
☑			Work up numbers for MasterCraft	In Progress	Tue 10/22/96	0%	Sales	2	
☑			Order lunch for Fall meeting	Not Started	Tue 10/22/96	0%	Admin	3	
☑			Reserve room and equipment for fall ...	Not Started	Tue 10/22/96	0%	Admin	3	
☑	↓		Prepare for weekly staff meeting	Not Started	Fri 10/18/96	0%	Admin	4	
☑	↓		Prepare monthly report	Not Started	Wed 10/23/96	0%	Sales	5	

 Note: When you add a new field, it is by definition a text field and is sorted and handled as text. When you put numbers in it, the numbers 10 and 11 are going to sort after 1 instead of after 9. Therefore, you must decide if you want more than nine numbers, and if so, you must consistently use two-digit numbers (01, 02, etc.).

? It's handy having my task list on the screen with my Calendar, but is there an easy way to create appointments with tasks or create blocks of time to work on the task?

You bet; you can do that by simply dragging a task to the Calendar. This causes an Appointment form to open, allowing you to identify some time you can spend on the task. Also, if you need a meeting to accomplish a task, you can set one up by dragging a task to the Calendar; after the Appointment form opens, use the Meeting Planner to schedule a meeting and invite those you want to come.

My boss is in another office, so I often get assignments via e-mail. How can I create tasks directly from e-mail?

You simply drag the e-mail message to the Tasks icon in the Outlook bar. When you do that, a task is created that contains the e-mail message and uses the subject of the message as the task subject. For example, say you get this message:

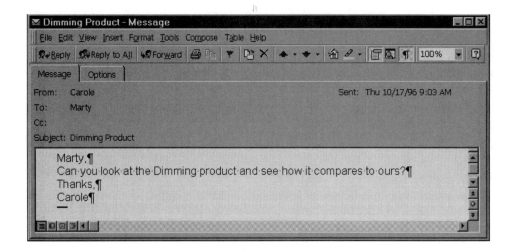

If you close the message and then drag the Inbox entry to the Tasks icon in the Outlook bar, you'll get a Task form that looks like Figure 7-22. The original e-mail message is copied to the notes part of the task, and the subject is copied to the task subject. The due date can now be set, as can all the other parts of a detailed task. When you save and close the Task form, you'll have a normal entry in your task list tied to the original e-mail message.

I have several tasks that I have to do every week. How can I make a task a recurring one?

Outlook has an option to make any task you enter a recurring task on either a periodic basis or upon the

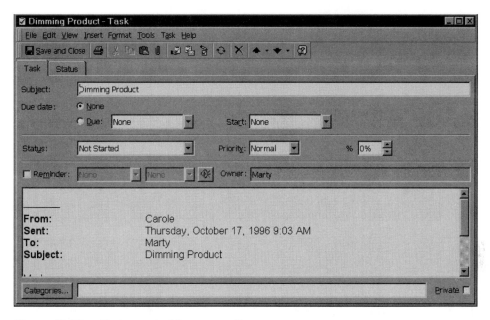

Figure 7-22: Task created from e-mail

completion of the previous task. In either case, the new task appears when the previous one is complete. If the recurrence is set for a periodic basis, after the last occurrence, the new task appears on the specified day of the week, month, or year. If the recurrence is based on completion, then after completion of one occurrence, the new task appears a fixed number of days in the future. Here's how this works:

1. In the Simple List view of a task list, double-click a task you want to recur to open its form.

2. Click the Recurrence button in the toolbar. The Task Recurrence dialog box opens, as you can see in Figure 7-23. Note the difference from the Recurrence dialog boxes you saw with the Calendar. With Tasks, you have the option to regenerate a new task a fixed number of days, weeks, months, or years (based on the setting on the left of the dialog box) after the current task is complete.

3. Click Daily in the upper-left column of the Task Recurrence dialog box. Click *Regenerate new task,* drag across the number in that line, type **7**, press TAB, type **2 weeks before** as the Start of the recurring pattern, and

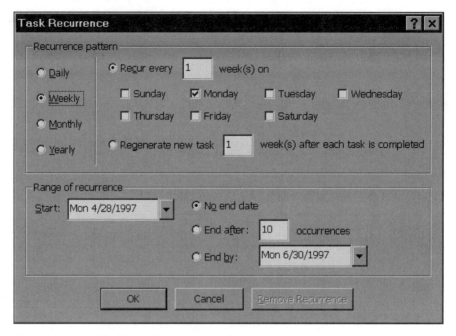

Figure 7-23: The Task Recurrence dialog box

click OK. Back in the Task form, you get a message that the task is overdue by 14 days.

4. **Click Save and Close. Click OK.** Back in the Tasks list, notice that the new task has a different icon and is a different color (typically red) because it is overdue. You'll fix the overdue status next.

5. Click the completion box in the second column of your task. The original task has a line drawn through it and a new task is created seven days after the day you clicked the completion box. In the entries shown next, the completion box was clicked on 10/17/96 (seven days before the next occurrence on 10/24/96).

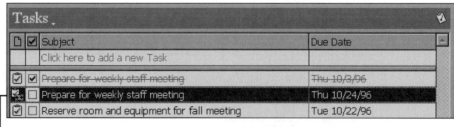

Task recurring on completion

6. Press DELETE to delete the new entry and click the completion box of the original again to uncomplete it, then double-click the task to reopen its form.

7. Click the Recurrence button to open the Task Recurrence dialog box and click weekly in the left column. The default pattern of *Recur every 1 week on . . .* the day of the original task should appear. If not, select it, click OK, and click Save and Close in the Task form.

8. Click the completion box of your task. This time, a new task is created one week after the original due date of the completed one (instead of seven days after the date it was marked completed, as we did earlier).

9. Click the completion box of the second copy of your task, and you see another task created one week after the due date of the second one:

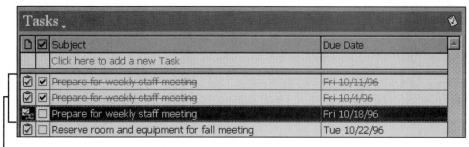

Tasks recurring on a fixed cycle

•••••• *Tip:* If you want to stop a task from recurring, double-click the task to open its form, open the Task Recurrence dialog box, and click Remove Recurrence.

❓ I want to **send a task to someone else**. How can I do that?

Outlook has included the capability to send a task to someone, allow them to accept or reject it, and keep a copy of it to track, all within Tasks. See how this is done with these instructions:

1. From the open Tasks folder, double-click the task you want to transfer to open it in the Task form. Click the

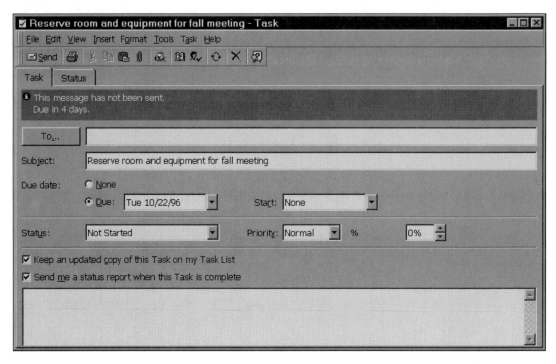

Figure 7-24: Sending a task to someone else

Assign Task toolbar button, and the Task form changes to a combination task form and e-mail form, as you can see in Figure 7-24.

2. Click the To button to open your Address Book and select who you want to send the task to. Make any other appropriate changes, such as the status and the priority or a note. Click one or both of the two check boxes if appropriate: One keeps the task visible to you in your list, and the other automatically sends you a status report on completion.

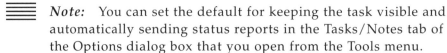
Note: You can set the default for keeping the task visible and automatically sending status reports in the Tasks/Notes tab of the Options dialog box that you open from the Tools menu.

3. When you are ready, click Send, and then click OK.

The recipient sees a message in his or her Inbox that makes it very clear that a task request has been received, as you can see here:

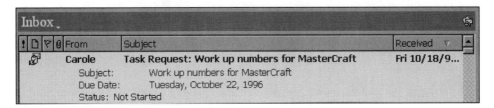

Also, upon receipt of a message request, a task is automatically added to the recipient's task list even if the message has not been opened. When either the Inbox message or the task is opened, the form shown in Figure 7-25 is displayed. Notice that the toolbar has two buttons: Accept and Decline. When one is clicked, a message of the decision is automatically sent back to the original sender of the task; a notice that the message is being returned is also sent to the recipient of the task and

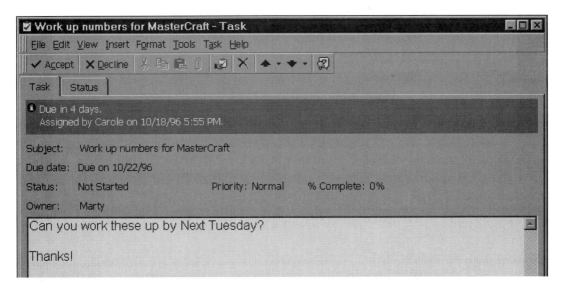

Figure 7-25:   A message requesting a task

the recipient is given the chance to add a note. Here are examples of such messages:

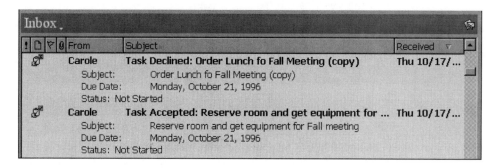

If the task-requesting message is accepted, the ownership of the message goes from the sender to the recipient, and the task becomes a permanent part of the recipient's task list. If the task is declined, the ownership stays with the sender and it is removed from the recipient's task list. Once the recipient has accepted a task, he or she can then change any of the settings, such as the due date and status. When such a change is made (for example, completing the task), the originator will be notified of the change with a Task Update message, like this:

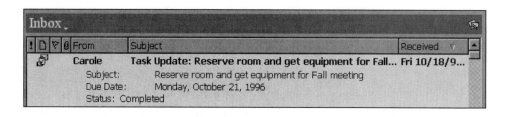

> **Tip:** You can tell who will get the automatic update information by looking at the Update list on the bottom of the Status tab of a task.

? I would like to order my tasks by something other than the Subject, Status, or Due Date. Is there some way to **sort by other categories** in Tasks?

Yes; if you select the Detailed List view of Tasks, you can put any information you want in the Categories field, and then use that information to arrange your tasks.

Note: You cannot sort by the Categories field, but you can group on Categories, which gives you almost the same results.

Add categories to your tasks with the following steps:

1. Right-click in the Categories field of a task, choose Categories from the context menu, and click Master Category List. Type **Admin** in the text box at the top and click Add. Type **Planning**, click Add, type **Sales**, click Add, and click OK. (The actual categories, of course, can be anything you want.)

2. Back in the Categories dialog box, click one of the categories you have just added and click OK. Repeat this last step for each of the tasks in your task list.

3. Select By Category from the Current View drop-down list (if you get a message asking if you want to save the current view settings, answer No), and click the plus button to open each group and see your tasks grouped by category.

Tip: You can have the groups all expanded (opened) by default by selecting Group By from the View menu, then opening *Expand/collapse defaults* and selecting *All expanded*.

4. Click the Due Date heading to sort by date within each category, and you'll get a result like this:

	!	@	Subject	Status	Due Date	% Complete	Categories
			Click here to add a new Task				
⊟ Categories : Admin							
	☑		Prepare for weekly staff meeting	Comple...	Fri 10/4/96	100%	Admin
	☑		Prepare for weekly staff meeting	Comple...	Fri 10/11/96	100%	Admin
	☑		Prepare for weekly staff meeting	Not Sta...	Fri 10/18/96	0%	Admin
	☑		Order lunch for Fall meeting	Not Sta...	Tue 10/22/96	0%	Admin
	☑		Reserve room and equipment for fall...	Not Sta...	Tue 10/22/96	0%	Admin
	☑		Order supplies	Not Sta...	Tue 10/22/96	0%	Admin
⊟ Categories : Planning							
	☑		Plan Fall meeting	Not Sta...	Fri 10/18/96	0%	Planning
	☑		Contact presenters for Fall meeting	In Prog...	Mon 10/21/96	25%	Planning
⊟ Categories : Sales							
	☑		Dimming Product	Not Sta...	None	0%	Sales
	☑		Work up numbers for MasterCraft	Not Sta...	Tue 10/22/96	0%	Sales
	☑		Prepare monthly report	Not Sta...	Wed 10/23/96	0%	Sales

Note: To manually arrange your tasks, you must first clear all sorting and grouping parameters by clicking Clear All in the Sort and Group By dialog boxes from the View menu.

 I would like to track the time spent on a task, as well as other information. Is there a way to do that?

Yes. The Status tab of the Task form allows you to enter billing, mileage, and contact information, as you can see here:

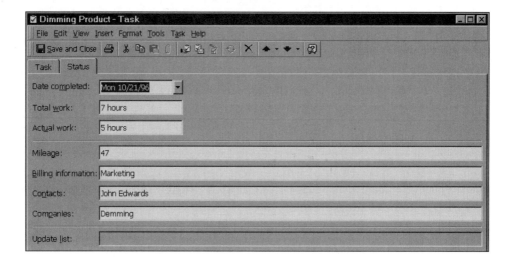

With this information, you can create a custom view to see this information for all your tasks, or you can export it to Excel, where it can be summarized.

 Note: The total and actual work time collected in Tasks is exported in minutes, so you may want to adjust for that. Also, the mileage is exported as a text field and needs to be converted so it can be summarized.

While I'm entering due date for tasks, I sometimes need to double-check a date. Is there some way to view a calendar while entering due dates for tasks?

Yes, the date can be entered using the AutoDate described earlier in the "Using the Calendar" section of this chapter under the discussion of **date and time abbreviations.** For example, you can type **next tue** to get the date for next Tuesday, or you can type **10/23** or **oct 23** for that date. Also, you can click a date field and click its drop-down arrow to open the Date Navigator, which gives you a calendar to look at:

KEEPING A JOURNAL AND MAKING NOTES

Outlook Journal and Notes

The Outlook Journal is the central collection point for status information, not just within Outlook but for all of Microsoft Office 97 (see Figure 7-26). The Journal automatically collects information on a time line about the messages, phone calls, and documents you are handling. In particular, the Journal can be set to automatically collect information about the following:

▷ E-mail messages sent from or received by Outlook to or from individuals selected in your contact list

▷ Meeting requests, responses, and cancellations sent in Outlook to and from selected individuals in your contact list

▷ Task requests and responses to and from selected individuals in your contact list

▷ Documents created or revised with Microsoft Access, Excel, Office Binder, PowerPoint, and Word and other compatible programs

▷ Phone calls, faxes, letters, and other Office 97 documents sent to or, if electronic, received from selected individuals in your contact list

You can also manually create Journal entries for conversations or any of the above interactions with others, electronic or otherwise, or just to make a note. The Contact form has a page that displays all of the Journal entries for a particular contact—which can easily be all of the activities with that contact. Additionally, the Journal allows you to accomplish the following:

▷ Categorize your entries so that they can be grouped on some basis other than those built into Outlook

▷ Track the time spent on Journal activities, such as writing a report, making or taking a phone call, and holding a meeting

▷ Look up a document in the Journal based on its creation or revision date when you don't know its filename or subject

Outlook Notes are a computer version of 3M Post-it Notes. You can use them to quickly and briefly capture an idea, a name, a phone number, driving directions, a question, or any other brief note. You can keep notes on your screen and look at them as either a listing or as icons in Outlook. You can use notes of different colors and attach categories to them for easy sorting and grouping.

The default view of the Outlook Journal window is a timeline view of activities by type, as shown in Figure 7-26. In this view, you have the familiar choice of seeing a day, a week, or a month, similar to your options with the Calendar. The types of activities that can be included in Journal, their icons, and how they can get there are shown in Table 7-2.

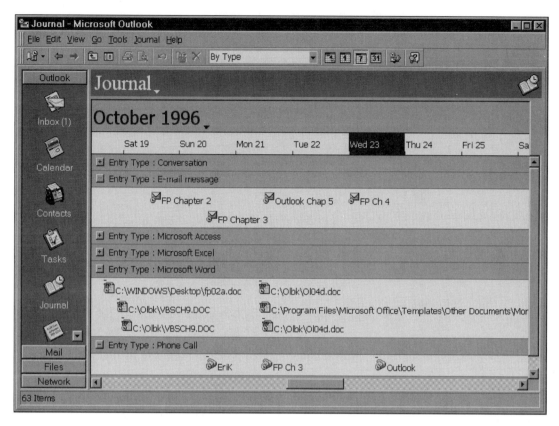

Figure 7-26:   Journal can collect and display activities on a time line

? In the Journal time line, what does the **bar over an activity** represent?

The bar above the icon in the Journal window represents the duration or length of time taken by the activity. In other words, it increases in length the longer the activity.

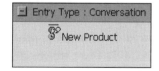

Table 7-2: Types of Journal Activities

Icon	Activity	How Journalized
	Conversation	Manually entered
	Document	Manually entered
	E-mail	By sending or receiving a message from or to Outlook, or manually entered
	Fax	Manually entered
	Letter	Manually entered
	Meeting	By sending or responding to a meeting request or canceling a meeting, or manually entered
	Note	Manually entered
	Office 97 application	By opening and closing a file in any Office 97 application, or manually entered
	Phone call	By placing a call with the AutoDialer, or manually entered
	Remote session	By initiating a remote session from Outlook, or manually entered
	Task	By sending or responding to a task request, or manually entered

? How can I **control what activities are Journalized?**

For the most part, Journal entries are created automatically: by sending an e-mail message, by creating an Office document, or by setting up a meeting, making a phone call, or a creating a task in Outlook. You can control which activities automatically create Journal entries in two ways: by selecting the type of activities or by selecting the contacts they relate to. See how with these steps:

1. From the Journal window, open the Tools menu and choose Options. This opens the Options dialog box with the Journal tab showing, as you can see in Figure 7-27.

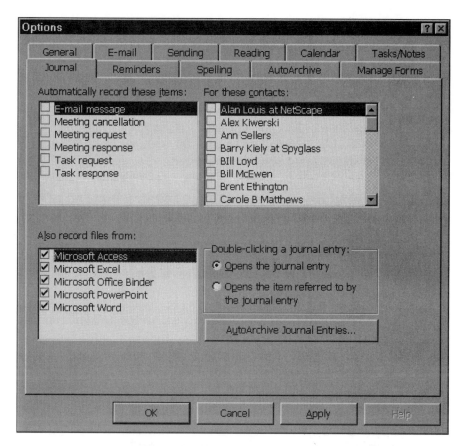

Figure 7-27: The Options dialog box determines what activities are Journalized.

2. In the *Automatically record these items* section, select the Outlook activities that you want Journalized for the contacts that you indicate in the next step.

3. In the *For these contacts* section, select the people in your contact list for whom you want to Journalize selected Outlook activities.

4. In the *Also record files from* section, select the Office 97 and potentially Office 97–compatible documents whose creation and modification you want Journalized.

5. In the *Double-clicking a journal entry* section, you have two choices: When you double-click a Journal icon (or when you select Open from the File or context menus), either the Journal Entry form or the original document that caused the creation of the Journal entry will open.

Select one of these two options. When you are done, click OK to close the Options dialog box.

 Note: If you choose to open the original document when you double-click a Journal entry icon, you will have no way to open the Journal Entry form for that document. On the other hand, if you choose to open the Journal Entry form for the item, you'll see an icon for a shortcut to the item that will immediately take you to it.

? I like the idea of using Outlook Notes instead of sticking the little yellow paper ones all around my screen, but usually when I want to write myself a note, Outlook is not running and so it is easier to just write myself a paper note. Is there a way to create a note quickly without starting Outlook?

Yes, if you have another note on your screen. You can create a note any time, without having either Outlook or its Notes component open. If you have a note on your screen, you can click the icon in the upper-left corner and choose New Note.

? I had heard that I could drag Journal entries from one category to another to change the category, but this doesn't work. Did I just hear wrong?

No, but you can't do it in the By Category view of Journal entries. You must use the Entry List view and then group by categories. Use these steps:

1. From the Journal window, open the Current View drop-down list box and choose Entry List. This view shows all of your Journal entries as a list.

2. Add categories to all the Journal entries that you want to categorize by either directly entering the category or by right-clicking the entry, choosing Categories from the context menu, and then selecting a category from a list.

3. When you have finished entering the categories that you want, you can quickly look at the activities in each category by clicking the Group By toolbar button and then dragging the Categories column header to the Group By box. Your result should look something like Figure 7-28.

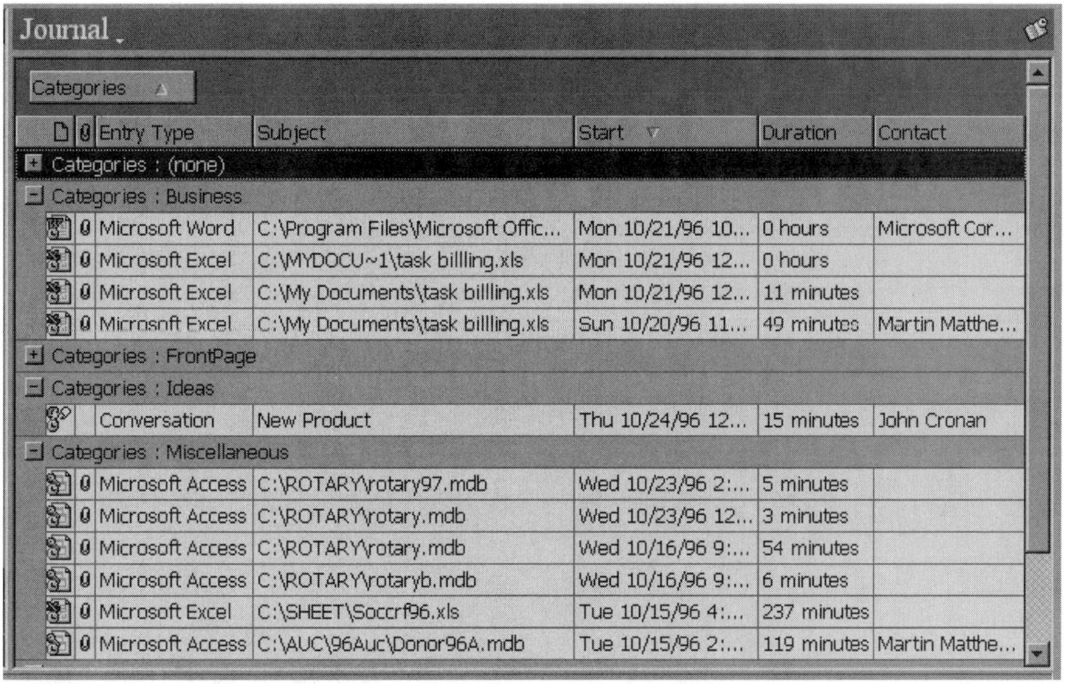

Figure 7-28:   List of Journal entries grouped by categories

With your Outlook window configured like the one in Figure 7-28, you can quickly add categories to entries by dragging them from the None group to the particular category group you want the entries to have, or you can change categories by dragging entries from one category to another.

Tip: You can also group by category by right-clicking the Categories column heading and selecting Group By This Field from the context menu.

?   **I can't seem to sort my Journal entries by contact and yet I want to view all the Journal entries related to a contact. How can I do that?**

You are correct that you cannot sort on Contact or Categories using either the column headers or the Sort dialog box. You can use the Journal views By Contact or By Category to group your Journal entries by either Contact or Category. Also, the Contact form includes a Journal tab, in which all the Journal entries for a particular contact are displayed. This page, which is shown in Figure 7-29, not only displays Journal entries but also allows you to control what is displayed, to sort the display, and to add and delete Journal entries.

 Note: If you select *Create new Journal Entry when starting new call* from the Contacts New Call dialog box, you can time your call and keep notes about it.

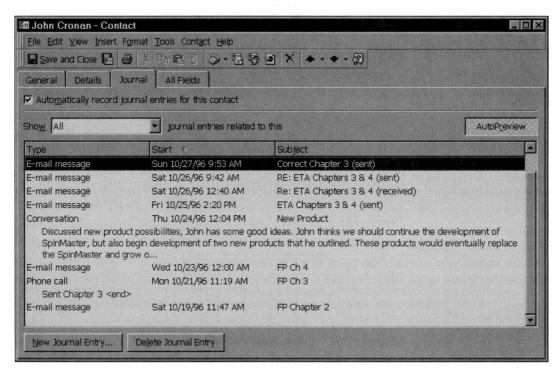

Figure 7-29: A contact's Journal entries

Integrating Office Documents

Answer Topics!

Integrating
@ a Glance

Office Professional 97 provides a number of ways in which you can easily combine files created in the various applications.

☞ The **merge function** in either Word or Access provides a way to combine an Access database with a Word mail merge main document to produce large mailings, including printing envelopes and labels.

☞ A **PowerPoint presentation file** can contain files that have been created in Word and Excel. It can also contain information from Access; however, this information must first be embedded in a Word or Excel document, then inserted in PowerPoint.

☞ The **cut and paste functions** can be used to combine information from an Excel worksheet with text and graphics that were created in a Word document in order to produce various documents such as company reports or newsletters.

☞ **Object Linking and Embedding (OLE)** is used to insert information from a file in one application into a file in a different application. When the information is embedded, the functions of the embedded application can be used to edit it in the destination document. If the embedded data is linked, changes in the original document are automatically updated when displayed in the linked document.

☞ The **Binder** application is used to combine documents from several applications into one document such as a large report or a book. These documents can be rearranged or modified within the binder file, and page numbering and common headers and footers can be added.

SHARING FILES AND FOLDERS

 I was unable to insert an Access report in a PowerPoint presentation. Is there a way to do this?

The best way to display an Access report in PowerPoint is to first send the report to Word. Then import the Word file into PowerPoint. To send the report to Word, do the following:

1. In Access, open the database and select the report that you want to send to Word.

2. Choose Office Links from the Tools menu.

3. Click *Publish It with MS Word*. The report is then displayed in a Word document window.

4. Save the document.

To Insert the report in a PowerPoint presentation,

1. Open the PowerPoint file into which you want to insert the report (or create a new file).

2. Choose Object from the Insert menu.

3. Click *Create from File.*

4. Click Browse. The default folder window is displayed. If the Word document containing the report is in a different folder, locate this folder.

5. Select the filename. Be sure the file you select has a Word file icon in front of it.

6. Click OK to return to the Insert Object dialog box, shown here:

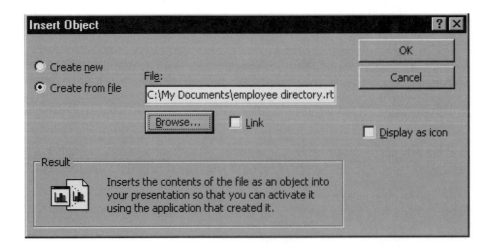

7. If you like, turn on Link. This will allow any edits that are made in PowerPoint to change the original file in Word.

Tip: If you select *Display as icon,* an icon will be inserted. In the presentation, you can double-click the icon and the file will be opened in Word.

8. Click OK to insert the object in PowerPoint, and save the PowerPoint file.

? I know how to produce a mail merge output in Word using an Access database, but I work primarily in Access. Is it possible to merge from Access?

Yes, you can do the following to start a mail merge from Access.

1. Open the table in Access from which you want to start the merge.

2. Choose Office Links from the Tools menu.

3. Select *Merge It with MS Word* to go to the Mail Merge Wizard shown here:

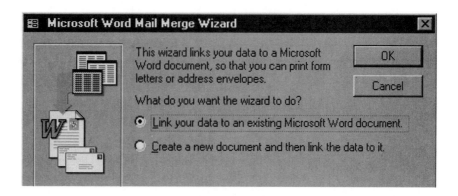

4. Select one of the following and then click OK.

> ⊳ *Link your data to an existing Microsoft Word document.* If you select this option, the field names must match in both documents. The merge can then be

performed from Word in the usual way. See Chapter 3, "Writing with Word," for more specific information about this.

▷ *Create a new document and then link the data to it.* This will open a new Word mail merge document, the top of which is shown here:

Mail Merge toolbar

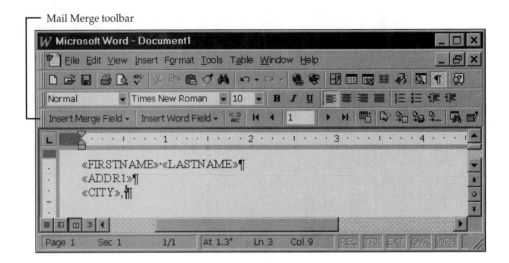

If you selected *Create a new document,* do the following.

5. Click the Insert Merge Field button, and select the fields to be inserted at specific locations. Type text and insert graphics as appropriate.

6. Save the main document and perform the merge. You can choose from the following options:

    ▷ Merge to New Document to display the output in a new document window

    ▷ Merge to Printer to send the output directly to the printer

    ▷ Mail Merge to select only specific records to merge or to sort the records to be merged

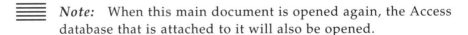 *Note:*   When this main document is opened again, the Access database that is attached to it will also be opened.

? **I want to use an Access database in a merge in Word, but the field names are different in each application. How can I merge when the field names aren't the same in Access and Word?**

To rename the fields in Access with field names that match those in Word, do the following:

1. Open the Access table that you want to use in the merge.

2. Move the insertion point into the first field and choose Rename Column from the Format menu.

3. Type the new field name. Repeat for all the remaining fields.

4. Save the edited database. You can then perform the merge, either from Word or from Access.

If you start the merge from Word,

1. From the Tools menu choose Mail Merge and click Get Data.

2. Select Open Data Source. The Open Data Source window is displayed as shown in Figure 8-1.

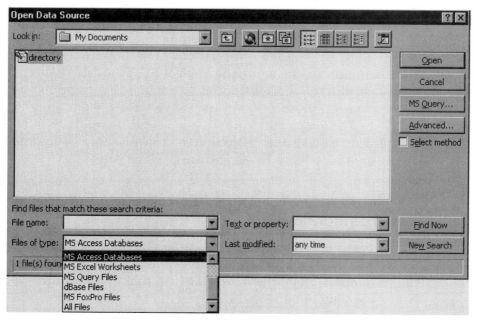

Figure 8-1: The Open Data Source window

3. Select MS Access Databases in the *Files of type* dialog box to display the filenames of the databases.

4. Select the database containing the table you want.

5. Click Open to see the Microsoft Access dialog box.

6. Select the table and click OK.

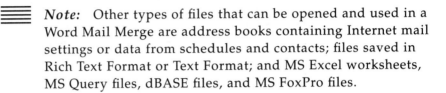 *Note:*   Other types of files that can be opened and used in a Word Mail Merge are address books containing Internet mail settings or data from schedules and contacts; files saved in Rich Text Format or Text Format; and MS Excel worksheets, MS Query files, dBASE files, and MS FoxPro files.

See Chapter 3, "Writing with Word," for more specific information about performing a mail merge in Word.

PASTING, EMBEDDING, AND LINKING BETWEEN APPLICATIONS

What are the **advantages of using embedding rather than linking?**

Use embedding without linking if it is not essential that the data in the original document be available when you work on the embedded information. This allows the document containing the embedded object to be moved to another computer, where edits can be made if that computer has the same application that was used to create the original object. Embedding without linking is useful if you frequently want to take a document home to work on it or to give it to another person to edit or use in some way.

What are the **differences between pasting, linking, and embedding?**

Pasting, linking, and embedding are three ways in which you can transfer information from one application to another. Also, they are related in that you begin by copying or cutting the information to be transferred in the originating application. They differ only in how the information is handled in the receiving application.

Pasting inserts a copy of information into another location in the same document, into another document in the same application, or into another document in another application. In any of these cases, a copy of the information becomes an integral part of its new document and is edited in the receiving application. Pasting is accomplished by selecting the information, cutting or copying it (depending on whether you want to move or copy it) to the Clipboard, and pasting it into its destination. For example, if you paste a range of cells from Excel into Word, the data is inserted as a Word table that is integral to the receiving document and is edited using the Word table functions.

Linking places a link to information created in one location from another location in the same document, from another document in the same application, or from another document in another application. In any of these cases, the information stays a part of its original document and is edited in the original application. Any change made to either the original document or the link is reflected in both areas. There are two ways to do this:

➤ After copying the information to the Clipboard, in the receiving document's Edit menu, select Paste Special and check the *Paste link* option, as shown in Figure 8-2.

➤ *Without* originally copying the information, select Object in the receiving document's Insert menu, select the *Create from File* tab, enter or browse the filename, and choose *Link to file* (see Figure 8-3).

Embedding places a copy of information created in one location into another location in the same document, in another document in the same application, or in another document in another application. In any of these cases, a copy of the information physically resides in the new document, but it is edited in the originating application. Also, the information is not linked to the original document, meaning that any changes made in the original document

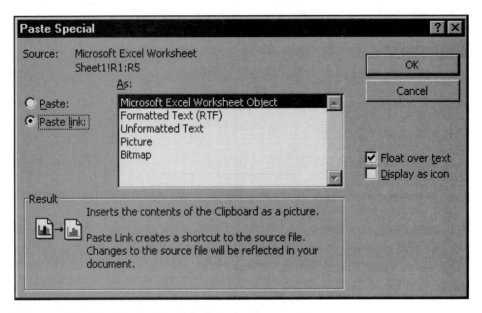

Figure 8-2:   The Paste Special dialog box

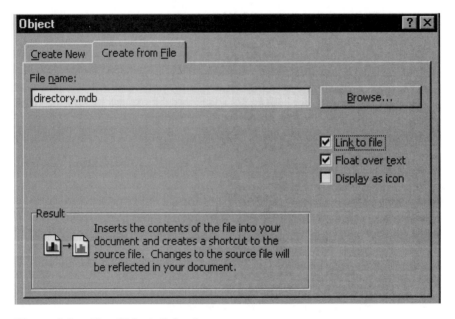

Figure 8-3:   The Object dialog box

will not be reflected in the embedded object. As with linking, there are two ways to do this:

 After copying the information to the Clipboard, in the receiving document's Edit menu, select Paste Special without checking the *Paste link* option.

 Without originally copying the information, select Object from the receiving document's Insert menu, select the *Create from File* tab, enter or browse the filename, and *don't* check *Link to file*.

? It seems fairly easy to link objects in Excel or Word, but I am unable to use these steps to embed tables or text in Access. How do I do this?

You first have to format a field in an Access table as an OLE Object field. Then you can choose Object from the Insert menu in Access to link to an Excel or Word document. An example of this is when a company logo created in Word is used in an Access form or report. If changes are made to the original logo in Word, they are reflected in the Access form or report.

Note: Also refer to Chapter 6, "Organizing with Access," for information about exporting and importing Access files.

Linking an Excel or Word Object in Access

Prior to bringing a linked object into Access, you must format a field in Access as an OLE Object field. You can then insert a linked object into that field. Use the following steps to do that:

1. Open the Access table to which you want to link an Excel or Word object in Design View. To do this, open the table, click the Design button, and select Design View (or create a new table in Design view).

2. Move to the field that you want to format as an OLE Object field. Type a field name and press TAB to go to the Data Type column. Click the down arrow to display the list of choices and select OLE Object as shown next:

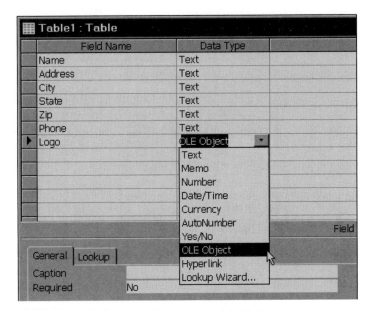

3. Close Design View, name and save the table, if necessary, and open the table in Datasheet View.

4. Move to the field that has been formatted as an OLE Object field and choose Object from the Insert menu to display the Insert Object dialog box.

5. Select *Create from File* and type or browse for the filename, and select Link:

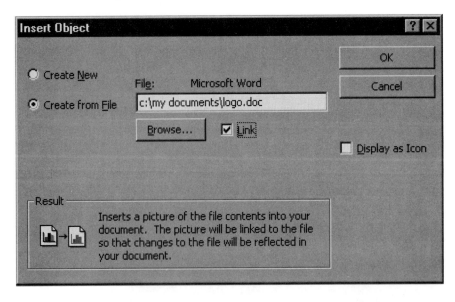

You may also select *Display as Icon,* if you wish. Click OK.

 Note: If you choose *Display as Icon,* in Form View this will display an icon rather than the actual text or table. If you don't select it, the actual text or table will be displayed when you are in Form View. When you are in Datasheet View, only the name of the type of file being embedded will be displayed.

? I selected and copied a range of cells in Excel and pasted it into a Word document; however, the information was inserted as a Word table, not as an Excel worksheet. Isn't it possible to actually paste an Excel worksheet into Word that is not formatted as a Word table?

Yes, if you choose Paste Special from the Edit menu (rather than just Paste) and select Microsoft Excel Worksheet Object, the data will be inserted in the Word document as an Excel object. You can then double-click it to display the Excel toolbars and work on the data in Word using the Excel functions.

Using Paste Special

To copy data from an Excel worksheet to a Word document using Paste Special, do the following:

1. Open the worksheet in Excel, select the range of cells to be copied, and click Copy, or choose Copy from the Edit menu, to copy the range to the Clipboard.

2. Open the Word document.

3. Move the insertion point to the place where you want to insert the data.

4. Choose Paste Special from the Edit menu. The Paste Special dialog box is displayed as shown next:

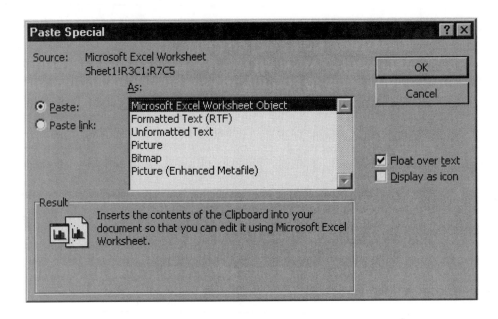

5. Choose Paste, select Microsoft Excel Worksheet Object, and click OK. The worksheet is inserted in the Word document. When you click the object, handles will be displayed, and you can work with it as you might work with other objects such as pictures, WordArt, or AutoShapes.

 Note: If you select RTF format, the selection that is inserted is in a Word format only, and you will not be able to double-click it to edit it in Excel.

6. To use Excel to edit the embedded object, double-click it. The Excel toolbars are displayed, as you can see here, giving you all the capabilities you would have in Excel itself.

Excel menus   Excel toolbars

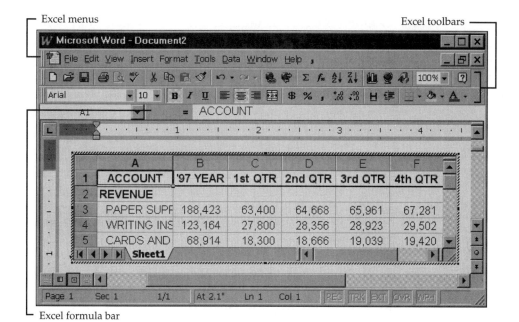

Excel formula bar

7. When you have finished editing the Excel object, click anywhere outside the table to close the Excel menus and toolbars and return to Word.

When you use Paste Special, the embedded object is not necessarily linked to the original Excel worksheet (although it can be). If the Paste Link option is not selected, changes made to the worksheet in Word will not be reflected in the worksheet in Excel.

I used the Paste Special function to move information between Word and Excel; however, when I tried this same procedure to move a table from Word to Access, a message was displayed saying my text was too long to insert in Access. How can I paste text or data from Word or Excel into Access?

Use Paste Append in Access rather than Paste Special. The following steps show how to do this.

1. In either Word or Excel, select the text or table, and click the Copy button or choose Copy from the Edit menu to copy the selection to the Clipboard.

2. Open the Access table and move the insertion point to where you want to insert the selected block.

3. Choose Paste Append, rather than Paste Special, from the Edit menu in Access. When you do this, a message will be displayed telling you that you are about to paste a number of records and asking if you are sure you want to do it. Click Yes. The selected text will be inserted.

This text is not linked to the original text in either Word or Excel; therefore, any edits will not be automatically applied to the text copied to an Access table. For information about linking text imported into Access from either Word or Excel, see the question in this section on **embedding tables or text in Access.**

Tip: Numbers moved or copied from an Excel table may not be formatted as they were in Excel. It is therefore a better idea to create a link to a worksheet from Excel.

❔ Can I **resize or crop an object?**

Yes—you can do both. Resizing changes the overall size of the object without changing the amount of data, text, or image contained in it. Cropping actually cuts some of the data, text, or image from what is displayed.

▷ To resize an object, select the object to display the handles, and then point to any of the handles and drag it to a different size.

▷ To crop the object, select the object and display the Picture toolbar by choosing Toolbars from the View menu and selecting Picture. Then click the Crop button, as shown next, and position the Crop mark on any of the handles to drag it to a different position.

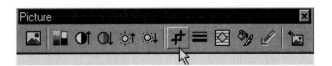

Tip: The Picture toolbar can also be displayed by clicking with the right mouse button on any toolbar to display the Toolbar menu, and then choosing Picture.

There are times when I do not want Excel data that is embedded in a Word document to be changed, even though I have changed the data in Excel. Can I update linked data in Word if I need to do this later?

Yes, the default setting for linked data is to automatically update the information; however, you can change this so that you can control when the data is updated. To turn off the automatic update option, do the following:

1. Select the linked object and choose Links from the Edit menu to display the Links dialog box shown in Figure 8-4.

2. Select Manual for the type of Update, and click OK. Now any changes made in the original document will not be displayed in the embedded object unless you manually update it.

To manually update the object, select it in the destination document, choose Links from the Edit menu, and click the Update Now button. Any changes that have been made in the original document will now be reflected in the linked object.

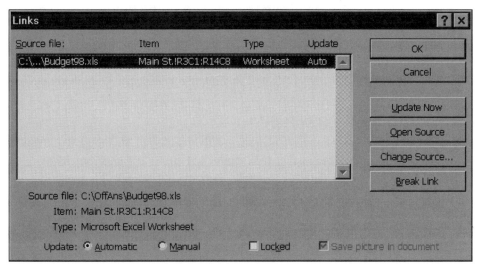

Figure 8-4:   The Links dialog box

Tip: The Break Link button will remove the link from the object. If you want to re-establish the link, delete the object and reinsert it by choosing Object from the Insert menu and choosing *Link to File.*

USING BINDERS

I know that either a binder or the Briefcase can store files from various Office applications. Why should I create a binder, when I can store all the files I want to work with in the Briefcase?

A binder is used to combine files that you want to group together, such as a company report or a project. The following features that make it easy to combine files are available in the Binder.

➤ The files—each in a separate section—can be arranged in the order in which you want to present them, and the page numbering will be consecutive throughout the binder when it is printed. The page numbering that is used in the binder does not change the original page numbering in each individual document when it is opened in its own application.

➤ You can create headers and footers that apply to the entire binder and will be printed on each page in every section.

➤ You can rearrange the order of the files by simply dragging to a different position the icon that represents each section or file. See Figure 8-5.

➤ These documents can be opened and edited; however, they are usually inserted in a binder after they are completed in their own application.

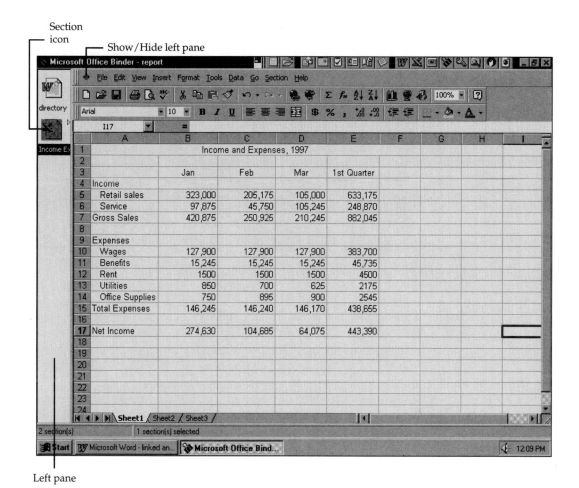

Figure 8-5: The Binder window

? **I don't see an option in any of the Office applications that allows me to create a binder. How do I do this?**

The binder is created from Windows. To do this,

1. Click the Start button in the Windows Taskbar.
2. Select Programs and click Microsoft Binder. The blank Binder window is opened, as you can see next:

Tip: If the Binder button is displayed in the Office Shortcut Bar, you can click it to open the binder. If it is not displayed, refer to the sidebar "Adding a Binder Button to the Office Shortcut Bar" for steps for doing this.

3. Choose Save Binder As from the File menu, type a name, and click Save. The binder is stored in the default My Documents folder unless you choose a different drive or folder, and in the *Save as type* box, it is saved as a Binder File.

You can now create files within the binder by choosing Add in the Section menu, or you can add existing files to the binder by choosing *Add from File* in the Section menu. See the next section, "Adding and Modifying Documents Within a Binder," for more specific information about this.

Note: To open a saved binder, open Microsoft Binder, choose Open Binder from the File menu, and select the binder you want.

❓ I saw only one supplied template in the Binder tab. Are there more, or can I **create a custom binder template**?

There is one supplied template that can be used for a binder; however, you can create your own template fairly easily by adding new documents or adding documents from

Adding a Binder Button to the Office Shortcut Bar

Use the following steps to add a Binder button to the Office Shortcut bar:

1. Right-click on any of the spaces between buttons on the Shortcut Bar as shown next, and a context menu will be displayed.

2. Click Customize and select the Buttons tab in the Customize dialog box, as shown here:

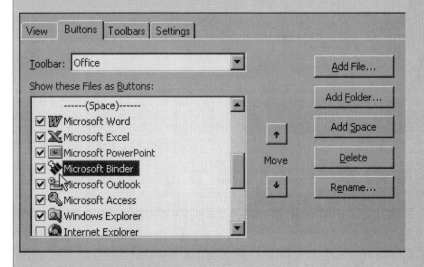

3. Scroll down through the list in the *Show these Files as Buttons* dialog box, and click Microsoft Binder. As soon as you do this, the Binder button shown on the left is added to the Shortcut Bar.

a file to a new binder. Then save the binder as a template. The following steps outline the details of doing this:

1. Open the Binder application and choose New Binder from the File menu.

2. In the General tab, select Blank Binder and click OK.

3. Add documents or templates from various applications. Also create new documents, if you like. See the next section, "Adding and Modifying Documents Within a Binder," for specific steps for doing this.

4. To save as a template, choose Save Binder As from the File menu, type a filename, click the down arrow in the *Save as type* list box and select Binder Templates, click Save, and close the binder.

   To use the new template choose New Binder from the File menu. The icon representing the new template and its filename are displayed in the General tab.

? **What happens to the headers and footers that are created with the original documents if I use a common header or footer in a binder, and how do I do that?**

They are not changed, just as the original page numbering remains unchanged in the original documents. To create a common header and footer in a binder, use the following steps:

1. Open the binder file in which you want to add a header or footer.

2. Select Binder Page Setup from the File menu, and click the Header/Footer tab if it isn't already open, as shown in Figure 8-6.

You can either choose one of the default headers or footers from the drop-down list, or create a custom header or footer by clicking one of the Custom buttons to open the Custom Header or Footer dialog box shown here, and then typing or inserting what you want in each of the three sections.

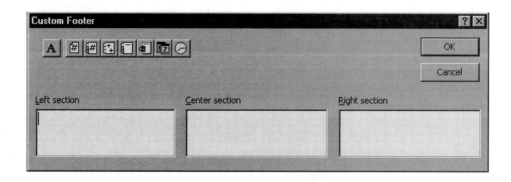

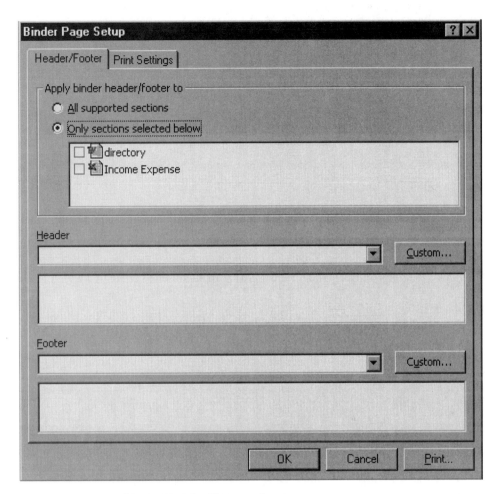

Figure 8-6:   The Binder Header/Footer tab

Once you have entered text, you can format it by clicking the Font button and choosing the font name, style, and size that you want. You can also insert a number of other items in the section boxes by clicking the appropriate buttons, as listed in the following table.

Button	Function
A	Opens the Font dialog box
#	Inserts the page number
#	Inserts the section number

Button	Function
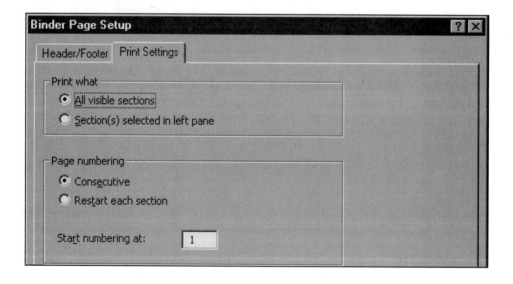	Inserts the number of sections
	Inserts the section name
	Inserts the binder name
	Inserts the current date
	Inserts the current time

? I want to **start page numbering at a number other than 1.** How do I do that?

To start page numbering at something other than 1, do the following:

1. Choose Binder Page Setup from the File menu of a binder, and select the Print Settings tab.

2. In the *Page numbering* box, choose either Consecutive or *Restart each section,* and then enter the starting page number that you want to use.

3. Click OK when you're done.

When I first opened a new Binder window, I wanted to use a supplied template to create it, but I didn't see any listed. Where can I find them?

To start the Binder application with a template do the following:

1. Click the New Office Document button in the Office shortcut bar.

2. Select the Binders tab to see the templates. An example of this tab is shown here (you may have more or fewer tabs in your New Office Document dialog box depending on the options you chose during installation):

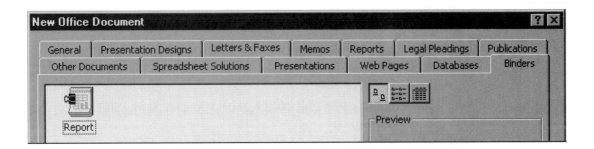

3. Select the template you want and click OK.

Note: You can also open the Microsoft Binder window, choose New from the File menu, click the Binders tab, and select the template you want.

ADDING AND MODIFYING DOCUMENTS WITHIN A BINDER

How can I add Access files to a Binder?

Access files cannot be copied directly to the Binder; however, you can embed an Access file in a Word document,

in an Excel worksheet, or in a PowerPoint presentation, and
then add that file to a binder. To do this,

1. Open the database table in Access that you want to be the
   binder.

2. Select Office Links from the Tools menu and choose either
   of the following:

    > *Publish It with MS Word* to copy the file to a Word
      document

    > *Analyze It with MS Excel* to copy the file to an Excel
      worksheet

≡ *Note:*   The Office Links option *Merge It with MS Word* is not
an appropriate choice here because that option attaches the
Access table to a merge main document in Word.

3. Save the table in the application in which it is linked.

4. Open the binder you want, and choose *Add from File* in
   the Section menu.

5. Select the file that contains the Access table and
   click Add.

≡ *Note:*   Refer to the section "Sharing Files and Folders" for
information about inserting an Access report in PowerPoint.

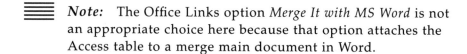 **In the Binder Section menu, how should I decide whether
to choose Add or *Add from File*?**

Choose Add to create a new document from within the
Binder. Choose *Add from File* to insert a document that
already exists in Excel, PowerPoint, or Word.

Adding a New Document

To add a new document to a binder,

1. Choose Add from the Section menu to display the
   various templates, as shown next:

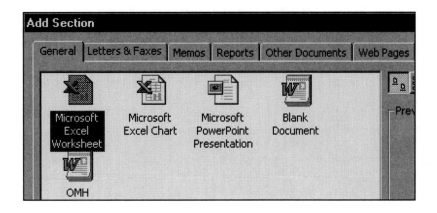

The General tab displays Word, Excel, and PowerPoint Presentation templates and possibly others. Click the other tabs to see additional templates, if you like.

2. Select the type of template you want to use for the document in the current section.

3. Click OK. The Binder window changes to the application used to create the document in this section.

4. Create the document.

5. Repeat steps 1 through 4 for additional documents that you want to create in the binder. You can also add documents that have already been created (see the next section for details).

6. When you're done, choose Save Binder As from the File menu, type a name, and click Save; or choose Save Binder if you have already named the file.

Tip: Each section can also be saved as a separate document. To do this, select it, choose Save As File from the Section menu, type a filename, choose the location, and click OK.

Adding a Document from a File

To add an existing document from a file,

1. In the Binder window, choose *Add from File* in the Section menu to open the *Add from File* dialog box shown in Figure 8-7.

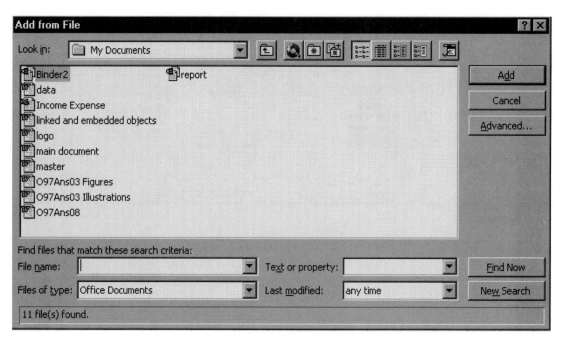

Figure 8-7:   The *Add from File* dialog box

2. Select the file you want and click Add. The document is shown in the window, and the appropriate toolbars, depending upon the application used to create the file, are displayed.

3. Repeat steps 1 and 2 for inserting additional documents, or add (create) new documents in the binder.

4. Choose Save Binder As from the File menu, type a name, and click Save; or choose Save Binder if you have already named the file.

? If I edit documents in a binder will this change the original file in the application in which it was created?

No—they are not linked when you choose *Add from file* in the Section menu, although you can link them if you wish. To link a document in the binder with a document in the original application, do the following:

1. Choose Add in the Section menu.

2. Select a template from the application that was used to create the document to be linked, and click OK.

3. Insert the document by choosing Object from the Insert menu and selecting the file.

4. Click *Link to file,* and then click OK. The menu bar, standard toolbar, and formatting toolbar from the application used to create that document will be displayed. Now changes in the original document will be reflected in the linked document in the Binder.

 Note: Changes to Binder page numbering and headers and footers do not apply here. Those functions are part of the binder file, not the separate document files combined in the Binder; therefore those changes are not reflected in page numbering and headers and footers in the individual files when they are opened in their own applications.

? **I inserted an Excel worksheet in a binder that had an extra blank page. I tried to use the Page Break Preview option in the View menu in the Binder, but it was dimmed. How can I edit Excel worksheets in a binder?**

You will have to delete the file from the binder, then edit the worksheet in Excel and add it to the binder again. To delete and re-add the file, do the following:

1. Select the icon, and click the right mouse button to display the list of options shown here:

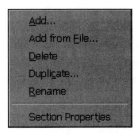

2. Choose Delete from the context menu and click OK when prompted.

3. Open the worksheet in Excel, choose Page Break Preview from the View menu, and drag the right edge of the extra page to the left to remove it.

4. Save the file, return to the binder, and choose *Add from File* in the Section menu to reinsert the file.

WORKING WITH THE BINDER FILE

? I inserted a Word document in a binder, but when I opened the binder the next time, I didn't see the document. How can I display an unseen document in the Binder?

The document has been hidden. To display the document again do the following:

1. Choose Unhide Section from the Section menu to display the Unhide Sections box, which lists the sections in the binder:

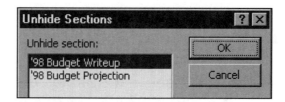

2. Select the name of the section you want to see and click OK.

Tip: To hide a section, select the section and choose Hide from the Section menu.

? I tried to drag an icon in the left pane to a different position in the binder, but I was unable to do this. How do you move a section from one position to another in a binder?

There are two ways to do this. Either drag an icon to a different position in the left pane, or choose Rearrange from the Section menu. To drag the icon to a different position, use these steps:

1. Click the icon for the document that you want to move to make it active. This is essential. The document cannot be moved unless it is active.

2. Point to the icon and drag it to the position you want.

Tip: If all icons are selected, you will not be able to drag just one of them. To remove the selection, choose Unselect All from the Section menu. Then you can select the file you want to move and drag it to a different position.

To move a section by using the Rearrange command,

1. Select any section and choose Rearrange from the Section menu. The Rearrange Sections dialog box is displayed, as shown here:

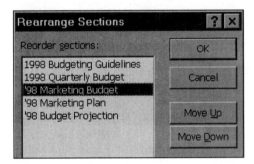

2. Select the section you want to move, and click either the Move Up button or the Move Down button to move it to the place where you want it in the binder. Click OK when done.

? I decided I wanted to move a file to a different binder so I chose Delete from the Section menu. I then opened the other binder and chose *Add from File* from the Section menu to insert it. Is there an easier way to move files from one binder to another?

Yes; you can drag the file icon from one binder to another. Use the following steps to do this:

1. Open both binder windows, displaying the left pane in each window.

2. Reduce the size of one of the windows, and rearrange them so that you can see both.

3. Drag the file icon from one binder left pane to the left pane in the other, as shown in Figure 8-8. Make sure you save the changes.

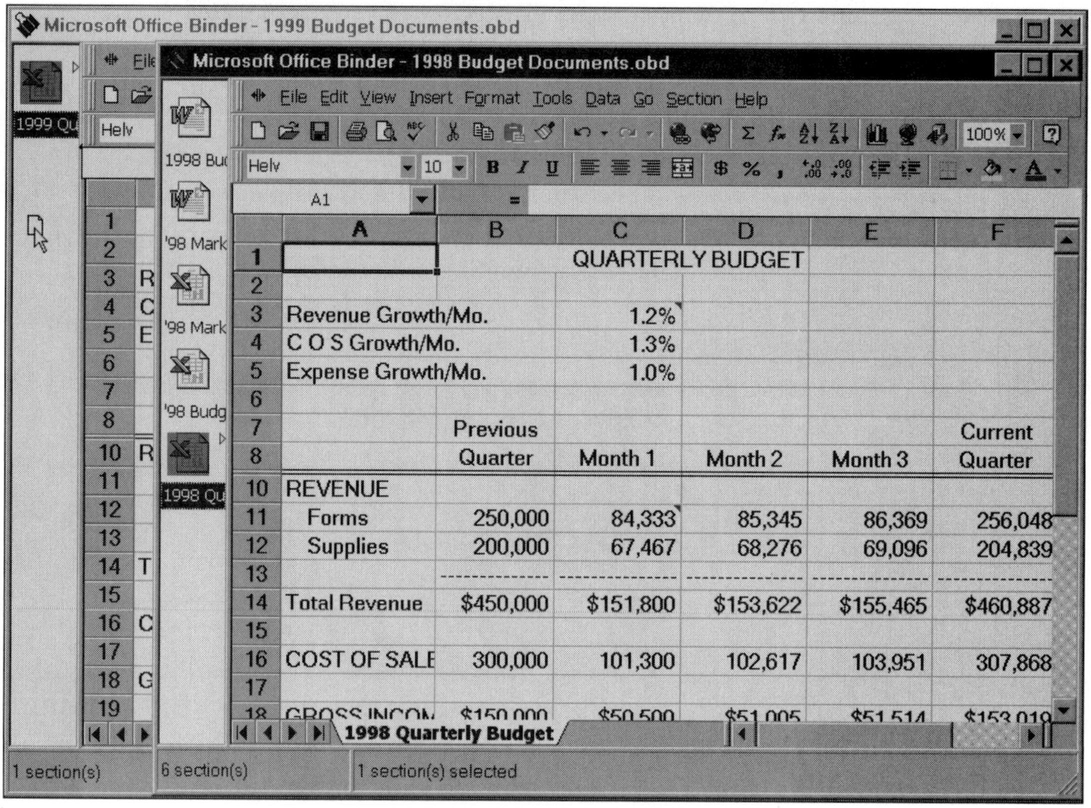

Figure 8-8:   Dragging a section between Binder windows

? When I opened a binder we had been using in our office, I noticed that the pane showing the icons disappeared from the left of the Binder window. What happened?

The Show/Hide Left Pane button has been turned off. To display the left pane, which contains the icons, click the Show/Hide Left Pane button again. This button, shown on the left, is located in the menu bar to the left of File. If the Show/Hide Left Pane button is not showing in the menu bar, choose Binder Options from the File menu, click the *Show left pane and left pane button* check box shown next, and click OK.

When I was in Binder Print Preview, I wanted to print the entire binder, but the Print button was dimmed so that I couldn't print from there. I exited from Binder Print Preview and clicked the Print button, but only the current section was printed. How do I print an entire binder?

Exit from Binder Print Preview and choose Print Binder from the File menu to open the Print Binder dialog box as shown in Figure 8-9. The option *All visible sections* is the default for printing, and it prints all sections *except those that are hidden*. If you want to print only several selected sections, choose the option *Section(s) selected in left pane.* This will print only the sections that you have selected.

To select more than one section, do either of the following:

▷ To select *nonadjacent* section icons in the left pane, hold down the CTRL key and click each of the sections.

▷ To select *adjacent* section icons, click the first icon that you want to select, hold down the SHIFT key, and click the last icon that you want to select.

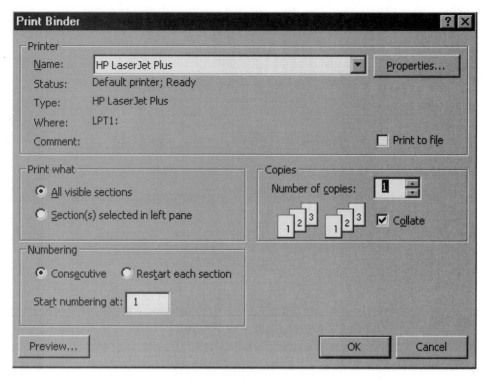

Figure 8-9:   The Print Binder dialog box

 I clicked the Print Preview button when I was in a binder, but the only document I could view was the one in the current section. Is there a way to view all the pages in a binder in Print Preview?

Yes, do the following:

1. Choose Binder Print Preview from the File menu. A Print Preview dialog box is displayed, as shown here:

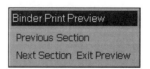

2. Click Next Section or click Previous Section to display other documents in the binder.

3. Click Exit Preview to leave the Preview window.

SHARING BINDERS

 I would like for others to see the contents of a binder, but I want to prevent others from changing anything in the binder file. I didn't see any options when I saved my binder that would allow me to do this. Is there a way to do this?

Yes, you can save the binder with the Read-only attribute for the entire file turned on. To do this use the following steps:

1. Open Windows 95 Explorer and right-click the filename of the binder.

2. Choose Properties, select the General Tab (shown in Figure 8-10), select Read-only, and click OK.

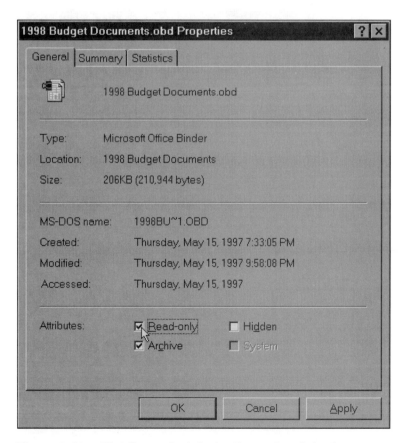

Figure 8-10:   The General tab in the Properties dialog box

Note: If a binder is saved with the Read-only attribute turned on, it can be opened and saved with another name without the Read-only attribute applied to it. Edits can then be made to this new binder.

Is there a way to prevent others from changing the contents of a section in a binder?

You can turn on Protect Document and enter a password that is required in order for the document in that section to be opened and edited. The procedure that is used to do this depends upon the type of file to which you want to apply the password. See the following sidebars, "Protecting an Excel Document" and "Protecting a Word Document," for specific information about each.

• • • • • • • • • •

Protecting an Excel Document

Use the following steps to protect an Excel document in a binder:

1. In the binder, select the Excel document, point on Protection in the Tools menu, and select Protect Sheet. A Protection dialog box is displayed, as shown here.

2. Select the options you want—Contents, Objects, or Scenarios—type a password, and click OK. Another password dialog box is displayed.

3. Type the password again and click OK.

To remove the password protection in the Excel file,

1. Select the Excel document and choose Protection from the Tools menu.

2. Click UnProtect Sheet, type the password, and click OK.

● ● ● ● ● ● ● ● ● ●

Protecting a Word Document

You can protect a Word document in a binder with these steps:

1. In the binder, select the Word document and choose Protect Document in the Tools menu. The Protect Document dialog box shown next is displayed.

2. Select the options you want—Tracked changes, Comments, or Forms—type a password, and click OK. Another password dialog box is displayed.

3. Type the password again and click OK. You can then make edits in the Word document; however, they will be marked either as deleted text or added text, and you cannot change this. The marks can be neither accepted nor rejected, as they are in a protected Word document in which *Track changes* is turned on.

To remove the password protection in Word, do the following:

1. Select the Word document and choose Unprotect Document from the Tools menu.

2. Type the password and click OK. Edits can now be made without being marked as tracked changes.

Note that you can also use the steps just given for protecting Excel and Word documents when they are created in their own applications before adding them to the binder.

chapter
9 Answers!
Using Office with the Internet and Intranets

Answer Topics!

Networking
@ a Glance

Office 97 provides several new and useful features, but none as apparent as the tools to enhance integration of desktop computing with the online world of the Internet and local intranets. From within the Office 97 programs you can

▷ Access the World Wide Web (WWW)

▷ View HyperText Markup Language (HTML) documents

▷ Jump to other Office documents and objects using hyperlinks

▷ Use Word as your e-mail editor

The Office 97 programs incorporate many similar methods to simplify creating online documents across the suite, such as inserting hyperlinks, as shown in Figure 9-1. However, due to the different objective of each program in the suite, there are unique capabilities provided for in each program that expand upon the standard methods. For example, after inserting a hyperlink into a PowerPoint slide you can determine what mouse action, a click or a simple point, activates the hyperlink jump in a slide show. Following are some other examples of inherent online capabilities found in the individual Office 97 programs:

▷ Word provides an easy means to create individual Web pages. Using many standard word processing features you can quickly create quality online documents without ever knowing how to spell HTML. Additionally, using Word as your e-mail editor provides the full range of its features to your communication channels.

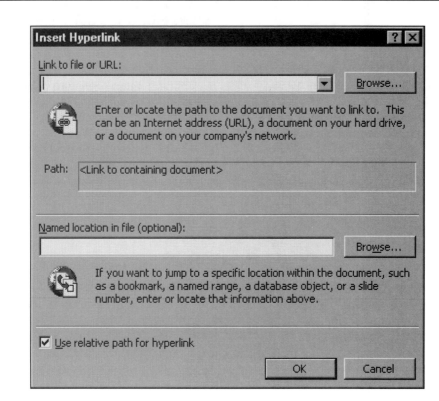

Figure 9-1:   The Insert Hyperlink dialog box

▷ PowerPoint easily transfers its powerful presentation features to HTML, providing ready-to-run online presentations that only require you to edit some sample text.

▷ Excel seamlessly converts ranges of data from worksheets to graphic tables in HTML documents. As with Access, you can create forms that receive user information and store that data in a convenient format for tabulation.

▷ Access offers dedicated hyperlink fields where you can display jumps to Internet addresses such as vendor home pages, where with one mouse click your employees can gather the information they need.

▷ Outlook stores the online particulars of contacts so you can effortlessly send e-mail or view any Web pages or other HTML documents associated with that person or organization.

CREATING INTERNET AND INTRANET DOCUMENTS

 I've created several HTML documents in Word and saved them in a cryptic filename convention that I've been using for years. I posted these files on my Web site and heard from others that my filename was appearing as the title for these pages when viewed in their browsers. Is there a way I can change the title, but not the filename, of an HTML document?

Yes. Choose Properties from the File menu to open the Document Properties dialog box shown in Figure 9-2. Enter a more descriptive name for your document in the Title box and click OK. The new name you chose for a title will now appear in the title bars of Word and browsers when the document is opened.

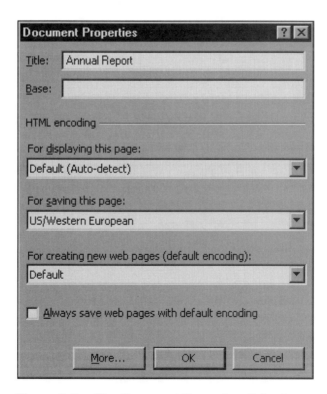

Figure 9-2:   The Document Properties dialog box

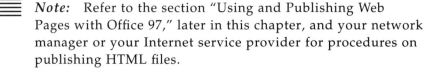   *Tip:*   The Document Properties dialog box that initially appears for an HTML document doesn't contain the usual wealth of information you're accustomed to seeing. To display the standard Properties dialog box for a file, click the More button.

? I didn't see a Web Pages tab when I created a new Excel workbook. Can I create a Web page in Excel with a template?

There is not a specific template that you can choose when you create a new workbook; however, you can convert an existing workbook, or selected parts of that workbook, to an HTML file. Do the following:

1. Open an Excel worksheet that you want to publish.

2. Choose *Save as HTML* from the File menu to display the Internet Assistant Wizard shown in Figure 9-3.

3. Select the range of cells that you want to display, or select charts. If a range is not automatically displayed, enter a new range. You can also remove any item that you do not want to be included in the HTML file, or you can change the order in which they will be presented. Click Next when you have selected the items you want.

4. You can now choose to create a new file, or you can combine this information with an existing HTML file. Click Next to go on.

5. The next wizard window is where you can enter information such as titles, header text, and other information that will appear with the file when published.

6. The final window is where you enter a filename and location for the file. Click Finish when you're done.

Note: Refer to the section "Using and Publishing Web Pages with Office 97," later in this chapter, and your network manager or your Internet service provider for procedures on publishing HTML files.

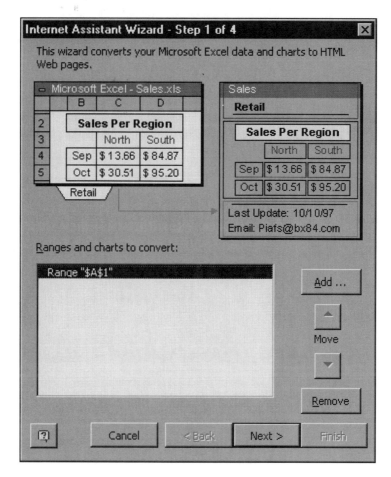

Figure 9-3:   The Excel Internet Assistant Wizard

? I want to use the Drawing tools in Word to create a graphic, but the Drawing toolbar doesn't offer the standard selection of tools. How can I create graphics for Word HTML documents?

You can still use the drawing tools you are familiar with, but you have to do it in a roundabout way. Use these steps to create graphics in HTML documents:

1. Open the HTML document in Word, choose Object from the Insert menu, and select Microsoft Word Picture from the *Object type* list box. Click OK. A new picture window appears with a drawing area in the center, the Edit

Edit Picture toolbar

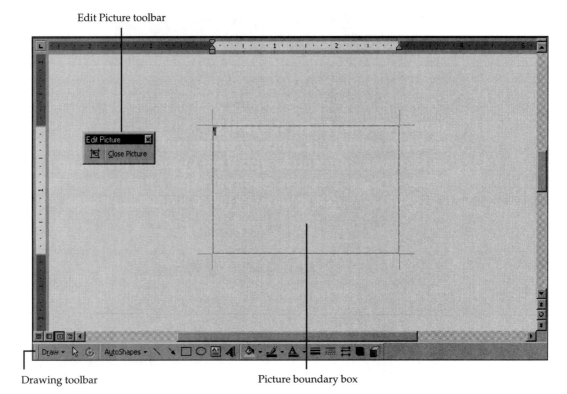

Drawing toolbar   Picture boundary box

Figure 9-4:   Use Microsoft Word Picture to create graphics for HTML documents

Picture toolbar displays, and the standard Drawing toolbar, as shown in Figure 9-4.

2. Use the Drawing toolbar to create your graphic. Don't be concerned about trying to fit the graphic in the boundary box; when you are finished creating the graphic, click the Reset Picture Boundary button on the Edit Picture toolbar and the boundary box will resize to enclose any objects you've made.

3. Click Close Picture in the Edit Picture toolbar and the graphic is inserted in the HTML document. You can reposition the graphic by using the alignment buttons on the Formatting toolbar or by dragging the graphic to a new paragraph location.

When you close the HTML document the graphic is converted to a .gif image, a graphic format that HTML supports. You won't be able to edit the graphic with the drawing tools once the graphic has been converted.

●●●●●● *Tip:*   You can choose how text flows around a picture by right-clicking the graphic and choosing Format Picture from the pop-up menu.

❓ When I open or create an HTML document in Word, I notice several changes in the toolbars and menus. One is that I cannot seem to change the font size of text. How can I adjust the **font size in Word HTML documents?**

You can still change the font size, but you are limited to seven point sizes that HTML recognizes. When an HTML document opens in Word, the Formatting toolbar replaces the Font Size list box with two buttons that increase or decrease the font size of selected text, as shown here:

Each time you click one of these buttons you increase or decrease the font size by one increment. Alternatively, by choosing Font from the Format menu you can specify one of the seven font sizes from the Size box, shown here:

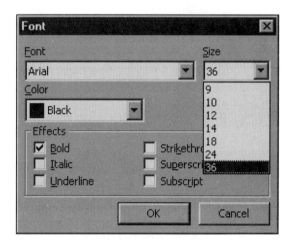

See the sidebar "What Has HTML Done to Word?" for other feature changes made to Word that support the creation of HTML documents.

▪▪▪▪▪▪ *Tip:* Always preview your HTML documents in a browser to see how they will appear to other users before you post them for public viewing. Displaying a file in more than one browser, such as Internet Explorer *and* Netscape Navigator, will let you know if there are any features you've added that aren't supported by the more popular browsers.

● ● ● ● ● ● ● ● ● ●

What Has HTML Done to Word?

The current version of the HyperText Markup Language that is used to code documents for the Web and intranets does not support as many features as we've come to expect from a full-service word processor such as Word, nor is it as flexible. However, once recognized, these limitations are more a way of looking at how to do things differently than you're used to than a true hindrance. Also, HTML provides some features that aren't supported in standard Word. The following table describes the more prominent of these changes.

	Question	Answer
A▲ A▼	How do I change font size?	Use the Increase and Decrease Font Size buttons on the Formatting toolbar or choose Font from the Format menu.
	How do I display the ruler?	Point to the gray band at the top of an HTML document.
	How do I control page numbering?	You don't; an HTML document is one page, regardless of its length. A good Web-page designer will break a long document into several documents and hyperlink them together.
	How can I create newspaper-type columns?	Use a table to create a similar effect.

	Question	Answer
	How do I create the horizontal bar that I see in many Web pages?	Click the Horizontal Line button on the Formatting or Drawing toolbar to insert a basic line. Choose Horizontal Line from the Insert menu to select a more fancy bar.
	How do I view the document's HTML code in its native form?	Choose HTML Source from the View menu. Click Exit HTML Source on the toolbar to return to standard viewing.
	How do I animate text?	The standard animation feature isn't supported; instead, choose Scrolling Text from the Insert menu to create a moving marquee effect.
	How do I set tabs?	You can't; however, you can use tables to line up columns of items.
	There isn't a Paragraph dialog box. How do I control spacing between paragraphs?	Use a table.

? Are there special **templates or wizards for creating PowerPoint HTML files?**

If Web Page Authoring is installed, there will be several prebuilt presentation templates available for online use, as well as the opportunity to use the AutoContent wizard to create your own presentations in HTML. Or you can create a presentation using any template and, when done, save the file as an HTML file.

To use a template to create an HTML file, use these steps:

1. Open PowerPoint, select Template, as shown here, and click OK.

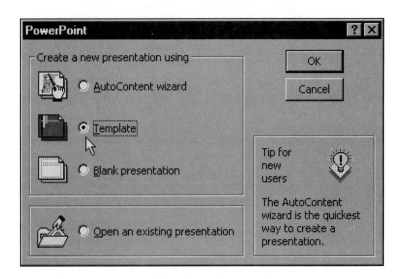

The New Presentation dialog box is displayed.

2. Choose a template by one of the following methods:

☞ Click the Web Pages tab and select the template you want.

☞ Click the Presentations tab and select a professionally designed presentation for online use.

☞ Select any other template from the Presentation Designs tab.

Tip: The templates included on the Web Pages tab help you prepare PowerPoint presentations in a layout that is effective when published on the Internet.

You can also convert any standard presentation for use on the Internet or an intranet with these steps:

1. Create the presentation, and when done, choose *Save as HTML* from the File menu. The *Save as HTML Wizard* is displayed next.

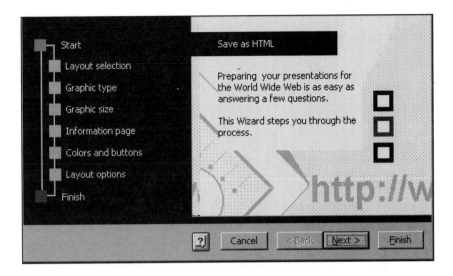

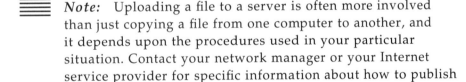

2. Respond to each prompt and click Next to go on.

3. When you've responded to all the prompts, click Finish. The file will be saved as an HTML file and will be ready to upload to an Internet server or to your company's intranet network server.

Note: Uploading a file to a server is often more involved than just copying a file from one computer to another, and it depends upon the procedures used in your particular situation. Contact your network manager or your Internet service provider for specific information about how to publish your file, and review the section "Using and Publishing Web Pages with Office 97" later in this chapter.

Can I use templates or wizards other than those in the Web Pages tab to create files to display on the Internet?

Yes, you can. If you choose other templates, just be sure that when you save the file you save it as an HTML file. See the sidebar "Saving Existing Documents as HTML" for more information.

Saving Existing Documents as HTML

Office 97 provides easy conversion methods to save your existing work in HTML format. Saving the file as an HTML file is necessary so that the file is compatible with and can be published on the World Wide Web or a local intranet.

➤ In Word, choose *Save as HTML* from the File menu, type a name, and click OK. Note that when you save a file as HTML, the formatting of the document may not be the same as it is in the original application, because HTML does not support all of the functions that the application provides.

➤ In Access, Excel, and PowerPoint, you also choose *Save as HTML* from the File menu, but a wizard will be displayed, as discussed in other questions in this chapter, that guides you through the procedure of saving the file as an HTML file.

The reason for using a Web Pages template or a wizard is that either can help you design a file that is professional looking. They provide you with choices to help you display information in an attractive format and format the document as it will look on the Internet or a network-based intranet.

? **I want to use a Web-site template to create a document in Word, but I don't see one in the New dialog box. Are there any templates and wizards for this? If so, where are they?**

If you can't find a template or wizard for creating a document for a Web site, it means that they weren't installed when Office Professional 97 was installed. Run Setup again and install those templates and wizards. See the following sidebar, "Installing Web-Page Authoring," for more information.

To create the file for the Web site in Word, do the following:

1. Choose New from the File menu.

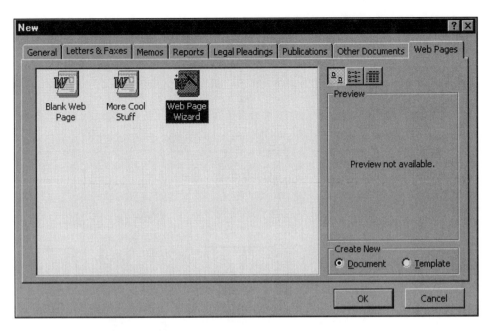

Figure 9-5:   The Web Pages tab in Word

2. Select the Web Pages tab, and select the template or wizard you want. Figure 9-5 shows the Web Pages tab in Word.

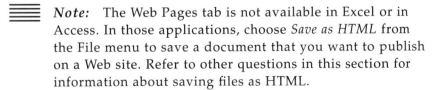 *Tip:*   If you double-click More Cool Stuff, you will see information about additional features that you can use if you installed Office Professional from a CD, or that you can find on the Microsoft Word Web site.

3. Create the document as you usually do.
4. When you're done, choose Save As from the File menu. Notice that the file type is an HTML document. If you like, you can also save it as a Word document.

≡ *Note:*   The Web Pages tab is not available in Excel or in Access. In those applications, choose *Save as HTML* from the File menu to save a document that you want to publish on a Web site. Refer to other questions in this section for information about saving files as HTML.

Installing Web-Page Authoring

First, you must run Setup again. If you are rerunning Setup
from a floppy drive, insert the disk in the drive and follow
these steps:

1. Click the Start button in the Windows Taskbar.

2. Select Settings, and select Control Panel.

3. Double-click Add/Remove Programs.

4. Select Install/Uninstall, and click the Install button. Then
   follow the instructions on the screen.

5. When the Microsoft Office 97 - Maintenance window
   is displayed, select Web Page Authoring (HTML). See
   Figure 9-6.

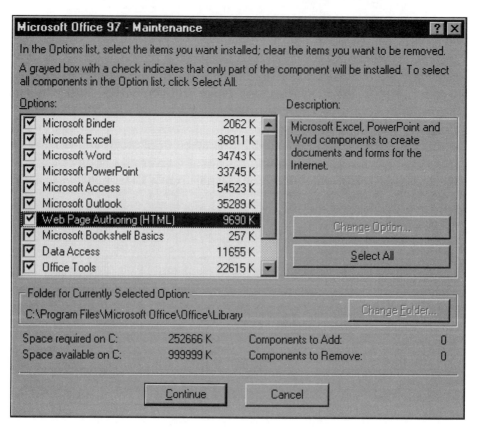

Figure 9-6: The Microsoft Office 97 - Maintenance window

6. Click Continue and respond to the prompts to install the additional option.

If you are rerunning Setup from a CD-ROM drive, insert the CD and follow these steps:

1. When the Office 97 Pro window is displayed, double-click the Setup icon.

Setup

2. At the prompt suggesting you close any applications that may be running, close the applications and, when you return to this point, click OK. The Setup window will be displayed.

3. In the Setup window, click the Add/Remove button. You will go to the Microsoft Office 97 - Maintenance window.

4. Click Web Page Authoring (HTML). See Figure 9-6.

5. Click Continue and respond to the prompts to install the additional option.

ADDING HYPERLINKS TO OFFICE DOCUMENTS

I want to create a hyperlink to text in another Word document. What is the easiest way to do this?

To insert a hyperlink to a block of text in a document, do the following:

1. Open both Word documents and choose Arrange All from the Window menu to display both.

2. Select the block of text that you want the hyperlink to go to.

3. Drag the selected text with the right mouse button to the location in the other document where you want the hyperlink to appear.

4. Release the right mouse button and choose Create Hyperlink Here from the pop-up menu.

5. A few words from the selected text will appear as a hyperlink. Use SHIFT and the LEFT and RIGHT ARROW keys to select the hyperlink text, and type in words that are more meaningful.

Tip: You can also copy the selected text to the Clipboard and use Paste as Hyperlink to insert it in the other document. This same technique can be used to insert graphics (from PowerPoint and other Word documents), ranges in an Excel worksheet, and Access objects into a Word document.

What's the difference between **hyperlinks and linked documents?**

A *hyperlink* will take you immediately to a block of text, an Office 97 object, a document file, or a Web site.

The primary purpose of *linking* is to allow editing in an original file to be automatically reflected in the linked data that is pasted into other files. See Chapter 8, "Integrating Office Documents," for more information on linking.

How do you use **hyperlinks in Access forms or reports?**

The procedure for inserting a hyperlink in either a form or a report is basically the same.

Note: Hyperlinks created in reports don't work when viewed in Access; however, they will work if the report is outputted to Excel or Word or converted to HTML.

There are two types of hyperlinks you can use:

 Hyperlinks that are stored in the table that the form or report is based upon

 Hyperlinks that are attached to labels or pictures in forms and reports, and to command buttons in forms

To use a hyperlink field in a form or report, be sure you have added a hyperlink data type field to the table on which your form or report is based. (Refer to the section "Inserting a Hyperlink in an Access Table" in the question on **inserting a hyperlink in an Access database** for specific steps for doing this.) Then do the following:

1. Create the form or report the same way you usually do, or open an existing form or report based on a table that contains a hyperlink field in Design view. Refer to Chapter 6, "Organizing with Access," for specific information about creating forms and reports.

2. If the list of field names is not displayed, choose Field List from the View menu.

Tip: You can also click the Field List button to display the list of field names.

3. Select the hyperlink field name from the list and drag it to the position you want it in the form or report.

4. Save and close the form or report design. Then you can open the form or report, click the hypertext name, and go directly to the file or Web site to which it is linked.

   To add a hyperlink to a label,

1. In Design view, click the Insert Hyperlink button.

2. Enter a URL, UNC address, or path in the *Link to file or URL* box. If you are hyperlinking to a location or object within an Office 97 file, browse to its location in the *Named location or file* box.

3. Click OK. The URL or path appears on the form or report as a label in the default hyperlink color. Move the label into position and change the text and background color to what you want the user to see in Form view.

4. Switch to Form view to test the hyperlink.

   To attach hyperlinks to a picture or command button, insert the picture or command button and open its Properties window. In the Hyperlink Address property box, click the Builder button to open the Insert Hyperlink dialog box, and navigate to the URL or file you want to open when the picture or command button is selected.

I tried to insert a hyperlink in an Access database the same way I did in Word, but the Hyperlink option was dimmed in the Insert menu. How do I do this?

This requires two basic steps:

1. Select the table and go to Design view to insert a new field in the table, and choose Hyperlink as the data type.

2. Go to that field in the table, choose Hyperlink from the Insert menu, and insert the URL if you are linking to a Web site on the Internet, a UNC (Universal Naming Convention) address or path for intranet documents, or a path and filename if you are creating a hyperlink to another file on your local drive. See the sidebar "Addressing" for a further description of addressing formats.

Tip: You can also insert a hyperlink field when you open the table in Datasheet view. To do that, move the insertion point to the place where you want to insert a new field. Choose

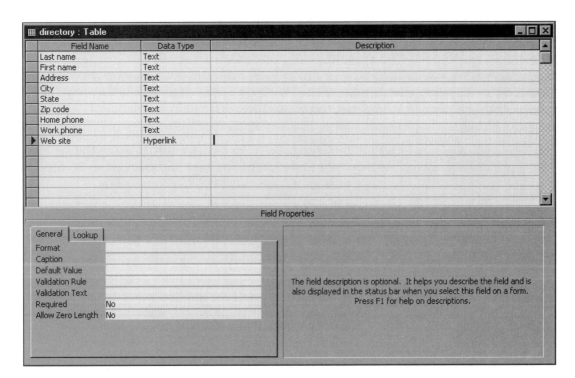

Figure 9-7:   Access Design view

Hyperlink column from the Insert menu. Then you can choose Rename Column from the Format menu to give the field an appropriate name. The sidebar "Inserting a Hyperlink in an Access Table" gives specific steps for doing this.

Inserting a Hyperlink in an Access Table

To add a hyperlink field to a database table, do the following:

1. Open the database, select the table that you want to contain the hyperlink field in the Database window, and click the Design button to go to Design view. See the example in Figure 9-7.

2. Move to the first vacant cell in the Field Name column, and type a field name.

3. Press TAB to move to the Data Type column and click the down arrow to display the list of field-type choices shown here:

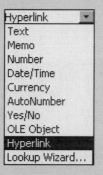

4. Select Hyperlink.

5. Close Design view and return to the Database window.

To add a hyperlink to the table, use the next set of steps.

1. Open the table in Datasheet view and move to the cell in which you want to enter a hyperlink.

2. Do either of the following:

    ➤ If you know the name, type in the hyperlink: either a URL, a UNC address, or a path and filename. See the sidebar "Addressing" for a further description of addressing formats.

● ● ● ● ● ● ● ● ● ● ●

▷ Choose Hyperlink from the Insert menu to go to the
Insert Hyperlink dialog box, shown in Figure 9-8.

Tip: You can also click the Insert Hyperlink button shown on
the left to go to the Insert Hyperlink dialog box. This button is
active only when the insertion point is in a hyperlink field.

3. Click the down arrow to see a list of locations and select
one (the sites listed depend on what you have been
working with). Or click the Browse button to locate the file
or Web site that you want. If you are linking to a specific
location or object within an Office 97 file, use the second
Browse button to find it. When you are done, click OK to
insert the hyperlink in the cell.

4. Save the table. To go to the site or file, just click the
hyperlink name.

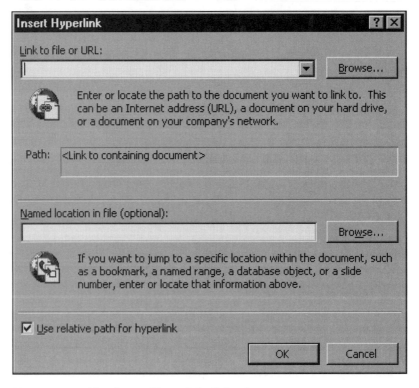

Figure 9-8:   The Insert Hyperlink dialog box

? **I don't see how to insert a hyperlink in an Excel worksheet.** The Hyperlink option in the Insert menu is dimmed, as is the Insert Hyperlink button. Is there a way to do this? If so, how?

If the Excel worksheet is a shared worksheet, the Hyperlink option in the Insert menu is dimmed, and you will have to remove the Shared attribute before inserting a hyperlink. See the sidebar "Removing a Shared Attribute from a Worksheet in Excel" for instructions for doing that.

Removing a Shared Attribute from a Worksheet in Excel

You cannot insert a hyperlink in an Excel workbook that is shared. Clear the shared attribute with these steps:

1. Open the worksheet, and choose Share Workbook from the Tools menu to display the Share Workbook dialog box.

2. On the Editing tab, clear the *Allow changes by more than one user at a time* check box, and notify any users who may have the workbook open to close it before you remove the workbook from shared use.

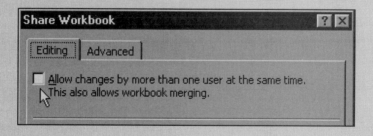

3. Click OK, and when prompted, click Yes to remove the workbook from shared use.

I inserted a hyperlink successfully in a Word document, but when I tried to use the same steps to insert a hyperlink in a PowerPoint presentation, nothing happened. How do I insert a hyperlink in PowerPoint?

Use the familiar Insert Hyperlink dialog box to link to another file, Internet, or document location. Note that in PowerPoint, if you are in Slide view when you click the hyperlink, you will not jump to the linked file or object. To activate the hyperlink, click the Slide Show View button, shown here, or choose Slide Show from the View menu. Click the hyperlink. Refer to other questions in this section for more specific steps to create a hyperlink to a Web site or to another document. Also, see the sidebar "Using Action Settings to Create a Hyperlink in PowerPoint."

Using Action Settings to Create a Hyperlink in PowerPoint

Normally, you initiate a hyperlink by clicking text or an object when the mouse pointer changes into the "pointing" hand, shown below.

In PowerPoint you can also initiate a hyperlink by just moving the mouse pointer over the hyperlinked text or object. Use these steps:

1. Select the text or object that is to be the hyperlink in the PowerPoint presentation.

2. Choose Action Settings from the Slide Show menu.

3. Select *Hyperlink to* in the Mouse Click or Mouse Over tab, depending on how you want the user to be able to activate the hyperlink.

4. Click the down arrow in the *Hyperlink to* box to display a list of choices as shown here:

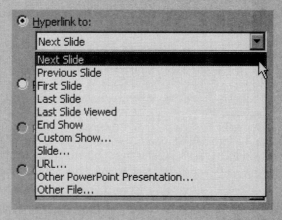

5. Select the option you want and supply location information as prompted.

6. Click OK in the Action Settings dialog box to insert the hyperlink in the presentation. To see the link, go to Slide Show view and click or pass the mouse pointer over the hyperlink text.

I know I can insert a hyperlink in Word that can be used to go immediately to a Web site, but are there any other uses for hyperlinks?

Yes; the most frequent use of hyperlinks is to go to a Web site on the Internet, but you can also insert a hyperlink to another document that others on a network can open. The following steps show you how to do either of these.

1. Open the document that is to contain the hyperlink, and select the text that will be formatted so that you can jump to the referenced document or URL.

2. Choose Hyperlink from the Insert menu. The Insert Hyperlink box is displayed.

3. In the *Link to file or URL* box, you can click the down arrow to display a list of Web sites and documents that

may have been used as hyperlink references. Select one of these, or click the Browse button to go to the *Link to File* box, and locate a document from a folder.

4. Optionally, in the *Named location in file* box, you can locate a bookmark that may have been inserted in the document or Web site that you selected. Click the Browse button to display the Bookmark box. Bookmarks in the file or URL that is selected in the *Link to file or URL* box will be displayed. Select the bookmark you want and click OK.

5. Select *Use Relative path for hyperlink* if the file you are linking to may be moved later. If you deselect this option, the hyperlinked file will be opened only when it is in its current folder.

6. When you're done, click OK to leave the Insert Hyperlink dialog box. The hyperlink will be displayed in your document. Now, when users open this document, they can click the hyperlink text to go immediately to the referenced document or URL.

What are some **reasons for using hyperlinks in Access?**

Creating hyperlinks to Web sites can be especially useful in an Access database. For example, if your company buys products from a number of different manufacturers, you can create a database table that contains company names, addresses, and names of sales reps for each supplier and create a hyperlink field that contains the address (the Uniform Resource Locator, or URL) of each manufacturer's Web site (if they have one). This would allow the user to go directly to that Web site to see the latest product updates and information. An educator can create a table with a hyperlink field to publishers' Web pages, where the latest textbooks that are available from each company are listed.

A hyperlink to a file on a network also provides an easy way for users to share information without duplicating files. See the related Access questions in this section for information on creating hyperlinks in Access.

ACCESSING THE WEB AND INTRANETS WITH OFFICE 97

I'd like to access the Web from Office 97 in much the same manner that I use Internet Explorer. What is the best way to go online from within an Office 97 application?

Display the Web toolbar from the View menu Toolbar option (or click the Web Toolbar button on the Standard toolbar in Excel, PowerPoint, or Word). The Web toolbar buttons are essentially the same as those on the Internet Explorer toolbar. The following sidebar, "The Web Toolbar," describes what each button does.

Tip: Besides using the Web toolbar to open a Web document, you can enter the document's address in the *File name box* of the File Open dialog box and click Open. See the sidebar "Addressing" for information on proper addressing syntax for the Web and intranets.

The Web Toolbar

The gateway to the World Wide Web and corporate intranets is through the buttons on the Web toolbar, shown here:

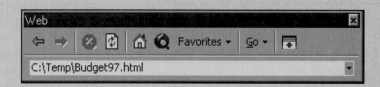

The Web toolbar is available in all Office 97 products except Outlook (you can get to the Web in Outlook by other means). Display the toolbar by opening the View menu, choosing Toolbars, and clicking Web. The buttons in the Web toolbar are described in Table 9-1.

Table 9-1: Web Toolbar Buttons and Their Functions

	Button name	Description
⬅	Back	Allows you move backward through previously opened Web pages or hyperlinks once a page or document has been opened
➡	Forward	Allows you to move forward through previously opened Web pages or hyperlinks once a page or document has been opened
⊗	Stop Current Jump	Ceases the process of finding and displaying a Web page or hyperlink document
⟳	Refresh Current Page	Updates the display of the current document
⌂	Start Page	Displays and allows you to modify the Web page or document that is first located
◉	Search the Web	Opens Internet Explorer and connects to a Microsoft Network (MSN) search palette, where you can type in a keyword and choose a search engine
Favorites ▾	Favorites	Allows you to add frequently visited sites to an easy access list
Go ▾	Go	Provides a drop-down list of the buttons on the Web toolbar. A good one-stop button if you're trying to reduce the number of buttons on a toolbar.
⬆	Show Only Web Toolbar	Hides other toolbars to gain maximum viewing area
C:\Temp\Budget97.html	Address box	Provides a means to type a Web-page address or an intranet or local computer document address; pressing ENTER takes you to the specified location.

• • • • • • • • • •

Note that here are many terms used to describe what you access when going online, such as *Web page, Web site, online document, spreadsheet, presentation, table,* and so forth, as well as other variations of nononline items. Generally, the HTML files found on the World Wide Web are referred to as Web pages; those items found on an intranet or on a local computer are called HTML documents.

? **I want to change the search page that I use from within Excel so that it will be different from the one I use in my browser. Can I have different search pages for Office 97 and my browser?**

No. "One for all" is the motto in this instance. (This is also true for the Start page.) Several of the Web features that are a part of Office 97 programs are shared components with your browser (assuming your browser is compatible with Office 97).

? **I'm trying to find an HTML-format marketing analysis spreadsheet on one of our servers, but I don't know what the URL is. Can I open an HTML document without knowing its URL?**

Sure; actually, you don't need to use URLs to open HTML documents stored on a network. You can just navigate normally (using the Open dialog box in Excel or Windows Explorer, or the Find feature in Windows 95) to find the file's location and double-click its filename. The spreadsheet should open in Excel as it would appear in a browser, as shown in Figure 9-9. For a review on addressing conventions used for online documents, see the sidebar "Addressing."

• • • • • • • • • •

Addressing

Different addressing conventions are used depending on where you're searching for an online item:

▷ To open a Web page, type in its address, or URL (Uniform Resource Locator), in the Web toolbar Address box. A URL takes the form of *protocol://domain/path*; for example, http://www.microsoft.com/office.

▷ To open a document on a LAN-based intranet or on a local drive, type the UNC (Universal Naming Convention) or a standard *drive:\path* designation. A UNC takes the form of *computername\drive\path*; for example, \\marty\c\office97\chapter9.

Using either convention, press ENTER after typing in the address.

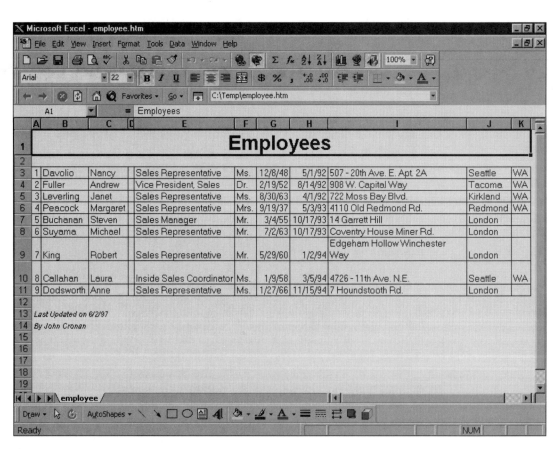

Figure 9-9:   An HTML document opened in Excel

? I understand I should view my HTML documents in a browser to see how they will look to users on the Web. How can I quickly preview HTML documents in a browser from Office 97 programs?

Word offers the best route to preview its HTML files. When an HTML document is opened in Word, you can choose Web Page Preview from the File menu or click the Web Page Preview button on the Standard toolbar to open the document in your default browser. In the other Office 97 programs, you need to use the Web toolbar to display the browser and then open the HTML document from within the browser. See the related questions in this section that discuss accessing the Web.

? I need to transfer a file to a client using FTP (File Transfer Protocol). Can I transfer files and access FTP sites from Office 97 applications?

Yes, you can; however, before you begin the file transfer process you have to provide the Office application with the necessary information to connect to the FTP site. Add a site to your FTP Locations list with these steps:

1. Open the document you want to transfer and then open the Save As dialog box from the File menu Save As option.

2. Click the down arrow next to the *Save in* list box and click Add/Modify FTP Locations. The Add/Modify FTP Locations dialog box opens as shown in Figure 9-10.

3. Type in the FTP site name; choose to log on either as Anonymous or, if you have a user name, choose User and enter the name; and type in the applicable password (*guest* is a common password for Anonymous logons).

4. Click the Add button and then click OK.

The FTP site is now listed in the Save As (or Open) dialog box as you can see in Figure 9-11.

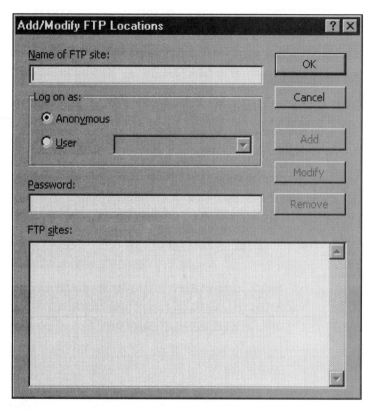

Figure 9-10:   The Add/Modify FTP Locations dialog box

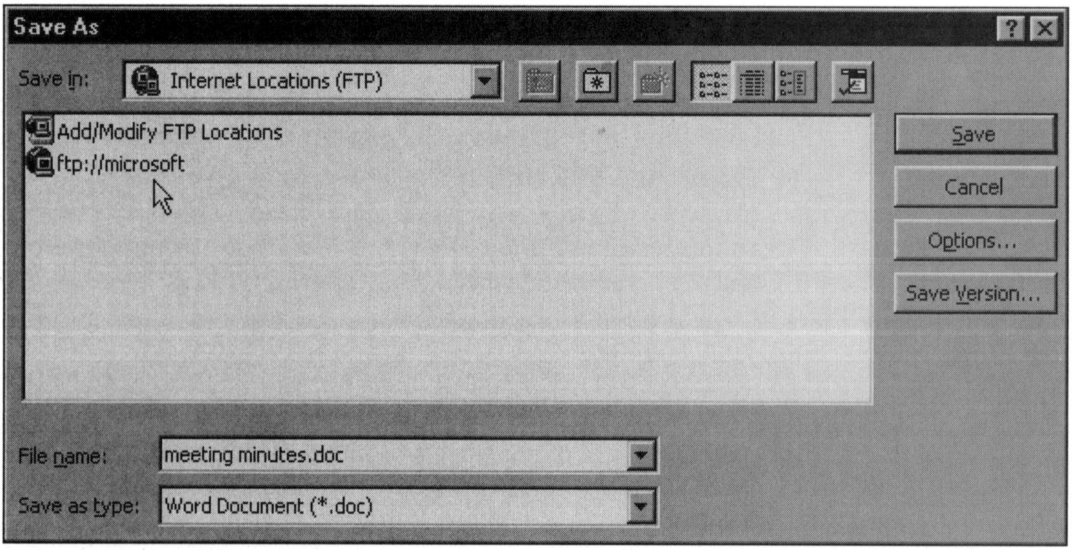

Figure 9-11:   Transferring a file to an FTP site

To transfer a file to an FTP site,

1. Log on to your Internet service provider (ISP).
2. Open the Save As dialog box if it's not already displayed.
3. Open the *Save in* list box, select the site name, and you will connect with the FTP site.
4. Navigate to the folder where you want to transfer your document and click Save.

Note: To transfer a document from an FTP site to your local computer, use similar steps, except operate from the Open dialog box instead of the Save As dialog box.

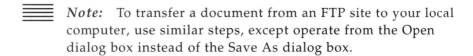 I don't see a **Web toolbar in Outlook**. Does this mean I can't access the Web in Outlook?

No, you can access the Web from Outlook, but in a different manner than from the other Office 97 products. Using the Contacts folder you can open a contact window that has an associated home page, as shown next, and then click the Explore Web Page button on the toolbar.

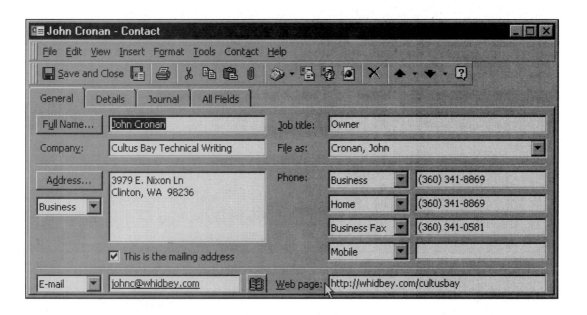

Tip: You can also right-click a contact and click Explore Web Page in the pop-up menu.

Your browser will open and display the contact's home page. From the browser, you now have access to other Web pages and HTML documents.

Also, in any messages you receive in Outlook that have hyperlinked text (usually identified by the color blue) to Web pages, you can click the text to open your browser and jump to the page.

USING AND PUBLISHING WEB PAGES WITH OFFICE 97

? **I have installed Web Page Authoring (HTML) in Office Professional 97; however, there is not a Web Pages tab in the Access New dialog box when I create a new database. Is there a way I can put an Access database on a Web site?**

Yes; do the following:

1. Create a database as you usually do, or open an existing database.

2. Choose *Save as HTML* from the File menu to display the *Publish to the Web Wizard,* as shown in Figure 9-12.

3. Read the information that is displayed in the opening window, and then click the Next button.

Tip: If you have used the Wizard previously and saved the settings, you can check the *I want to use a Web publication profile I already created with this wizard* box that is in the opening window. If you do this, you will be able to skip some of the wizard windows and your database will be formatted in the same way as previous databases saved as HTML files.

Respond to the prompts in each window to make various choices in the wizard. In the window showing the database objects, you will be required to select at least one—table, form, report, or query. When you select the object, a check will be placed in the check box. Then click the Next button to go on. You will be able to choose a template for preparing the file, and you can also choose the type of format for saving the file. The wizard will prompt you to save the file to a folder, and if data is

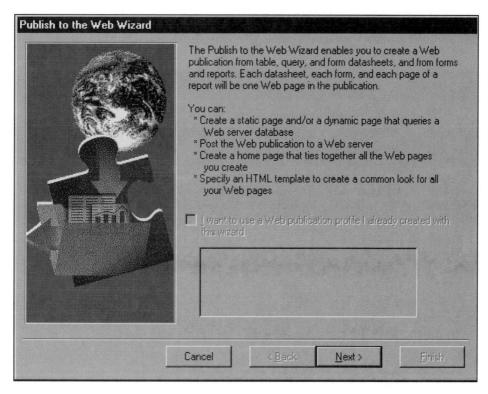

Figure 9-12:   The Access *Publish to the Web Wizard*

stored on a Microsoft Internet Information Server (IIS) or Microsoft Personal Web Server (PWS), you can also publish the file directly to the server. And finally, you can choose to create a home page for your file.

4. When you reach the last page in the Wizard, click Finish. The database is now ready to be published either to an Internet site or on your company's network.

? I've created a Web document in Word 97 that I want to view in Internet Explorer to see how it will look on our company's intranet. After I open Internet Explorer I always find it cumbersome to have to type the path to an HTML document on my hard drive in the Address box. Is there a better way to access local HTML documents from Internet Explorer?

Yes. As in other Windows programs, Internet Explorer has an Open option on the File menu. Choosing this option displays the Open dialog box, shown here, which has a different appearance than most Open dialog boxes:

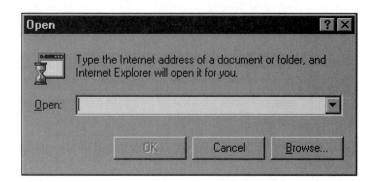

You have three methods to locate a HTML document:

▷ Type in the address/path in the Open box.

▷ Click the down arrow in the Open box and select an address or path that has been used previously.

▷ Click the Browse button to display the more familiar Open dialog box, where you can navigate to the file.

?   I want to be able to send my Web documents to my Internet service provider so I can publish them on the Web. Does Office 97 provide any tools or features that assist me in publishing Web documents?

Yes, there are publishing wizards available to guide you through assembling and copying the necessary files to display your documents on the Web.

Once you've created HTML documents in Office 97 you'll want to get them out to the rest of the world, whether that's really the rest of the world via the Web, or a subset of the world on an intranet. In either case, Office 97 can help you out, and with a little help from some free Microsoft software, you can even create your own intranet on your personal computer.

To be able to publish Web documents beyond your own hard drive you need Internet server software to handle the communication of TCP/IP from one computer to another and across the Web. Internet service providers such as America Online and large corporate intranets rely on sophisticated programs such as Microsoft Internet Information Server running on a Windows NT server that can handle the heavy volume of activity they experience. For the rest of us using Windows 95, there is a way to have use of a server to handle most of the operations that a small networked workgroup or individual user will need. Microsoft offers the Personal Web Server, packaged in several of their Internet products (for example, FrontPage and the Internet Starter Kit). It supports many advanced features used in Web pages, such as data collection and access, and is used in developing, testing, and staging Web applications. The Personal Web Server Properties dialog box is shown in Figure 9-13.

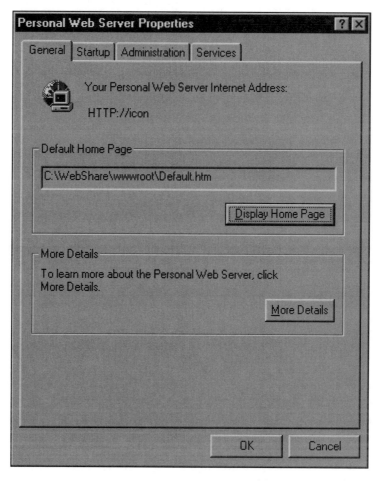

Figure 9-13:   The Personal Web Server Properties dialog box

In order to get your HTML documents and associated files to a server for publishing, Office 97 provides the Web Publishing Wizard on the Office 97 CD-ROM (run Webpost.exe from \Valupack\Webpost to install the wizard). Once installed, the wizard will walk you through the process of copying all the necessary files to the Internet server. Most of the Office 97 products require you to run the Web Publishing Wizard manually after you create HTML documents; however, in Access when you choose to save an object as HTML, its own *Publish to the Web Wizard*, shown in Figure 9-14, provides a lead-in to the Web Publishing Wizard.

 Note: Although Office 97 offers many features to make creating and publishing online documents easy, it cannot do the job of dedicated Web-authoring programs such as Microsoft FrontPage. For more information on creating your

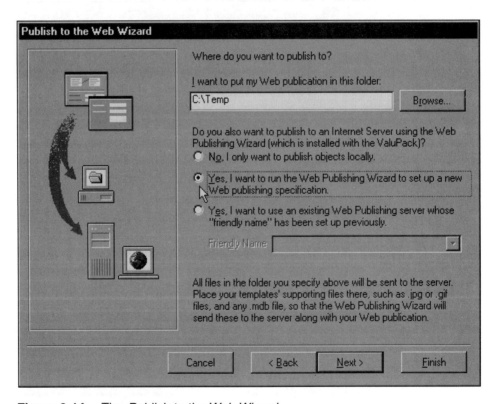

Figure 9-14:   The *Publish to the Web Wizard*

own Web pages and Web sites, read Osborne/McGraw-Hill's *Web Publishing with Microsoft FrontPage,* 2nd edition, by Martin Matthews.

 A friend of mine raves about Web Find Fast as a great way to help her search for HTML documents. I've never seen this feature offered for use. What is Web Find Fast and what do I have to do to use it?

Web Find Fast is similar to Find Fast, which allows you to search for documents using criteria you select from the Open dialog boxes of the Office 97 products, shown here:

Find files that match these search criteria:			
File name:	Northwind.mdb ▼	Text or property: ▼	Find Now
Files of type:	Microsoft Access Databases (*.mdb) ▼	Last modified: any time ▼	New Search
3 file(s) found.			

Web Find Fast extends this capability to search over an intranet for HTML documents. Unfortunately, unless you're connected to a Windows NT network you won't be able to use Web Find Fast, as it only works on Windows NT servers (or Windows NT workstations configured as servers) that have an installed Web server.

≡ *Note:*   The Web Find Fast software is located on the Office 97 CD-ROM. Before you run Web Find Fast Setup, check out the readme.txt file in the \Srvpack folder to ensure that you have the necessary hardware and software in place to support this feature.

USING WORD AS YOUR E-MAIL CREATOR, EDITOR, AND READER

 What is the advantage of using Word to create e-mail when basically all I want to do is type the message?

If all you want to do is type a message, and you are not going to edit a shared document or you are not particularly concerned about formatting, then you probably do not need the Word functions. However, using Word as your e-mail editor makes more Word functions available in addition to the features such as spell checking, autosignature, and font and paragraph formatting that are available in the default editor. See the sidebar "WordMail Functions" for specific uses of Word in e-mail messages.

● ● ● ● ● ● ● ● ● ●

WordMail Functions

The following is a sampling of Word functions you can use in the e-mail message window.

Use the Edit options to

➤ Paste a Hyperlink.

➤ Find, Replace, and Go To text in the message. Without Word, only the Find and Find Next options are available.

➤ Repeat an edit. Without using Word, only the Undo option is available.

Use the View options to

➤ Display the message in Normal, Online Layout, Page Layout, or Outline view.

➤ Display the Word toolbars. If you are not using Word, only the Standard and Formatting toolbars are available.

➤ Use the Document Map feature.

Use the Insert options to

➤ Insert page, column, and section breaks.

➤ Insert date and time, fields, symbols, comments, footnotes, captions, cross-references, bookmarks, and hyperlinks.

➤ Add a table of contents or an index, if you like.

Use the Format options to

➤ Format text in newspaper-type columns.

➤ Format text with bullets or numbers, borders, or shading.

➤ Set new tab stops. If you are not using Word, default tabs are set every half-inch, but you are not able to set new tab stops.

> Use styles. The choices here are limited and are not the same as those available in Word 97.

> Use AutoFormat. The choices here are to automatically format the message as e-mail, as a letter, or as a general document.

> Format the background with colors.

Use the Tools options to

> Use a grammar checker, select a language, use the Thesaurus, or use word count.

> Use automatic features such as AutoSummarize, AutoCorrect, and AutoSignature.

> Track changes.

> Run macros. You cannot, however, create a macro in e-mail.

> Use templates and add-ins.

> Use the Table function to create and edit tables.

Note that many of the special formatting and other features that WordMail can add to e-mail are not observable by recipients over the Internet. If you are on a network with an Exchange server, then the additional formatting will be transferred to the e-mail recipient within the network. Otherwise it will be stripped out.

? **I know I can choose AutoText from the Insert menu and insert my signature, because it is displayed as a user signature, but I would like to have my signature formatted differently. Can I create a new signature in Word that will be added automatically to my e-mail messages?**

Yes; you can create a new signature in Word, save it as an AutoText entry, and name it *signature.* If you do this, either in Word 97, or in the Exchange or Outlook message window when you are using Word as your e-mail editor, the new signature will be displayed automatically in your message window whenever you open it. If you open the message window without using Word as your e-mail editor, the signature will not be displayed automatically. See the sidebar "Creating an AutoText Entry with the Word E-Mail Editor in Exchange or Outlook" for specific steps.

You do not necessarily have to use the AutoText New entry function to create a signature in Exchange or in Outlook. You can use AutoSignature, which is quicker, if you are using Word as an e-mail editor. Use the following steps:

1. Open a new message window.

2. Type and format the text for the automatic signature, and then select it.

3. Choose AutoSignature from the Tools menu to display the AutoSignature box shown here:

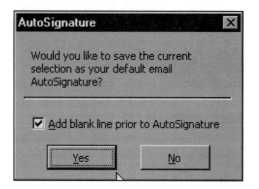

4. Click Yes. A prompt is displayed, telling you the signature is saved.

••••• *Tip:* If you are not using WordMail as your e-mail editor, you can still use AutoSignature to create and save entries in either Outlook or Exchange. To do this, choose AutoSignature from the Tools menu, type and format the text in the text box, select *Add this signature to the end of new message,* if you like, and click OK when you're done.

● ● ● ● ● ● ● ● ● ●

Creating an AutoText Entry with the Word E-Mail Editor in Exchange or Outlook

To do this, use the following steps:

1. Create the text and select it.

2. Choose *AutoText entry* from the Insert menu.

3. Choose New to display the Create AutoText box shown here:

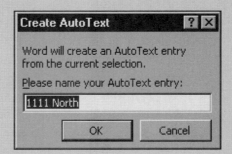

4. The first couple of words of the selected text will be displayed; however, you can type a different name for the entry, if you like.

5. Click OK when you're done.

To use an AutoText entry in Exchange or Outlook, do the following:

1. Move the insertion point to the place where you want to insert the entry.

2. Type the name of the AutoText entry and press F3.

AutoText entries are not limited to signatures. You can create any type of text—for example, a company logo, memo headings, return addresses, technical or scientific terms, terms that are in a foreign language, or any other block of text that you use repeatedly. By creating it as an AutoText entry, you can ensure that it will always be the same and that it will be correct (unless there is an error in the AutoText entry—check it well). Plus, it's a quick way to enter text.

? **I thought that when I connected to the Internet using either Microsoft Exchange or Microsoft Outlook that I would automatically be able to use Word to create e-mail messages, but I don't see any Word functions. How can I create e-mail messages with Word functions if they are not showing?**

If the Word functions are not available, it means that they were not installed when Office 97 was installed originally. You need to run Setup again and install WordMail. To do that,

1. Follow the procedures to run Setup to Add/Remove components described in several other questions in this and previous chapters.

2. In the Maintenance dialog box, select Microsoft Word in the list of items, and then click the Change Option button.

3. Select WordMail in Exchange, click OK, and then click Continue to install it.

To use WordMail in Microsoft Exchange, do the following:

1. Open Microsoft Exchange.

2. Choose WordMail Options in the Compose menu.

3. Select *Enable Word as e-mail editor.* Your message window should now look like the one shown in Figure 9-15.

⋯⋯ *Tip:*   If you do not want to use WordMail for writing your e-mail messages in Outlook, you can turn that option off by choosing Options from the Tools menu, clicking the E-mail tab, and clearing the *Use Microsoft Word as e-mail editor* check box. Turning off WordMail in Outlook may also turn off the use of WordMail in Exchange.

? **How is editing an e-mail message with Word different from editing without using Word?**

Three of the most useful Word features that you can use are the following:

Track Changes is a function that is available when you use Word to edit a message. When you use this function, you

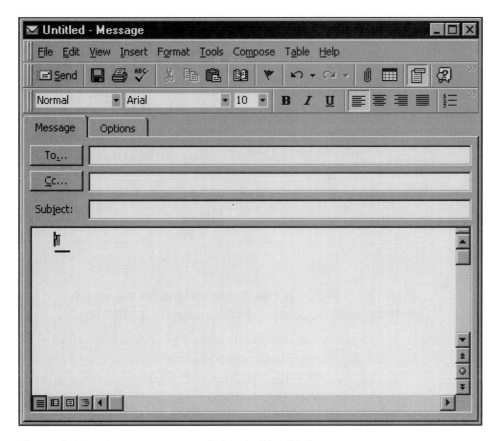

Figure 9-15:   A new message window in WordMail

can mark any changes that you make to an e-mail message so that it is easy for a reader to see the edits you have made. Refer to Chapter 3, "Writing with Word," for more information about using Track Changes when editing.

Highlighting text is an advantage, especially if you are sending a long message. Specific sections can be highlighted so that the reader can pick out especially significant portions of the text.

Comments that can be questions, suggestions, or references can be inserted the same way they are inserted in a Word document.

I have been told that reading e-mail in Word is easier. I don't see much difference except for changes in formatting. Are there other differences?

When you use Word as your e-mail editor, you have Word's various view options available. If you choose Online Layout view, it enlarges the text so that it is easier to read. To use this view, just click the Online Layout View button located at the bottom of the text area, shown here, or choose Online Layout from the View menu.

 If I send a Word e-mail message to someone who doesn't have Word, what happens to the text?

The message will be displayed as text only, without any of the formatting that may have been applied if Word were used to create the message. For example, symbols that may have been inserted will not be displayed as symbols; if you have entered a table, the text in the table will be displayed as tab-delimited text, not in a table format; and text in newspaper-type columns will no longer be formatted in columns.

Working with the Rest of Office

Answer Topics!

Extra Office Features
@ a Glance

Office 97 includes several applets, or subapplications, that add considerably to the power of Office 97:

☛ **Bookshelf** provides a group of reference books: a dictionary, a thesaurus, and a book of quotations. From a list of topics, words, or phrases, references are provided in text, audio, video, or a combination of all three. Additional references, such as maps and encyclopedias, are available by subscription.

☛ **Drawing,** available in Word, Excel, and PowerPoint, supplies a group of tools for drawing and formatting shapes, such as standard rectangles, squares, and circles; lines and arcs; and freeform drawing, as well as automatically drawn shapes of all types. The drawings can be modified with color, line style, shadow, 3D effects, and more.

☛ **Graph** is a charting tool used in Word, PowerPoint, and Access (Excel has its own graphing feature that is separate from this one).

☛ **Clip Gallery** contains clip art, pictures, sounds, and video clips that can be inserted into your Office documents and presentations.

☛ **Equation Editor** allows you to create complex mathematical expressions.

☛ **Organization Chart** provides the tools to create organization charts.

BOOKSHELF

?   ### What is **Bookshelf** and where do I find it?

Bookshelf is a set of references available in Word, Excel, or PowerPoint or on its own. Office 97's Bookshelf comes with three references: *The American Heritage Dictionary, The Original Roget's Thesaurus,* and *The Columbia Dictionary of Quotations.* You can also review and then subscribe to other references, including *Address Builder* (to locate an address), *Bookshelf Internet Directory, The Concise Columbia Encyclopedia, The Concise Encarta World Atlas, The People's Chronology,* and *The World Almanac and Book of Facts.* You can order a one-time upgrade or subscribe to get a new upgrade and additions to Bookshelf's information and features every year. The ordering procedure can be displayed as you review the Microsoft Bookshelf Basics.

Follow these steps to get into Bookshelf:

1. Insert the Office 97 CD into your disk drive.

2. From the Office Shortcut Bar, click Microsoft Bookshelf Basics. Or, in Word or PowerPoint, from the Tools menu select Look Up Reference, and then Microsoft Bookshelf Basics.

3. Click OK and the screen shown in Figure 10-1 will be displayed. (First-time users will first get the *Preview of the Day* screen until they choose the check box to not show it again.)

?   ### How can I **copy a video** into a document?

When an article contains a video or animation, you must copy it in a different way. In this case, follow these steps:

1. Right-click the article and choose Create Shortcut. A shortcut to the article will be created and placed on the desktop.

2. Open the document that will contain the copy and drag the shortcut into it.

3. Double-click the shortcut icon. Bookshelf will be loaded and the article containing the video or animation opened. You can then play it as usual.

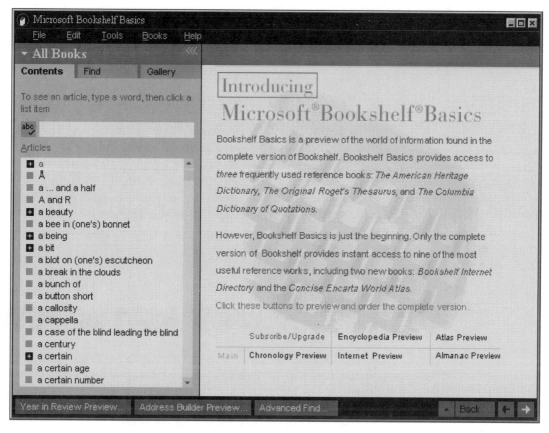

Figure 10-1: Microsoft Bookshelf's introductory screen

❓ How can I **copy an entire article**, not just selected parts of it?

Copying the entire document can be done by right-clicking the article to be copied. The article must be opened first. A pop-up menu will be displayed, as shown here:

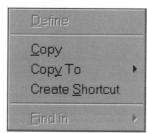

Select Copy to place it on the Clipboard. Then go into the other application and Paste it from the Clipboard.

Caution: For the Copy command to work, you must be sure that nothing is selected or highlighted in the article; otherwise only that part will be copied.

If you choose Copy To, you place the article in a specific Word, Excel, or PowerPoint document. That application will be loaded and, if no document is open, the article will be pasted to a new one. If a document is already open, you will be allowed to select a New Document, Current Location of an open document, or the End of an open document.

Note: When you copy an article, Bookshelf automatically includes a copyright notice that is part of the article. In Excel it is placed in the cells following the article, in PowerPoint it immediately follows the text, and in Word it appears as a footnote.

? I have trouble seeing the small text in Bookshelf. Is there a way to **enlarge the font**?

Yes; from the Tools menu, select Options. The screen shown here will allow you to select a Text Size of Normal, Larger, or Largest:

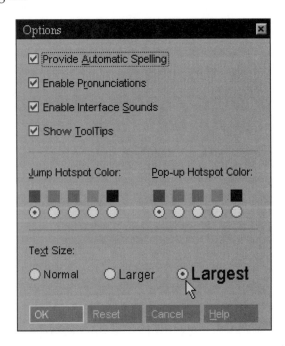

••••• *Tip:*   You can also use the Options dialog box on the Tools menu to change your Bookshelf environment. You can switch colors for jump and pop-up hotspots; enable or disable word pronunciations, automatic spelling, and interface sounds; and show ToolTips.

? **When I click the Microsoft Bookshelf Basics button, I get an error message: "The file or folder 'BS96SE.EXE' that this shortcut refers to cannot be found." What's the problem?**

You must not have the Office 97 CD-ROM in the disk drive. The CD must be inserted before Bookshelf will run.

? **Where are the front matter and special sections that come with the Dictionary and Thesaurus?**

The front matter for the Dictionary includes the Guide to the Dictionary, which contains an explanation of syllabification, pronunciation, variants, and other language characteristics; introductory remarks on the edition and history of the Dictionary; and the Guide to Indo-European Roots. The Thesaurus includes a classification explanation, organization overview, and other useful information.

Follow these steps to find the front matter for the Dictionary or Thesaurus:

1. From the Help menu, choose Help Contents.

2. Select the Index tab.

3. Type in **Dictionary** or **Thesaurus** and then click Display.

4. For the Dictionary, select *Front matter-The American Heritage Dictionary, Third Edition* as shown below, and click Display. For the Thesaurus, select *Roget's Thesaurus of English Words and Phrases-Overview* and click Display.

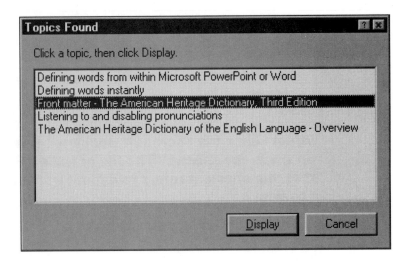

? **How can I look up references in just one book?** The first screen is displayed with the Contents showing All Books and I can't see how to get just one.

Next to the words *All Books* is a downward-pointing arrow. Click it and you will be able to choose from a drop-down list the specific book or preview you want to see, as shown here:

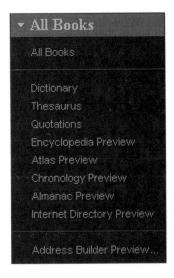

How do I return to a previously viewed article without looking it up again?

On the lower right of the Bookshelf Basics window is the Feature Bar, which contains the Back button. Click the arrow to the left of the Back button to see a list of articles you have looked at, an example of which is shown here:

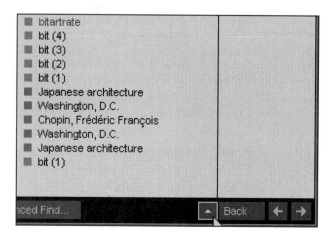

DRAWING

I want to add several **callouts with varying background colors** to a document. How do I do this?

Follow these steps to draw and then add text and color to callouts:

1. In Excel and Word, display the Drawing toolbar by right-clicking a toolbar and selecting Drawing. In PowerPoint the Drawing toolbar is displayed on the bottom of the screen.

2. After clicking the AutoShapes button select Callouts as shown here, and then select the shape of callout you want.

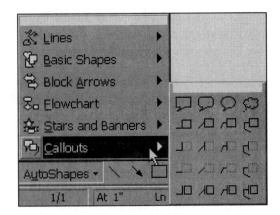

The mouse pointer will become a crossbar.

3. Place the pointer on the document where you want the callout and drag it to about the size you want.

▷ To alter the size of the callout, place the pointer on one of its control handles. When a two-arrow pointer appears, as shown below, drag it to the size you want.

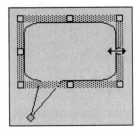

You can also use the Format AutoShape dialog box if dragging seems difficult.

▷ To change the placement of the callout, place the pointer on the border of the callout but not on a control handle. When a four-arrow pointer appears, as shown here, drag the callout where you want it.

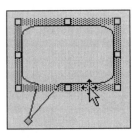

▷ To change the position of the callout leader, place the pointer just above its tip until the adjustment handle becomes a yellow, diamond-shaped icon, as shown below. Then drag the tip to a new location.

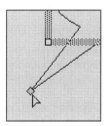

4. Select all the callouts that you want to have the same color. Do this by either surrounding them with a selection rectangle or by clicking each one while pressing SHIFT. Figure 10-2 shows three callouts selected at once.

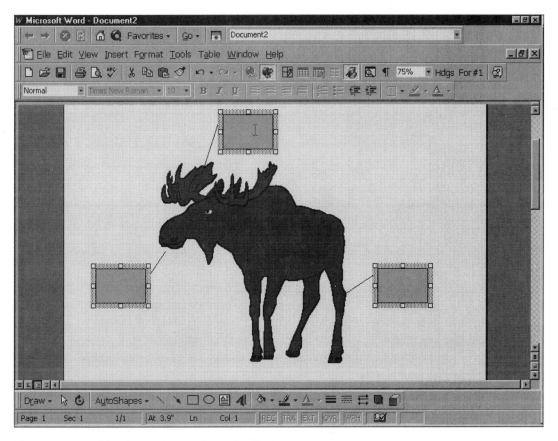

Figure 10-2: Simultaneously selected callouts

5. From the Drawing toolbar, click the Fill Color icon, as shown here, and select a color.

? How can I **draw a circle** quickly?

While you are dragging the Oval tool, press SHIFT for a perfect circle. To draw a perfect square, drag the Rectangle tool while pressing SHIFT.

 Tip: To draw images from the center out, press CTRL while dragging the Rectangle or Oval tool. To draw a perfect circle or rectangle from the center out, press both CTRL and SHIFT while dragging the Rectangle or Oval tool.

? How can I **manipulate the shapes of letters** in a title?

You can use WordArt on the Drawing toolbar (found in Word, Excel, and PowerPoint). Follow these steps to create and then manipulate a title:

1. Click the Insert WordArt button, shown here, and a menu of styles is displayed, as shown in Figure 10-3.

2. Select a style and click OK. A text box is displayed, where you can type your text as shown here:

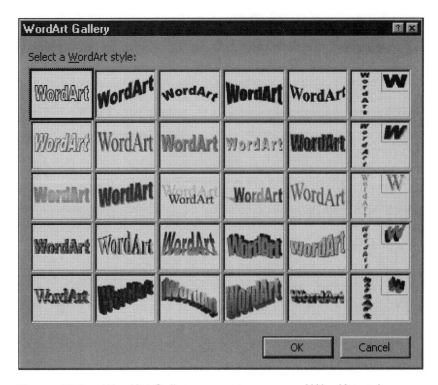

Figure 10-3:   WordArt Gallery presents a menu of WordArt styles.

3. Type your title and click OK. The WordArt is inserted into your document.

4. You will now have a graphic that can be manipulated using the WordArt toolbar. In addition to using the buttons in the toolbar, you can stretch and skew the letters by pulling on the control handles of the selected object. Figure 10-4 shows an example of a title manipulated with WordArt.

❓ How can I **protect my drawings** from being changed or used by others?

You can apply password protection to a graphic in Excel and Word, just as you do a spreadsheet cell or document. The procedure varies slightly for each application.

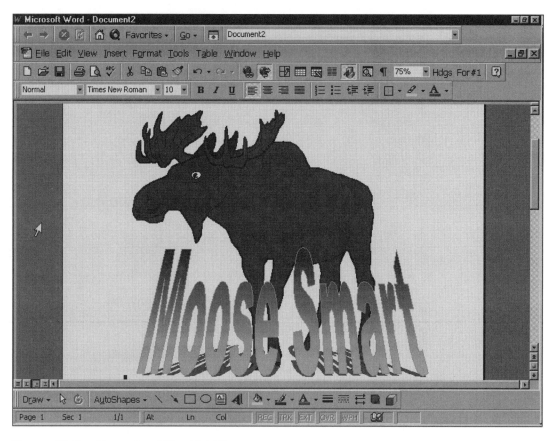

Figure 10-4:   Example of WordArt title

The Drawing Toolbar

Drawing tools are found in Word, Excel, and PowerPoint. You access the tools from the Drawing toolbar. The Line, Arrow, Rectangle, Oval, Text Box, and AutoShapes tools enable you to draw lines and shapes. When you click one of these tools, the pointer changes to an I-beam that you drag to form the line or shape. Except for the WordArt tool, the remaining tools, which alter shapes or lines, require that you select an object before clicking it. The functions of the Drawing tools are described in the following table.

	Tool	Description
Draw ▾	Draw	Displays a menu with options to group, order, nudge, align, rotate or flip, edit control points, change an AutoShape, set AutoShape defaults, or create a grid
▷	Select Objects	Selects drawn objects
↻	Free Rotate	Rotates a drawing around a central point
AutoShapes ▾	AutoShapes	Displays a selection of predefined shapes
╲	Line	Draws a straight line
↘	Arrow	Draws an arrow
▢	Rectangle	Draws a rectangle (or square with shift)
◯	Oval	Draws a circle (with shift) or ellipse
🔠	Text Box	Draws a text box for entering text
🄰	Insert WordArt	Provides a selection of text styles
🎨 ▾	Fill Color	Displays a palette of colors that fill closed shapes when they are clicked
✏ ▾	Line Color	Displays a palette of colors to apply to selected lines
A ▾	Font Color	Displays a palette of colors to apply to selected text
≡	Line Style	Displays a selection of line styles to apply to selected lines

	Tool	Description
	Dash Style	Displays a selection of dashed-line styles to apply to selected lines
	Arrow Style	Displays a selection of arrow styles to apply to selected arrows
	Shadow	Displays a selection of shadow styles to apply to selected objects
	3D	Displays a selection of 3D styles to apply to selected objects

Word

In Word, to protect the graphic you must protect the whole document, as follows:

1. From the Tools menu, select Protect Document. The Protect Document dialog box will be displayed.
2. Select Forms.
3. Enter a Password and click OK.

Excel

In Excel you protect the drawing as you do for a cell, as follows:

1. Right-click the graphic.
2. From the pop-up menu, select Format Object and click the Protection tab.

 Note: The Format option changes name according to what is selected and right-clicked. For a circle, the option is called Format AutoShape, for clip art it is Format Picture, and so on.

3. Turn on the Locked option and click OK.
4. From the Tools menu, select Protection and then Protect Sheet.

5. In the Protect Sheet dialog box, shown here, type in a password and click OK.

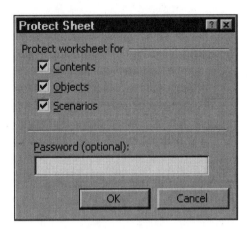

? **When I work with a document or spreadsheet with graphics in it, the response time is slow because of the time it takes to redraw the graphics. I want the graphics for display purposes, but don't need them while I am working on it. What can I do to increase my response speed?**

You can hide the graphics while you are working on a Word document or Excel spreadsheet with these steps:

1. From the Tools menu, select Options.

2. In Word, on the View tab under Show, place a check mark on the items you want to show in the document. Remove the check mark on Drawings (and any other items you want to hide), as shown in Figure 10-5. Click OK. In Excel, in the View tab, click *Hide all* under Objects (or click *Show placeholders* to display the placeholder graphics, which are important while you are working).

When you have finished working on the document or spreadsheet, you can reverse the process and place check marks next to the graphics you want to see, or next to *Show all* in Excel.

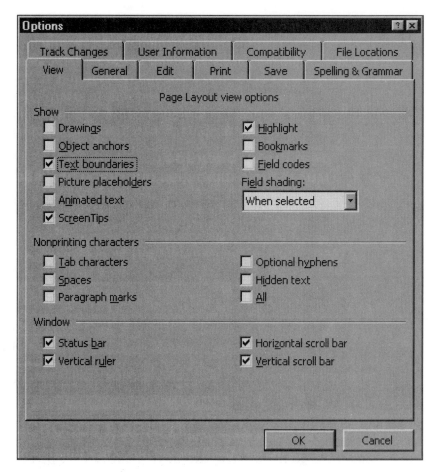

Figure 10-5:   Hiding graphics makes your response time faster.

MICROSOFT GRAPH

> *Note:*   The terms *Chart* and *Graph* are used interchangeably; they mean the same thing.

How do I **add rows or columns to the Graph datasheet?**

The original datasheet displayed when you first bring up Graph appears to have a limited number of rows and columns. You can extend it by simply placing the pointer on the edge and dragging the border of the datasheet down or to the right to increase its size. If you need to add rows or columns in specific places, follow these steps:

1. Select a cell in the row below or the column to the right of the one to be inserted.

 Note: If you select the entire row or column, choosing Cells from the Insert menu adds another row or column without bringing up the Insert dialog box; if you only select a cell, then the dialog box is displayed.

2. Select Cells from the Insert menu. (You can also right-click the datasheet and select Insert.)

3. In the Insert dialog box, click *Entire column* or *Entire row,* as shown here, and click OK:

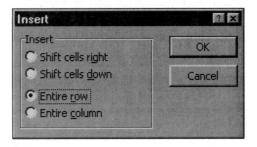

 Tip: If you want to insert more than one row or column at a time, select the number you want inserted, and then choose Insert Cells.

? Why is there more than one graph package? Which is the best graph package?

There are really only two graphing capabilities in Office 97. One is the graphic feature within Excel and the other is Microsoft Graph, used within Word, PowerPoint, and Access (Access's version is very similar to Word's and PowerPoint's although not exactly the same).

The question of which is best is difficult to answer since it depends on what you need graphing for and what your experience is. The Excel feature is more comprehensive and, consequently, more complex, as well. The data to be graphed needs to be developed within Excel on a worksheet. This feature offers flexibility and capabilities not found in Graph. Graph, on the other hand, is easy to use, although limited in its capability. If you want a quick chart or are new to graphing, Graph will serve you well. If you are comfortable with Excel and need a more comprehensive charting tool, Excel's charting features are best.

? How can I **change the size of a chart?**

1. Click the chart to select it, and control handles will appear.

2. Place your pointer on the corner control handles until a two-headed arrow (or a plus sign) appears. Drag the image in the direction you want the size to be changed.

   ▷ If you drag toward the center of the graph, the image will be reduced; away from the center, increased.

   ▷ If you place the pointer somewhere within the graph, a four-headed arrow will appear. Drag the chart wherever you want it.

Tip: To crop using the keyboard, select Format and then Object. On the Picture tab you can enter precise measurements for cropping the graph. You can use Reset to restore the original values while you get the measurements correct.

? How do I **find and use Microsoft Graph?** I don't know where and how to start.

You must be in Word, PowerPoint, or Access to use Microsoft Graph. (Excel has its own charting capability.) It is a subapplication that is used within the larger Office 97 applications. However, it acts as if it is a part of the application in terms of how the menus and dialog boxes are presented to you. That is, a separate application is not started with its own environment, such as you might find with OLE. How you bring up the package and work with it varies slightly between the applications.

Follow these steps to bring up Graph:

In Word

1. Initiate the Graph feature by selecting Object from the Insert menu, and then choosing Microsoft Graph 97

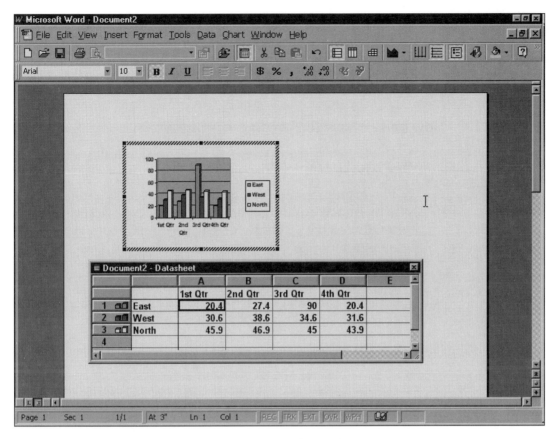

Figure 10-6: Microsoft Graph's sample chart and datasheet

Chart. A sample datasheet and sample chart will be displayed as shown in Figure 10-6.

2. Replace the words and numbers in the datasheet that is displayed with the numbers and labels you want.

3. When you have finished, click the View Datasheet button in the toolbar, as shown here. This will close the datasheet until it is clicked again. You can also just click outside the datasheet area to clear it from the screen.

Tip: If the View Datasheet button is not showing and you want to edit the data, right-click the chart and select Chart Object, and then Edit. If you cannot get the Chart Object option on the pop-up menu, double-click the chart first, and then right-click it and select Chart Object from the pop-up menu. The datasheet will be redisplayed. A third option is to select Datasheet from the View menu if it is showing.

4. From the Chart menu, select Chart Type to select the type of chart, and then Chart Options to add titles and perform other fine-tuning to the chart.

⬤⬤⬤⬤⬤⬤ *Tip:*   If the Chart menu is not showing, right-click the chart and select Chart Object and then Edit. The data will be displayed and the Chart menu will reappear.

In PowerPoint

In PowerPoint you have a quicker way to get charts. When you are building a presentation for the first time, you will be given a choice of several AutoLayout styles, as shown here:

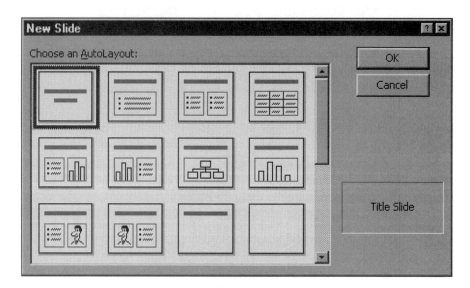

The second row contains three charting templates.

1. Select an AutoLayout slide with a chart placeholder and click OK.

2. Double-click the chart placeholder to get the Microsoft Graph datasheet and chart as described in the instructions "In Word."

⬤⬤⬤⬤⬤⬤ *Tip:*   If you are working with slides without chart placeholders, you can get to Microsoft Graph by clicking the Insert Chart icon on the toolbar, shown here.

In Access

In order to be able to use Graph, you must have installed Advanced Wizards. If you have not done this, bring up the Add/Remove Programs in the Control Panel and install it for Office 97. In Access the chart's data is created from an Access table or query rather than the separate datasheet you use in Word or PowerPoint.

1. To use the Chart Wizard, click the Forms tab in the Database window.

2. Click New and the New Form dialog box will open.

3. Select Chart Wizard from the list box, as shown below, and enter the name of the table or query to be used.

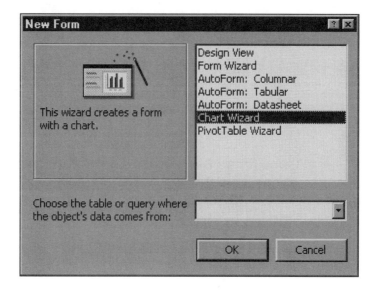

4. Click OK, and the wizard will start.

Tip: You can force the use of the separate datasheet by selecting Chart from the Insert menu.

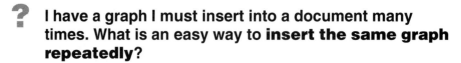

I have a graph I must insert into a document many times. What is an easy way to insert the same graph repeatedly?

The easiest way is to add the object to AutoText. Then, when you type its name and press F3, the graphic will automatically replace the name. Follow these steps to do it:

1. Select the graph.

2. From the Insert menu, select AutoText, and then New from the pop-up menu. The Create AutoText dialog box will be displayed, as shown here:

3. Type a name for the graph and click OK.

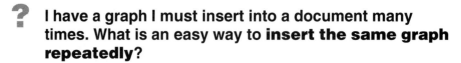

Once it has been closed, how can I redisplay a chart datasheet?

There are at least three ways to get the datasheet redisplayed, depending on what buttons and menus are available when you are trying to display it:

▷ Redisplay the graph datasheet by clicking the View Datasheet button on the toolbar, as shown here:

▷ Select the chart by double-clicking it. This method selects the chart with a striped line surrounding it and black control handles. Then either right-click the chart and select Datasheet from the pop-up menu as shown below or, from the View menu, select Datasheet.

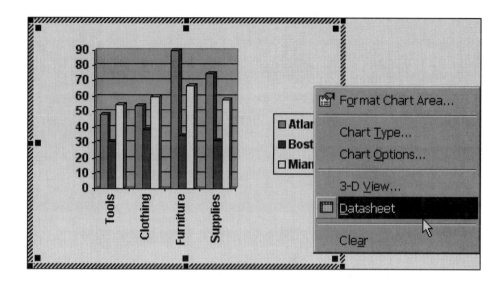

⊳ Select the chart by clicking it once so that clear control handles are shown, and then right-click the chart and select Chart Object to see the datasheet.

❓ How can I put **tick marks on an axis?**

You can insert tick marks on a selected axis so that it may be read more precisely. Follow these steps:

1. Ensure that the graph is selected with the black striped line surrounding it. If not, double-click it to select it.

2. Select the axis by clicking it. Control handles will appear on each end of the axis. You must click the axis, but not on a corner.

3. Select Selected Axis from the Format menu.

4. On the Patterns tab, click the type of tick mark you want in the *Major tick mark type, Minor tick mark type,* and *Tick mark labels* check boxes, as shown next.

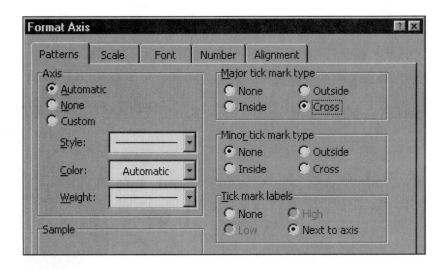

The Basics of Graphing

Microsoft Graph offers 14 types of standard charts. These 14 types are then extended by several 3D effects for each type, plus there are an additional 20 custom types. Each type of standard graph displays data in a slightly different way, allowing you to choose the type that is best for presenting your data. The standard types of charts are described in Table 10-1.

Graphs display data on two or three axes, as shown in Figure 10-7. These axes and their reference names are

▷ The vertical axis, also called the Y axis, or the value axis

▷ The horizontal axis, also called the X axis, or the category axis

▷ The depth axis, which gives a 3D appearance and is also called the Z axis, or the series axis

Note: The definition of which axis is used for Values and which for Categories can be changed.

Using the options in Chart Type and Chart Options, you can define the appearance of your chart. You format a chart by opening the Chart Options dialog box and selecting one of the tab names italicized below:

➤ Type the name for the chart and a *title* for each of the axes.

➤ Define which is the primary *axis* and define whether it is a category or time-scale axis, or whether Graph will assume the titles from the data.

➤ Designate whether major or minor *gridlines* are to be used for each axis.

➤ Stipulate where the *legend* is to be placed or whether to show it at all.

➤ Define whether to show data or value *labels* on the chart, or other measurements such as percentages.

➤ Stipulate whether to show the *data table* where the values and labels are defined.

Table 10-1:   Table Describing Standard Chart Types

	Type of Chart	Description
	Column	Displays the data in vertical bars or columns; compares values in one category to those in another
	Bar	Displays data in horizontal bars; compares values in one category to those in another

Table 10-1: (*Continued*)

	Type of Chart	Description
	Line	Displays data in lines with values plotted along the lines; used to show trends over time
	Pie	Displays the data as pieces of a pie, showing the relation of a part to the other pieces and to the whole
	XY (Scatter)	Compares pairs of values to show patterns or trends
	Area	Displays how a value contributes to a trend over time or categories

Table 10-1: (*Continued*)

	Type of Chart	Description
	Doughnut	Shows how a value compares to a whole; can display multiple series
	Radar	Connects values at various positions and frequencies compared with a central point and with each other
	Surface	3D surface; shows how values in a continuous curve contribute to a trend
	Bubble	Compares sets of three values
	Stock	Displays four values of a stock's daily price: opening, high, low, and closing

Table 10-1:   *(Continued)*

	Type of Chart	Description
	Cylinder	Same as Columnar but displays the columns as cylinders
	Cone	Same as Columnar but displays the columns as cones
	Pyramid	Same as Columnar but displays the columns as pyramids

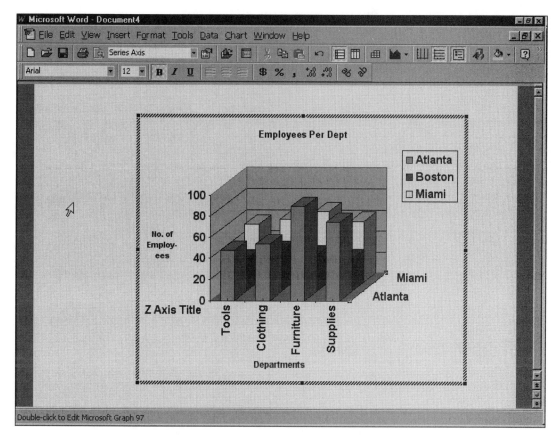

Figure 10-7: Example of a 3D column chart

CLIP GALLERY

❓ How do I **add clip art objects to the Clip Gallery?**

In Word, Excel, and PowerPoint, you can add new clip art objects to the Clip Gallery by importing them. First, bring up the Clip Gallery by selecting Picture from the Insert menu and then choosing Clip Art. When the Clip Gallery window appears, follow these steps:

1. Click the Import Clips button on the lower right of the Clip Gallery window.

2. In the *Add clip art to Clip Gallery* dialog box, find the file to be added and click Open.

3. In the Clip Properties dialog box, shown in Figure 10-8, type in the Keyword for the object and choose a category under which it will be found.

4. Click OK.

Note: In Access, you must be in Design for Forms/Reports and then select Insert Object to open the dialog box in which Microsoft Clip Gallery can be selected.

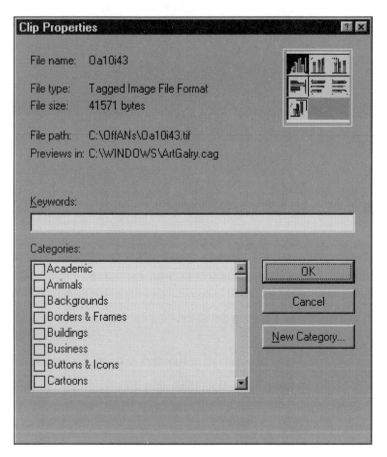

Figure 10-8:   Clip Properties dialog box

? **I can't access the Clip Gallery.** Why not?

You probably have not installed it correctly. Follow these steps to install it again:

1. Insert your Office 97 CD-ROM into the disk drive.

2. From the Start menu select Settings, then Control Panel, and then double-click Add/Remove Programs.

3. On the Install/Uninstall tab, find and click Microsoft Office 97 or Microsoft Office 97 Professional Edition and click Add/Remove. Click OK to indicate that your CD-ROM is inserted.

4. Click the Add/Remove button on the Microsoft Office 97 Setup dialog box.

5. On the Microsoft Office 97 - Maintenance dialog box, click Office Tools and click Change Option.

6. Find Clip Gallery in the Office Tools dialog box, place a check mark next to it, as shown below, and click OK.

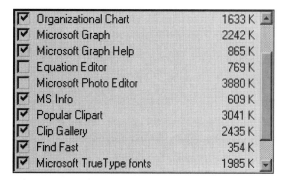

7. Click Continue.

Tip: In PowerPoint you can access the Clip Gallery quickly. You only need to select a slide with an AutoLayout style containing a clip art placeholder, such as the one shown below, and then double-click it to open the Clip Gallery dialog box.

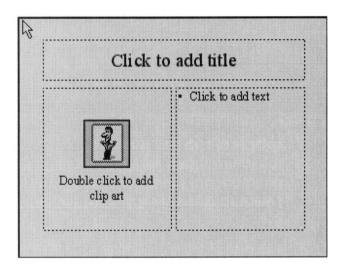

? **When I double-click clip art, normally the Clip Gallery window reappears so that I can replace it or select other clip art. But sometimes in PowerPoint it doesn't work.**

My guess is that you have converted the clip art object to a PowerPoint object that is no longer recognized as clip art. There is no way to restore the object to its previous status without exploring what has happened—perhaps it was included in a group. You will have to load the Clip Art Gallery again by selecting Picture from the Insert menu and choosing Clip Art from the submenu. If you want to replace the current clip art object with another one, you'll have to delete it first.

Tip: If you want clip art to be shown on all pages of a PowerPoint presentation, insert it on the Slide Master.

? **How do I modify clip art?**

You can isolate the individual parts of the clip art image and then change them by altering the image itself, changing the color of the lines or fill, or combining the individual elements of an image in a different way. To do any of these things, you use the Drawing toolbar:

1. Select the clip art image you want to change.

2. From the Drawing toolbar, click Draw and then select Ungroup. The image will be divided into groups, all selected, as shown here:

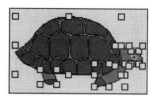

3. Click outside the image and again select just the parts of the image you want to change. Again click Draw and then Ungroup. Repeat this process until the element you want cannot be further ungrouped. For example, you can see how the previous drawing has been disassembled here:

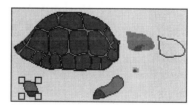

4. Use the menu options on the Drawing toolbar to change the image.

5. When you have finished, select the individual images and groups that you want to be considered as a single image, and then select Draw and then Group.

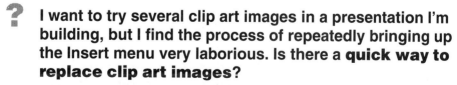

I want to try several clip art images in a presentation I'm building, but I find the process of repeatedly bringing up the Insert menu very laborious. Is there a quick way to replace clip art images?

The quickest way to replace clip art images is to follow these steps:

1. Double-click the image you want to replace. The Clip Gallery window will be displayed.

2. Find the image you want to use as a replacement.

3. Double-click the replacement image. Your original image will be replaced with the new one.

? Where are the **video samples** that come with PowerPoint 97?

You can find video samples on your own system by clicking Insert and selecting *Movies and Sounds,* and then *Movie from File.* Find and open the Media folder and select the video you want.

Office 97 comes with additional video samples. These can be found in the Microsoft Clip Gallery. Follow these steps to find and preview them:

1. Insert the Office 97 CD-ROM into your CD drive.

2. In PowerPoint bring up the Insert menu and select *Movies and Sounds.* Select *Movie from Gallery,* and the Clip Gallery will open.

3. Select the Videos tab, as shown in Figure 10-9.

4. Select a video and click Play to preview the video clip.

5. When you find one you want to insert in a presentation, click Insert.

Tip: Another location containing clips on the Microsoft Web site can be accessed from PowerPoint. From the Tools menu, click PowerPoint Central. This site contains free audio, video, photos, clip art, soundtracks, fonts, and movies that you can download (plus more stuff!).

To display a larger video thumbnail, as shown in Figure 10-9, place a check mark in the Magnify check box.

EQUATION EDITOR

? Where in Office can I **build equations**? I don't know where to find the symbols for building a mathematical expression.

The Equation Editor is a separate application that works with Office products for that very purpose. However, as

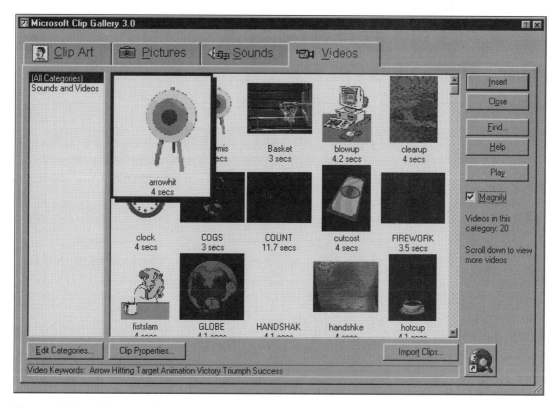

Figure 10-9: Microsoft Clip Gallery 3.0

with OLE applications, you load it into your current Office application and the Equation Editor will appear with its own menus and toolbar. To get to it, follow these steps:

1. From the Insert menu, select Object and click the Create New tab.

2. Select Microsoft Equation 3.0.

Note: If Microsoft Equation 3.0 isn't available to you, you will need to install it using Add/Remove Programs and the Office 97 CD-ROM.

3. Select or clear *Float over text* by clicking the check box. Click OK. The Equation toolbar will be displayed, as shown here:

Select *Float over text* if you want the equation to be an object over your document. If you intend to place the equation in a cell or on a Web page, deselect *Float over text* so that the equation is placed inline.

•••••• *Tip:*   To see the contents of the toolbar menus, place the pointer over the icons and their labels will appear.

4. Construct the equation by clicking the toolbar menus to select the symbol and expression templates and typing variables and numbers in the Equation Editor text boxes.

•••••• *Tip:*   A third-party product that significantly enhances the capabilities of Equation Editor is available. From the Equation Editor Help menu, select Equation Editor Help Topics, select the Contents tab, and then choose Upgrading Equation Editor for additional information.

? How does the Equation Editor **calculate**? I can't get it to solve even simple equations.

The Equation Editor is not designed to perform calculations at all. It is simply a tool for typing complex equations with all the symbols and constructs needed.

? When I want to **change an equation in a document**, is there a way to get the Equation Editor quickly without going through the Insert menu?

Yes—when you want the Equation Editor window to reappear, simply double-click the equation and it will be displayed.

? How do I **change the font and font size** used in equations?

There are three ways you can change fonts and sizes of equations:

▷ First, you can define the defaults for the fonts and sizes that will be used in equations. The fonts and sizes can be applied to the various parts of an equation (Text, Functions, Variables, Lower Case Greek, Upper Case Greek, Symbols, Matrix-Vectors, and Numbers). To change the defaults for fonts, select Define from the Style menu. The Styles dialog box will be displayed, as shown in Figure 10-10. Select the font by clicking the down arrow and choosing the font you want. To specify bold or italic, click the relevant check box to place a check mark in it. To change the default for the size of font used, choose Define from the Size menu. A similar dialog box will allow you to change sizes for character variations.

▷ Second, you can change the font for an existing equation. Select the expression or the part you want

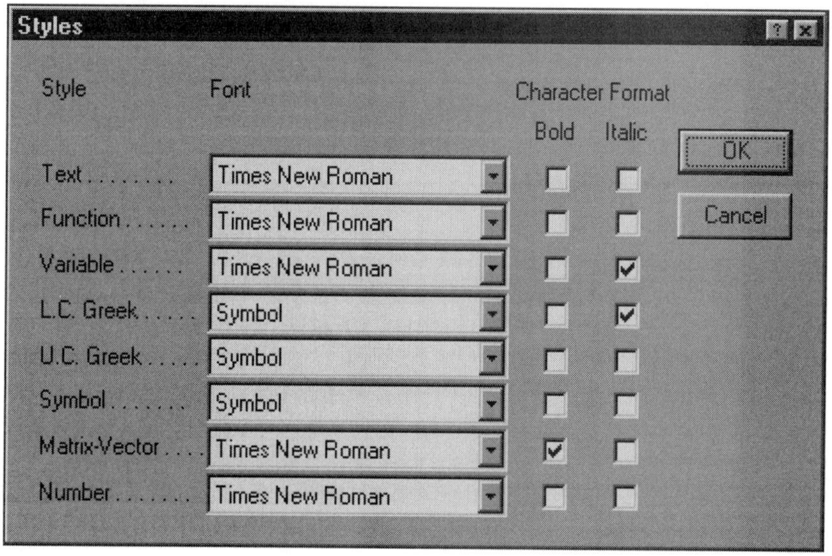

Figure 10-10:   The Styles dialog box

to change, choose Other from the Style menu, and select the font you want. In the same way, you can change the size for an existing equation by selecting Other from the Size menu.

☞ Third, the Equation Editor assigns a standard size to elements of an equation—the equation templates have "slots" that define an element and, therefore, its size. For example, subscripts are smaller, and brackets around summations are larger. You can also change the size of an element by selecting a standard size from the Size menu. This assigns a standard size to a specific type of element:

☞ **Full** pertains to normal-size characters.

☞ **Subscript** is used for subscripts and superscripts next to normal numbers. It is one size smaller than Full size. It can also be used for other situations requiring that size of character.

☞ **Sub-Subscript** is used for subscripts and superscripts assigned to sub- or superscripts. It is two sizes smaller than Full size and can be used for other elements requiring the smaller-size characters.

☞ **Symbol** pertains to oversized symbols that are part of the equations and their templates.

☞ **Sub-Symbol** pertains to oversized symbols used in subscript-size positions.

? **I find I am not as familiar with mathematical terminology as I need to be to use the Equation Editor easily. Where can I get some guidance?**

The Equation Editor has a glossary you may find helpful. On the Help menu, select Equation Editor Help Topics, Reference Information, and then Definitions. The Definitions screen will be displayed, as partially shown here:

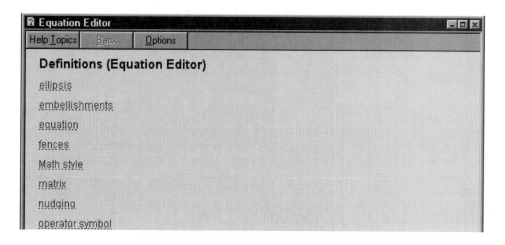

Click an item to see its definition.

❓ When I am nudging parts of an equation, I find it difficult because the size of the image on the screen is too small to place the symbols precisely. Can I enlarge it?

When you are making very precise changes to an equation's symbol and text positioning, you need to increase the size of the image on the screen. Since you must be in the Equation Editor window to have the magnification commands available to you, bring it up by selecting the equation, choosing Equation Object from the Edit menu, and choosing Open. Then you can enlarge the image on the screen by selecting a magnification size from the View menu. For example, select 400% to see the image enlarged four times. Then use these commands to move the items by one pixel:

▷ CTRL-LEFT ARROW to move left

▷ CTRL-RIGHT ARROW to move right

▷ CTRL-UP ARROW to move up

▷ CTRL-DOWN ARROW to move down

Tip: Use Redraw to redisplay the equation after you have made changes so that you will know where you are.

BUILDING ORGANIZATION CHARTS

What is a quick way to build an organization chart?

A separate miniapplication works with Office to design organization charts. To use it follow these steps:

1. Click where you want to insert the organization chart.

2. From the Insert menu, select Object and then choose MS Organization Chart 2.0 from the list. Click OK. The window shown in Figure 10-11 will be displayed.

3. Build the org chart by using these tools:

   ☞ Select the style of chart by selecting an option from the Styles menu.

   ☞ Select the magnification of the chart with the View options.

   ☞ Replace the text in the default boxes with your own.

   ☞ Add boxes by clicking a position button, shown below, and then placing the resulting icon on the box you want it connected to.

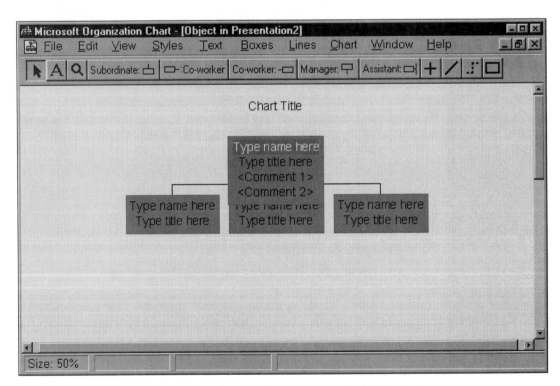

Figure 10-11:   The Microsoft Organization Chart program's initial display

> ▷ Add color, shadows, and borders to the boxes with the Boxes menu.
> ▷ Determine the thickness, color, and style of the box lines with the Lines menu.
> ▷ Use the Text menu to align the text and set its color and font.

4. Delete boxes by selecting them and selecting Cut from the Edit menu or pressing DEL.

How can I **change the initial default chart** display?

You can only change a limited number of characteristics of the default organization chart that is first displayed. You can choose whether the number of boxes initially displayed for new charts will be the current 4-box template or a 1-box template. The 4-box template will always contain sample text to be replaced. You can choose between having one box with text to be replaced, or preset text that you have established. Finally, you can select the magnification that will be used to display the org chart. Make your choices with the following steps:

1. Establish an organization chart as you would want to see it when the program is brought up each time.

2. From the Edit menu, select Options. The Options dialog box will be displayed.

3. Place a check mark next to the options you want to retain.

Note: Organization Chart is a simplified version of Org Plus for Windows. If you are interested in finding out about this enhanced organization chart program, look in the Help menu under About Microsoft Organization Chart for additional information.

How do I use **color in an org chart**?

You can place color in the background of the chart, as well as within the boxes. You might, for example, want to give the chart a more readable format with all of the same positions in one color and a contrasting background.

☞ For background color, select Background Color from the Chart menu.

☞ For colored boxes, select the boxes and then select Color from the Boxes menu. Select the boxes by clicking them, using SHIFT to select more than one box, or you can select specific positions from the Select option in the Edit menu.

❓ The boxes are so big on my screen that I cannot see them all. How do I **reduce the size of an org chart**?

To reduce the size of the organization chart on the screen, select *50% of Actual* from the View menu. If that is still too large to see all of the page, select Size to Window. When you want to return to the normal size, select Actual Size.

❓ When I **revise my org chart** I get some unexpected results. What are some guidelines?

When an Organization Chart is revised, it must rebuild itself according to the information it has. So when you want to delete a line of positions, either horizontally or vertically, you must select all of them before deleting them. When you move a position from one level to another, you must move it precisely. Here are some guidelines:

☞ If you delete a managing position, the subordinate positions will be moved up one position in the org chart, to the managing position. You can cut one box by right-clicking it and then and selecting Cut from the pop-up menu, as shown here:

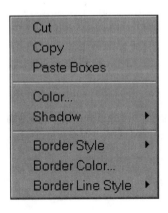

▷ To delete a manager and subordinates, you must select them all by selecting first the manager and then choosing Select from the Edit menu and then Branch. The whole line will be selected. Then select Cut from the Edit menu.

Tip: If you select Group, a horizontal line of positions will be selected; if Branch, a vertical line.

▷ To move subordinates from one position to another, select their boxes and drag them over the manager to which they will be subordinate.

Index

Action Index

To **speak to the support experts** who handle more than one million technical issues every month, call **Stream's** Microsoft ® Office 97 ® answer line! Trained specialists will answer your Office 97 questions regarding Word for Windows, Excel for Windows and PowerPoint for Windows.

Have all your questions been answered?

1-800-477-7613

For Word for Windows and PowerPoint for Windows Questions:
$34.95 per problem (Charge to a major credit card.)

1-800-477-7614

For Excel For Windows Questions:
$34.95 per problem (Charge to a major credit card.)

1-900-555-2007

For Word for Windows and PowerPoint for Windows Questions:
$34.95 per problem (Charge to your phone bill.)

1-900-555-2006

For Excel for Windows Questions:
$34.95 per problem (Charge to your phone bill.)

Visit our web site at www.stream.com.

Stream

The technical support specialists.

Instant Answers! Office 97

Toolbar Button	Shortcut	Product	Function	First Click Menu	Then Choose Option	Next
		Common	Add comment	Insert	Comment	
	CTRL-M	PowerPoint	Add new slide to a presentation	Insert	New Slide	Select layout
		Common	Add/delete buttons to toolbars	Tools	Customize	
		Excel/Word	Apply automatic formatting	Format	AutoFormat	Select type
	CTRL-1	Excel	Apply formatting to selected cells	Format	Cells	Select type
		Excel/Word	Apply style to selected text	Format	Style	Select type
		Common	Attach templates/use wizards	Tools	Add-Ins	
100%		Common	Change size of screen display	View	Zoom	Select magnification
	F7	Common	Check spelling	Tools	Spelling	
		Common	Choose errors to be corrected	Tools	AutoCorrect	Select types
A		Common	Choose font type and size	Format	Font	
		Common	Close application and return to Windows	File	Exit	
		Common	Close a current document	File	Close	
		Common	Close hyperlink	Edit	Paste Hyperlink	
	CTRL-V	Common	Copy clipboard contents	Edit	Paste	
		Common	Copy OLE object	Edit	Paste Hyperlink	
	CTRL-C	Common	Copy selected item to clipboard	Edit	Copy	
		Excel	Create and insert chart	Insert	Chart	Use Wizard
	CTRL-N	Common	Create new document	File	New	
		Common	Create/edit headers and footers	View	Header and Footer	
		Word	Create/insert AutoText	Insert	AutoText	Select Text
		Common	Create/run macros	Tools	Macros	
		Access	Delete row (record)	Edit	Delete record	
	DEL	Common	Delete selection	Edit	Clear	Contents
		Word/PoPt.	Display all open files	Window	Arrange All	
		Common	Display data—no page formatting	View	Normal	
		Common	Display full screen, no menus or toolbars	View	Full Screen	
		Access	Display hidden columns	Format	Unhide Columns	
		Excel	Display hidden row/column/sheet	Format	Row/Column/Sheet	Unhide
		Common	Display text in comments	View	Comments	
		Common	Display toolbar	View	Toolbars	Select toolbar
		Common	Display Web toolbar	View	Toolbar	Web
		Common	Duplicate window	Window	New	
		Common	Edit linked or embedded object	Edit	Links	
		Common	Edit selected object	Edit	Object	
	CTRL-D	Excel	Fill cells below	Edit	Fill	Down
	CTRL-F	Common	Find text in document or file	Edit	Find	
		Word	Format text in newspaper-type columns	Format	Columns	Select columns
		Common	Get help from the Internet	Help	Microsoft on the Web	Select item

Toolbar Button	Shortcut	Product	Function	First Click Menu	Then Choose Option	Next
	CTRL-G	Common	Go to page, section, line, etc.	Edit	Go To	
		Access	Hide columns	Format	Hide Columns	
		Excel	Hide row/column/sheet	Format	Row/Column/Sheet	Hide
		Word/PoPt.	Insert date/time	Insert	Date and Time	Select format
	CTRL-K	Common	Insert hyperlink to URL/document	Insert	Hyperlink	
		Access	Insert new record	Insert	Record	
		Common	Insert picture	Insert	Picture	Select picture type
	SHIFT-F7	Word	Look up synonyms and antonyms	Tools	Language	Thesaurus
		Excel/Word	Mark edits	Tools	Track Changes	Turn on highlighting
	CTRL-O	Common	Open existing document	File	Open	
	CTRL-P	Common	Print selected pages/area	File	Print	
		Access	Protect database	Tools	Security	Select protection
		Word	Protect file	Tools	Protect document	Enter password
		Excel	Protect/share workbook or sheet	Tools	Protection	Select item
	CTRL-X	Common	Remove selected item to clipboard	Edit	Cut	
	CTRL-Y	Common	Repeat last action	Edit	Redo	
	CTRL-H	Common	Replace text in document	Edit	Replace	
	CTRL-Z	Common	Reverse last action	Edit	Undo	
		Common	Save as web page	File	Save As HTML	
	CTRL-S	Common	Save current document	File	Save	
		Common	Save with new name	File	Save As	
		Common	See how page will print	File	Print Preview	
	CTRL-A	Word	Select entire document	Edit	Select all	
		Common	Set defaults for various functions	Tools	Options	
		Common	Set page features	File	Page Setup	
		Word	Sort paragraphs in table or selection	Table	Sort	Select A–Z or Z–A
		Access	Sort records	Records	Sort	Select A–Z or Z–A
		Excel	Sort selected data	Data	Sort	Select A–Z or Z–A
		PowerPoint	Sort slides	View	Slide Sorter	
		Common	Switch to different open document	Window	Document name	
		Common	Transmit document to e-mail address	File	Send To	Mail Recipient
		Common	Transmit document to Exchange folder	File	Sent To	Exchange Folder
		Common	Transmit document to routing list	File	Sent To	Routing Recipient
		Word/PoPt.	Type text in object	Insert	Text Box	
	F1	Common	Use Help	Help	Help	
	SHIFT-F1	Common	Use Help Assistant	Help	What's This	
		Common	Use Microsoft Bookshelf	Tools	Look Up Reference	